D0676966

A
JOURNEY
to the
DARK HEART
of
NAMELESS
UNSPEAKABLE EVIL

A
JOURNEY
to the
DARK HEART
of
NAMELESS
UNSPEAKABLE EVIL

Charities, Hollywood,
Joseph Kony, and
Other Abominations

JANE BUSSMANN

NORTIA
PRESS

www.nortiapress.com

East Baton Rouge Parish Library
Baton Rouge, Louisiana

www.nortiapress.com

2321 E 4th Street, C-219
Santa Ana, CA 92705
contact @ nortiapress.com

All rights reserved, including the right to reproduce this book or portions thereof.
For rights information please contact the publisher.

Copyright © 2014 by Jane Bussmann

MacMillan originally published a version of this book in the U.K. under the title *The Worst Date Ever: Or How It Took A Comedy Writer To Expose Africa's Secret War.*

Cover design by Naisola Grimwood.

ISBN: 978-0-9888798-4-3
LCCN: 2014936213

This book was printed by Worzalla in Stevens Point, Wisconsin, USA

To all of us comes a moment when we see ourselves clearly. Some of us reach this moment and realize, My God, I *am* awesome. I have improved the world, my jacket exemplifies all I have achieved, and my ass is just brilliant.

Some of us don't. For those of us who reach this moment and realize, My God, I am *still* like this, this book is for you.

Q: Out of every 100 Ugandans, how many do you think have a telephone?

A: Two.* And the tragedy is, they don't have each other's number.

* This may not be an accurate statistic.

CONTENTS

Note

In the Hollywood section, I've changed the order of some events to include more stupid encounters with celebrities. The events are irrelevant but they have famous people in them. In the Uganda section I've changed names, locations and anything else it took to avoid getting people into trouble. Any cock-ups I blame on drink.

I'VE MET SOME REALLY GREAT PRIESTS

I can pinpoint the moment it started: springtime 2003, and I was having lunch in Beverly Hills with the most fancied man in America. It was an intimate lunch outside a hilltop café, and I was gazing into the eyes of Ashton Kutcher, the actor, better known today as the bloke who took over from Bruce Willis on Demi Moore. Ashton's eyes were so picture-perfect dark and sexy that you felt guilty staring into them, the way you'd feel guilty stroking a naked ass if you found one in your bag. I felt I should apologize to everyone in the café. Everyone in the café agreed with me, from the waitress refilling my coffee cup with a look that said, *Nice going, sister*, to the veteran movie producer heaving his belly onto the table as he leaned round to see if it really was Ashton, really talking to someone other than him. The belly quivered in indignation: Ashton it really was, twenty-six and gorgeous, the breakout star of Hollywood, the hot one from *That '70s Show*, the maverick MTV rebel from *Punk'd*, and even this fat old straight man wanted to screw him. And as Ashton gazed back at me, I was thinking one thing: *There must be a way I can kill myself that wouldn't upset Mum. I'll save a drowning child. Yes. Beverly Hills Presbyterian Preschool & Kindergarten, I'll throw one in the river...*

Ashton didn't screw me. This was Hollywood: he hired someone else, and they screwed me, because I wasn't Ashton's girlfriend, I was the problem. It's the rule of talking to famous people, never bring up religion, they might have an opinion. But I'd run out of things I wanted to ask him. This happened a lot when I talked to celebrities. We'd already done his favorite blended coffee drink, phone handset and sneakers; there was nothing left.

And now here I was starting an argument about Jesus with Ashton Kutcher. Ashton said he was a Christian.

"Cool!" I said. "My favorite actor from Britain is a Christian!" *Oh good God I've lost my mind.*

"I'm not really religious... but I'm religious," Ashton explained. "Like, I don't congregate." He didn't go to church, for a reason: "I'd rather hang out with someone that doesn't have my beliefs and then maybe make them think about their beliefs." But surely... *then he means... yes he does but don't go there.* I went there.

"So could you convert me?" I said. He asked me my religion. Mine? That people are basically born... nice?

The conversation ran for much longer but I have condensed it because of space restrictions, and because I am a heathen.

"*Born* with that?" he said. "If we're born with it, do you think Hitler was born with all of that? Do you feel like Joseph Stalin was born with all of that?"

What have I done? He's going to use my own beliefs on me. I'm not going to apologize for being an atheist.

"No, no," I apologized.

"It all has to come from somewhere, right? So why not call that higher power God, which is the title of it?" he said. "This is the title of it, right? So it's God. You believe in God."

Then as he was talking, I saw myself from above. Ashton Kutcher was more use to the planet than I was. I wanted out, right now.

"I just don't like priests!" I said. "Creepy! Manipulative! Yuk!" He stared at me. "How many priests have you met?" he said.

"I... A dozen?"

"You can't generalize like that," he said. "I've met some really great priests. Two."

"Two great priests?"

"Yeah, but I've only met four priests... No, three priests... no, four priests. And one of them I didn't really know. But two of them were really great people... No, I've met four priests. I've met five priests and three of them were great."

I changed the subject to child abuse to lighten the mood. It didn't work.

"One of them still sends me a birthday card and I haven't seen him in twelve years," he said. "You know, I'll leave it open to your own judgment, but I think that you need to think about your thinking a little bit more."

Ashton later converted to Kabbalah.

Here's what I wrote: "Ashton really is the coolest person in America."

Welcome to my world. Celebrity journalism. Free lunches with the stars. The trouble was, Ashton was right: One of us made TV shows that entertained people, produced movies that premiered at Sundance and restored property with their father. The other was a celebrity journalist.

There were great celebrity journalists in Hollywood, and I wasn't one of them. I hated asking rude questions, I didn't know who was hot, and I thought fashion designers were uppity little freaks who made women look stupid on purpose. It was my own fault, the mistake that had stranded me in paradise surrounded by beautiful, sexy people—I'd run away. I'd run away to Hollywood to write movies. Unfortunately people who were good at writing movies got there first, so instead of writing *Casablanca* I found myself writing about what a fantastic bloke Ashton Kutcher was. Worse, I was by trade a comedy writer, trained to say the most inappropriate thing possible; now the reflex had mutated into some kind of cultural Tourette's, and I was scared, because sooner or later I was going to explode all over Paris Hilton.

If you think I'm complaining, I am. Please bear with me. I know that somewhere there's a little eight-year-old girl born with water on the brain who would have loved my job. But Sloshy never had to go on 400 blind dates with beautiful young millionaires who hate her and spend an hour telling her, "I can't find true love." (Subtitle: "I'm shagging Scarlett Johansson."[1])

---

1. Legal note: not Ashton Kutcher.

Back in the quiet farming state of Iowa where Ashton grew up, he would have been another lively guy in a bar. Except, as I'd learned over the years from talking to endless celebrities, fame arrests social development at the exact age it strikes. It's not the celebrity's fault; Britney is doing pretty well for an 11-year-old left in the care of pharmaceutical giants and K-Fed's winkle. Michael Jackson was completely normal for a five-year-old who loved pajama parties. On the reverse side, George Clooney famously slogged through twenty-odd guest roles, including "Lip-syncing Transvestite", before hitting it big with ER, so he'll be a graceful thirty-something for the rest of his days. In Ashton's case, throw a Calvin Klein underwear-modeling deal and a hit sitcom at a 19-year-old, and seven years later you had a school leaver apparently chosen by God to convert the heathens, specifically the Sodomites writing cover stories for British magazines. Because I'd asked him to. Conversation over, he sat back in victory. "So I don't go to church. But I'm in it every day."

I still didn't believe in God, but I'd had a revelation: Jesus, this is my life.

As luck would have it, P. Diddy texted. I don't think I will ever say that again and mean it. Ashton pulled out his phone and typed a reply to P. Diddy, aka Puffy, America's richest awful rapper. As Ashton started talking about his weekend with Diddy, I retooled my original make-it-in-Hollywood plan: *Leaving my organs for transplants. That's the only useful thing left I can do. But it mustn't look like suicide, because of Mum...*

"Puffy's got this thing... we have this, like, repertoire going... it's like the Rat Pack..."

But we're in Beverly Hills: what if Paris Hilton got my kidneys? I'll write on the donor card, "Any part of my body—except to celebrities."

"So I call him up and I call him Frank..."

What if it gets smudged and reads, "Any celebrities"? I'll end up in Simon Cowell.

"And he calls me Dean..."

I know. I'll put my donor card in a plastic bag and pin it to my shirt. Now I can die. Brilliant... Hang on. How does that not look like suicide?

Suddenly I realized Ashton was staring at me. I scrabbled in my torn Gucci bag for the package of Ashton Kutcher research. Balls. It was still on my doorstep unopened, where it had sat for a week after I'd used it to clean dog poo off my stilettos.

I had an emergency plan, however, because like anyone who hates their job, I had it down to minimum effort: I'd patented the Magic Questions for interviewing celebrities. Both of them.

Two magic psychological formulas to find out what makes anyone, say John Travolta, tick (in Travolta's case, it's airplanes and ▮▮▮. And why not? He's John Travolta). Magic Celebrity Question One: "You're in amazing shape, what's your secret?" To which the celebrity always replies, "Am I? Wow. Thanks. Because I never exercise and I live off cheese." A variation of Question One is crucial, because it allows the celebrity to relax and open up, like a bumhole on amyl nitrate. Ashton went one better: "I'm just happy. Happiness looks healthy," he said. "Yeah, you know depressed people don't look healthy—they're always, like, yeuch, that's in their face." Ashton ordered a kebab and got 20 percent better looking. I ordered three black coffees and got more yeuch.

Magic Celebrity Question Two: "We all know what you're most famous for," I said, hoping he didn't challenge me on this, "but how does it make you feel when you're not appreciated for your inner talents?" Magic Celebrity Question Two clinched it: Ashton relaxed and told me he was only truly himself doing altruistic work, citing the celebrity basketball match he was about to play with the NBA Entertainment League in front of thousands of sex-starved army wives. The Magic Questions would save my skin until I escaped.

That day, as I finished my lunch in Beverly Hills with the most fancied man in America, I finally faced reality. *OK, I have to escape from here. Because I have completely fucked up.*

I'd thrown away my life to scorn the theory of evolution in the hope that a former underwear model might like me. A former underwear model who thought I was an idiot. He had a point.

THE GOLDEN AGE OF STUPID

And what a time to be trapped in LA. This was the Golden Age of Stupid, and Hollywood was peaking; 2003-6 in Los Angeles was 1966-9 in London, without cool music, cool movies or people who did anything. Reporters fretted about Michael Jackson's duvet, chicken sneezes and cloned sheep, while "major social progress" meant a court had declared sodomy legal. You couldn't stop the President of the United States sneaking up on you with a $3 trillion war, but you sure could get taken from behind. We had a few years to go before the recession ("credit crunch"), high fuel prices and the decline of Los Angeles into full-blown mental illness, so for now it was all snort, fuck and buy another Chihuahua, a dog you'd surely only buy when blind drunk or on drugs.

Logically, this moment in history chose the It Kids to represent it; people who simply were. When you met the It Girls, Nicole Richie was warm and funny, Lindsay Lohan was wide-eyed and sweet, but worryingly surrounded by EuroToffs, and Paris Hilton dutifully kept up the "sexy" thing by being rude, which made you wonder how you'd bored her and struggle harder for her love. Dammit, I think I even fancied her. They were all smart, but boy, had they inspired a million Queens of Stupid.

Every weekend Sunset Strip was stalked by mannequins, running between the Skybar and the Standard with painted legs and no pubic hair. I know this, because this generation didn't burn bras, it spurned panties; the martinis hit their empty stomachs hard, and I'd watch them tumble giggling to the curb in front of a Maserati, child minges flashed to the whole town. As the world slid towards war, LA's rebellion wasn't to fight the system, it was to be sluttier than its wife.

They weren't disobeying their parents, who'd worked hard for what they had, they were disobeying the concept of giving a shit about anything at all. When I was with Mischa Barton, she cut the crap and bought a Girl Scout uniform. The behavior of hipsters in LA was childlike; they got tired like children and had temper tantrums, sobbing fits at the wheel of their cars. They sported wrist bandages and disappeared for vague hospital stays. Again, it was barely their fault; as responsible employees of the industry, Angelenos took drugs all day every day, much as Judy Garland had done, knocking back Ritalin, Adderall and Provigil—not because they were "concentration enhancers" (no use in the Golden Age of Stupid) but because they kept the weight off.

At night everyone took Ambien because it was marketed as a logical way to get to sleep, and no one was sleepy. Ambien fell out of favor when it was revealed that people were so perky they sometimes got out of bed and did things they didn't remember the next day. The New York press reported that people were taking Ambien, falling asleep and crashing cars. *That was a good night's sleep... Why's the car covered in teeth... ? No!* In LA, there was a different slant: people were taking Ambien, falling asleep and eating food. *That was a good night's sleep... Why's the bed covered in peanut butter... ? NoooOOO!* In short, we were a city fried.

The It Girls continued to hit the headlines, suffering tragically from confusion. Nicole pulled out the wrong way onto the freeway. Britney got married for less than three days, the annulment petition arguing that she "lacked understanding of her actions," while Paris explained her arrest for suspicion of DUI with "Maybe I was speeding a little bit... I was just really hungry and wanted an In-and-Out Burger." All of this was overseen not by their parents, but by their baffled, boggly-eyed pets.

Their parents had indeed worked hard for what they had. When Paris Hilton's ex Rick Salomon released *1 Night in Paris*, a DVD featuring his true love thrashing around in his groin like a rat going through the bins, Paris was the one who got the porno rep, a bad image that didn't help when she faced jail, while mum Kathy Hilton walked free into her own reality show. Lindsay Lohan got rehab and a drug rep, Dina Lohan got a reality show for the whole family. Britney got gurney straps and a paparazzo boyfriend; Lynne Spears got a book deal and *let her daughter out the house again.*

The Golden Age of Stupid exploded as a newsless phenomenon that the media found amazing news. My job: to pretend this nothing was something. Something great.

I was summoned to spend a day in the life of Nicole Richie for a women's magazine. The angle: *Look How Nice and Thin Nicole is Now.* The summer story was "Swimwear," gearing up for the winter story, "Stop Eating All That Food or You'll Never Get Into Your Swimwear." It had been raining all spring, and palm fronds and trash littered the road as though there'd been a riot. When it rains, this most uptight of cities collapses, gibbering, Chevrolets weaving across the freeway, stilt houses panicking and falling down the hills. That day, the city felt even more unhinged than usual. I drove along Hollywood Boulevard, past a man cycling with a parrot on his handlebars. A gold tramp in a gold suit jacket jitterbugged down the sidewalk. Oh, and there's Spiderman, strolling in his blue and red Lycra... *Christ...*

The sun was climbing and the non-airconditioned population was hot. So hot I was using a tea towel to hold the steering wheel. I wondered why actresses never had sweat patches, and remembered the insect-like surgeon I'd interviewed for *Marie Claire* who said that in the run-up to the Oscars he injected sixteen doses of Botox into actresses' armpits to paralyze their sweat glands. Probably with his proboscis. Today, thirty-two injections seemed like a fair trade. I knew I had no right to criticize any of this. I had no qualifications except A-Level art. *Maybe if I'd gone to a different school, maybe if I hadn't chosen physics, maybe if I'd done any revision at all instead of eating Kit-Kats in the Parliament Hill San Siro café for two years, then maybe I might not be on my way to the Tracey Ross boutique on Sunset Boulevard to write about how great it is to wear a bikini.*

Tracey Ross's boutique was hipper than hip, a place where a young starlet could lose pounds of ugly money by buying lime-green snakeskin passport covers, bracelets saying, "ASK FOR WISDOM," and brooches that looked for all the world to me like diamanté iron crosses. I picked up a bracelet made from old string.

"It's adorable," said the assistant quickly, a warning I should buy it.

"Doesn't look very hardwearing," I said even quicker, a warning I wouldn't.

"It's designed to break," she explained patiently, "so whoever finds it gets whatever you put into it. It's a pay-it-forward bracelet." My phone rang.

"OK, so this is going to be a long day," the magazine editor chirped.

You said it.

My interviewee stepped out of the changing room. After *The Simple Life*, Nicole went stellar, a subversive new personality. But that wasn't enough for Hollywood and Nicole had been taken under the wing of a Hollywood player—the stylist. Nicole looked amazing. At least that's what I wrote; I have no idea whether she did or not. She was freshly fatless and sprayed brown, so she looked healthy at least. By the following summer, when I interviewed her again—the angle: *Look How Far Too Thin Nicole is Now*—I wrote, "Nicole is not emaciated." Yes, and she was beautiful, but she'd been completely fatless for twelve months and a friend would have said, *Make her eat, you bastards, before she desiccates.*

I hoped Nicole didn't die. She was witty and disarmingly

friendly, with a nice smile, world-weary but still amused. Like Dolly Parton, Nicole was in on the airhead joke. Her excuse for arriving forty minutes late was, "Sorry, I crashed my car again." The adopted daughter of Lionel Richie, she tiptoed wide-eyed from one ludicrous LA scenario to another, a skinny princess in a magic kingdom.

"What was your most indulgent toy?" I asked.

"A bunch of Fabergé eggs," she said.

"Did your dad buy them for you?"

"No, I got them myself from Geary's," she said. Geary's, the Beverly Hills jeweller. "At the end of the year my dad got the bill and I've never had a charge account there since." I asked her how old she was then, expecting her to say sixteen.

"Eight," she said.

"How did you get there?"

"Drivers."

Yes, Nicole was great, but boy, did she have a cavalcade of cunts in her wake. Groomers, fixers and other random extras who'd all arrived that morning to be *there* for Nicole, arriving early enough to eat breakfast in the most visible seats of Hollywood's most visible breakfast joint.

Out of the dressing room came the woman who created size zero: stylist-to-the-stars Rachel Zoe herself, hovering over Nicole like a moth-eaten crow. Maybe crow is a little harsh; maybe boil-in-the-bag Brigitte Bardot getting done by a crow better describes Zoe. Either way, it didn't matter, because Zoe was heralded as a genius in Hollywood, a town where you're a genius for borrowing ideas from before 1990. Today she was styling Nicole Richie as a slut.

"OH MY GOD, EVERYBODY STOP WHAT YOU'RE DOING AND SEE HOW CUTE SHE LOOKS!" bellowed one of the cavalcade. The Crow had transformed the whip-smart Nicole into a child prostitute with a tattooist. Nicole pointed to a small pair of pointe shoes etched on her stomach.

"I got the ballet shoes when I was fourteen and I showed them to my dad," said Nicole, "and I told him I'd done it for him because of his song "Ballerina Girl.""

"What did he say?"

"Nothing." She looked at me with her huge "Who, me?" eyes. "Then he said, 'Please don't do me any more favors,' and burst into tears. When I was fourteen, I told him I was a lesbian. I make him cry all the time."

We wandered around the shop.

"How did you meet Rachel?" I asked Nicole, but before she could answer, Rachel swooped.

"I helped her choose an outfit for *Oprah* and we fell in love," Rachel said, staring me straight in the eye with no hint of humor. No one sees the funny side in Hollywood, unless they are lucratively contracted to do so by Paramount Pictures. "The clothes we chose got 'Look of the Week' in *US Weekly* magazine."

"How much does that cost? 'Look of the Week?'" I said. "What do you need to be in the running?"

"A Fendi or Marc Jacobs purse is fifteen hundred to three thousand dollars; shoes, Chloe or Stella, maybe five hundred to a thousand dollars; Oscar de la Renta cocktail dress... several thousand. The free samples don't fit Nicole; she's a straight size zero, twenty-four-inch waist," said Rachel. I hated her for being proud, I hated her because I could count Nicole's ribs, which would surprise you if you'd seen the huge plate of fried breakfast she'd eaten that morning. The cavalcade had all eaten huge breakfasts. I knew this, because they left me with the bill. Hollywood was notorious for "Celebrity Eating"—consuming a high-calorie meal in the presence of a journalist or paparazzo. I always played along, writing that the celebrity couldn't possibly have an eating disorder or drug problem, what with the big ol' plate of chow they just sucked up. I played along today because I liked Nicole and I reckoned that if I interviewed her every twelve months, she'd eat once a year.

"So Rolling Stones," exclaimed Zoe, pointing at Nicole's new outfit—clown pantaloons with a bikini.

"So Rolling Stones," deduced Zoe's assistant all by herself. I thought Zoe had made Nicole look like she'd tried to give Bill Wyman a blowjob. Wyman said no thanks. I wanted to run away. I had a part in this; I was complicit in her torture and demise. Right on cue I found a picture book about the Taliban, somehow stocked alongside all the Kabbalah literature. Nicole picked up the book, but Zoe snatched it away.

"No, Nicole! It might look political!" scolded Zoe, glaring at me for trying to damage her client. "Would you mind running to Coffee Bean? Nicole likes a black vanilla ice-blended. Anyone else? Get one for everyone. You don't need money, do you?" she said to an assistant, but aiming straight at me.

"So Rolling Stones," said Zoe's assistant.

"Black vanilla ice-blended, please," I said to the woman in the chrome-and-concrete Coffee Bean, ignoring Luke Wilson at the sugar stand because I fancied him after *The Royal Tenenbaums*.

"Dude... sorry... you're awesome," a man in wraparound shades said to Luke.

"Thanks, man," Luke said, blank-eyed, handing a girl who looked like Julie Christie a black coffee that she filled with saccharin. *Oh turds, now I don't fancy him; this keeps happening.*

We waited while they made Straight Size Zero Nicole her sugary drink. LA was hurting my logic boards and it wasn't even tea time. Trouble was, LA made the law, it was you that was crazy, and Coffee Bean on the crest of Sunset Plaza was not just another coffee house, it was the peak of LA's achievements, a sunbathed temple where you could worship the people you were supposed to aspire to. Right out front were three of the hottest girls in Los Angeles, and thereby the hottest girls in the world. Blonde, firm, smooth and long, they looked like Tara Reid in the days when partying still made her thin, and they all sat splayed in pastel Juicy Couture tracksuits, the high priestesses of Los Angeles. At their feet, they had pocket puppies, a strain of ultra-tiny Chihuahua that looked like a hamster being taken from behind; Chihuahuas had had to get thinner and stupider to keep up with the times. LA was infested with them; even Adrien Brody had a Chihuahua, and he'd done a movie about the Holocaust. I'd been trained to satirize stuff like this, but you couldn't satirize a creature stupid enough to strangle itself: the pocket puppies ran barking at each other, and as their leashes snapped tight, both dogs flipped up in the air with a yelp. You'd think they'd remember this happened the last time they picked a fight five minutes ago, but then you're not a Chihuahua.

The three girls were friends who'd come to suck iced coffee together. They all sat with their backs to each other, talking on their mobile phones to other people. *It's not them, it's me. They can do that if they like. Maybe they're retarded.*

"I am in such an angry place right now," said one of them. "Because she is coming into the workplace and using drugs in front of her coworkers. And that is totally selfish. I mean, I smoke pot at work, but she is just selfish."

"The blood tests are exhausting me. I am having a lot of blood work done and they're not finding anything wrong. I'm telling you, I'm going to find a new homeopath..." explained another. *Steady, Jane. Steady.*

"Black vanilla ice-blended for Jane?"

"Here! Thanks. Can I get a receipt? Brilliant, thanks, bye..." The assistant and I took the greasy cold coffees back to the cavalcade.

A GOOD CANDIDATE FOR A FACELIFT

The vibrant starving population of LA was just one conundrum in a bigger trend: *reality* was becoming optional. You don't like something the way it is? LA could cut it off and hush it up when things went wrong, unless you're Tara Reid and your fresh bad-surgery tit has flopped out on the red carpet. Fortunately she was too intoxicated by the giddy atmosphere of show business to notice. In the Golden Age of Stupid, LA's stupidest industry boomed and I covered it: plastic surgery became cooler than it had been since the 70s. You still saw its first wave around town, Farrah Fawcett noses, nipped in and painful-looking, on dowagers who creaked through Beverly Hills like brittle old Pekinese (a type of retro Chihuahua). I wondered if the dowagers sneezed like their dogs when they got a cold, spraying snot everywhere.

The cult nose of the day was the Mischa Barton—there were loads of them at Elton John's Oscar parties—but the real enemy of fabulousness wasn't a manly beak, it was adult thighs. The hot op was ultra-wet liposuction, which had gotten superfast, superpopular and supercheap. For a couple of grand, Hollywood girls went into surgery on Friday and were discharged the same day leaking a blood-streaked mixture of saline, Lidocaine and vasoconstrictor stress hormone onto their car seats. They leaked out of their puncture wounds for anything up to a couple of weeks, but mostly by Sunday morning they'd be out for brunch, putting it all back on. In LA, this was *normal*. My friend saw a woman in the changing room at Fred Segal (a "jean bar") ranting at the sales assistant that there was a red mark on the jeans she was trying on, before realizing it was her own lipo juice.

As a journalist, you get pumped with free stuff all the time. Mostly vanilla candles and mints. I was offered cut-price liposuction by Hollywood's top guy. He'd done the superstars of Hollywood and was getting ready to retire to a mansion spent, as lipo is a physically demanding op with lots of waggling and scraping out, especially if you have to waggle and scrape out every famous person in Hollywood every Friday afternoon. Standing in his treatment room, I thought, *Wow! I'll be all thin by Monday.* Then my friend heard the surgeon describing me as a "major operation." I was 125 lbs, and given my London drinking weight, I thought it wasn't that bad, like an idiot.

When I declined lipo, the surgeon didn't say much. He was stunned. I'd turned down a private sitting with the Canaletto of arse. "Well," he sighed eventually, "you'd be a good candidate for a facelift." I hoped it was an insult. It wasn't. At least now I knew why Hollywood people were so rude to me. I was a hideous freak.

SHE'S WAY MORE FAMOUS THAN HIM!
ASK HIM *WHY* SHE'S SHAGGING HIM!

Of course, it wasn't all bad. If every celebrity was Teri Hatcher, I could have stayed in my rut forever. Tiny Teri, one minute excited about *Desperate Housewives*, the next minute guilty that you could be doing something more productive than talking to her. Marilyn Manson, bounding through his Hollywood haunted castle, one minute showing off his collection of satanic knick-knacks, the next admitting he was so upset by the insanity of the Columbine witch hunt that he went into his attic and barely came down for two months. Dolly Parton, on stage for the audience in Tennessee a couple of days after her mum died, cracking jokes about "blocking the light" with her tits, then holding back tears as she sang about the coat of many colors that her momma really did make for her. These people were celebrities because they opened their hearts and let the audience in. As a journalist, you weren't just in their audience, you got to peek inside their world and see what made them brilliant.

And celebrity journalism used to be OK, seedy but affable, the pub's smelly old man buying you a drink. First the editor would call the journalist, and you'd have the following conversation:

"Fancy interviewing X on Tuesday?" says the editor.

"Why?" you say.

"X just made a film with Y; it's based on a really cool story. Did you read—"

"I can't, it's my mum's fiftieth," you say. "How much?" Result!

But then it started to change. There were clues I ignored.

"We've got Lucy Liu for the cover," said my editor. "Now, her parents were immigrants and she's got a really interesting story. We'd like you to do some investigating."

"Brilliant," I said. "Investigate what?"

"Get a good look at the scar on her breast and ask her if it was cancer." I was never going to ask that in a million years, but inevitably I found myself sitting opposite Lucy Liu. Nice, superpolite, up-for-work-at-3a.m., worked-in-a-warehouse-at-thirteen, fought-her-way-out-of-poverty Lucy Liu.

"It can be harder for a woman in this industry," said Lucy Liu. I, meanwhile, was staring at her tits. Celebrity culture had hit.

I think celebrity culture was started for a bet between some magazine editors who figured they could sell more copies if they printed more pictures with "Crikey! Why is he shagging this old scrubber?" as a caption. I think they justified it as tongue-in-cheek, ironic, post-modern. (NB: in TV and celebrity journalism there's no such thing as post-modern; it means dumb stuff made by clever people who feel guilty.) Soon celebrity journalism was seedy and postmodern, the pub's Paul Smith-wearing arsehole pretending he's bought you a drink, then pouring it on your feet.

Substitute the following conversation with the editor:

"Fancy interviewing X on Tuesday?" says the editor.

"Why?" you say.

"X just made a film with Y."

"Oh, that's based on a really cool story. Did you read—"

"Yeah. Ask him if he's really fucking her," says the editor. "In fact, fuck that, of course they're fucking fucking. But she's fifteen years older than him! Ask him why he's fucking her."

"The film—"

"Fuck the film. Just the fucking."

"I can't, it's my mum's fiftieth," you say. "How much?"

You always lied to your interviewee about why you wanted to talk to them. Interviews weren't just blind dates, they were dates where I turned up and talked about how it was, in fact, their friend I really fancied. The day that I was sent to interview Jared Leto, fiercely smart Jared had been told we gave a shit about Oliver Stone's *Alexander.* No one on God's green earth gave a shit about *Alexander,* but Jared did not deserve forty minutes of me repeatedly asking him whether or not he was shagging Scarlett Johansson. And that wasn't even what I was supposed to ask:

"She's way more famous than him! Ask him *why* she's shagging him!"

5

TUNNELS

I stuck it out because of Hollywood's manic drive. It was like a huge, unfriendly rave. With this much energy in one place, something would happen, it had to. It felt like a key moment in time, when the planets were aligning over the stylus on top of the giant LP stack that is the Capitol Records building, conducting the drive into everything.

There was notably less drive where I grew up in north London, a hinterland between Muswell Hill and Highgate. Muswell Hill had the sense of having been exciting once in some raw, punky British heyday, back when Suggs from Madness hung out there singing about his car and you could buy speed in a flat over the grocer's. Then property prices soared. Soon Muswell Hill sold nothing but croissants and baby clothes, while Suggs had gone to Camden. As for Highgate, no one lived there except Sting and teenage toffs on their way to Channing girls' school and Highgate boys' school, not bothering to look when they crossed the road because they were God's chosen people. Sting I'd never seen, unless he was a flasher with a scarf round his face in the mid-80s, in which case I saw quite a lot of him.

Our road disappeared into Queens Woods, an old plague pit where flashers would gather sociably to wait for schoolgirls in legwarmers taking a shortcut home. Any flashers left in the woods come 6.30 p.m. would see me stumbling back from judo in a brown duffle coat and Nana Mouskouri glasses and think, "Oh well, not exactly Claire Grogan, but I can't stand here with my knob out much longer: the mosquitoes are gathering. By the age of sixteen, between flashers and inedible prototype croissants, any drive I had left produced nothing but a collection of leaflets from pointless marches about cruise missiles and vivisection, and I was incapable of admitting I didn't really feel for antiwar protestors or white rats.

Here in California, every house oozed drive. The day of the Ashton/P. Diddy/donor-card-suicide nadir, I formed a plan. As I drove home through Bel Air, the afternoon sun gilded date palms and squat Mediterranean villas that looked like they could take some impact. But I kept driving. I'd lived in America long enough to know that you can change your life through sheer willpower. This was my escape plan: I'd dig a tunnel. *I will go home and write the greatest screenplay since* Peter's Friends.[2]

I let myself through a wooden gate on Fairfax Avenue into a lost pocket of Old Hollywood: a secret garden of lazy red hibiscus, purple bird-of-paradise flowers and banana palm leaves rustling in the warm air. This was home, a community of cottages built to house long-dead writers from Paramount Studios, we were told, cottages built deliberately munchkinsized so that resident writers were forced to write their way out or die on a fold-down Murphy wall bed. There was my tiny house. I'd found it in a classified ad: a twenties Spanish-style orange casita with a terracotta-tile roof. It was irresistible.

The little houses sat panting in the sun as their tenants typed. I wondered which script pages had been yanked out of typewriters in these small rooms, which producers had crashed out on the Murphy beds after eighteen-hour brainstorming sessions. Whether they'd woken up in the night, spinning from bourbon, and shuffled across the wooden floor through the writer's bedroom to use the bathroom. And whether, while peeing, they'd come up with the missing third act twist and decided to climb into bed with the writer to celebrate. This would make them gay, since most writers and producers are men, apart from Betty Comden, who got a writing credit on *Singin' in the Rain,* Frances Marion, who got an Oscar for writing *The Champ*, and Dorothy Parker, who got too drunk to write anything much. In fact, en suite bathrooms might explain why West Hollywood became the gay capital of the world. My neighbors included an angry gay designer with

---

2. This is a horrible movie.

a butterscotch-blond wedge and giant tawny muscles, who'd given up coke and left at five each morning to angrily pump iron with a closet gay cop. Then there was a gay session musician who slept with a gun, a gay bookseller and a straight wannabe-filmmaker guy who I sensed wouldn't last.

Today no typewriters clacked. Instead the muted tapping of Apple laptop keys came from the little arched windows. Hollywood, the industry town. In the street I'd left behind, Saltram Crescent, London W9, you'd see abandoned sideboards on the pavement. In Hollywood I once found a Macintosh G4 PowerBook. I booted up my computer. I had high hopes for this house, my seventh in two years. You tend to move a lot in Hollywood, as cities of dreamers attract a vast number of Bedlamites, most of whom rent property.

My first place was a guesthouse above the Sunset Strip that I rented from a boxy, middle-aged German woman called Helga. She had wild hair, a square black hole of a mouth where no teeth lived and clumps of brown slime on her chin. She claimed to have been abused by Gene Kelly's father, but didn't say in which hole. It took me six weeks to find out what the slime was. I moved out after I woke at 1 a.m. to find Helga climbing on my roof. As I left, I went into her house to claim the moral high ground with a few bons mots, but when I found her eating ice cream with her fingers, I felt this would be a hollow victory. And at last I knew what the slime was.

As the computer wittered to itself, I opened the fridge and drank a straight pint of cold coffee I'd saved from boot camp, where I'd been screamed at by a gay man for lacking the positive energy to really want to lose weight. He was a loveable gay man, and we all loved him, even more so when his own positive energy was later attributed to crystal meth. In fact, he got even more celebrity clients. Every time I got up at a ludicrous hour and did agonizing weighted squats when I could have been doing something constructive, I'd look up and see Mr. Big from *Sex and the City* on the treadmill beside me; the poor creature appeared to have no life at all.

I ripped open a new pack of paper, filled the printer and got typing. OK, so the Murphy bed was long gone. OK, so I was writing teenager-style under an IKEA platform desk/bunk that squeaked like a velociraptor with its nuts caught in a drawer. OK, so I was falling asleep because I'd been up since 6:14 a.m.— this was Hollywood, I'd overslept by two hours—but I was going to save the world with a movie.

In Hollywood, you begin with an idea that's easy to grasp. Mine would be *The English Patient* meets *Dr. Strangelove* meets *Casablanca* meets Monty Python's *Life of Brian*. A smash, and my tunnel out of here. I'd be Tim Robbins in *The Shawshank Redemption*, a model prisoner impassively buttfucked by the powerful, but behind the poster on my wall would be a dirty great hole I'd dug with a spoon. For a spoon I was using a copy of Hollywood's favorite scriptwriting manual, *Story* by Robert McKee. All young studio executives are made to attend McKee's seminars or be shot. McKee is the man Nicolas Cage's character tries to learn from in *Adaptation* before getting suicidal. McKee would make it simple.

McKee's simple advice was: "Protagonist seeks desire beyond reach. Consciously or unconsciously he chooses to take an action..." I decided I'd get the Ashton interview out of the way first.

At 4 a.m., I finished the Ashton piece, hit SEND and got back to my script, formatted a title page and fell asleep at my desk.

I woke to the phone ringing. The editor said the Ashton article was great, particularly the bit about charity basketball.

"I mean, who'd have known? That's a really sweet side to him..."

Aw, how did I fall asleep with my hair in my coffee?

"... So, we'll run Ashton as a cover, should be out in a few weeks..."

Call waiting. Another editor.

"... If you can do a face-to-face next Thursday, we've got someone else for you. It's really big; at this stage we couldn't say who..."

Good, because I couldn't give a crap. I can't believe I just sucked coffee out of my hair. Is that a piece of croissant... ? Yes, result. Mm.

Hang on, I never bought a croissant...

"... Oh, I can't keep it a secret. Jane, do you fancy a makeover?" the editor said. "Because we've got—wait for it—Rachel Zoe!"

Yes. Tell her to meet me outside Cedars Sinai. I'll drop my string bracelet, wait for her to pick it up, then back my car over her. Pay that forward. I stared at the title page of my script. It didn't even have a title. Tim Robbins would have been shagged to death at this rate.

6

I'VE GOT A SIX-FOOT RUBBER VAGINA
AND YOU'RE USING IT

I know successful people make a plan and follow through; I didn't plan any of this. I didn't start out in show business as one of those freakish little girls that interrupts her parents' dinner parties dressed in a tutu and lip gloss singing "The Sun Will Come Out Tomorrow," depressed because her dad doesn't fancy her. I had better aspirations: I wanted to be a physicist, but there was an obstacle. I was shit at physics. That's not a joke, it's a real tragedy, like a ballerina growing six foot tall; the older I got, the worse I became at physics. By the time I studied physics A-Level I could barely understand the questions. Not even the heroic quantities of beer mixed with cider and blackcurrant cordial I was consuming could clarify things. But then, as luck would have it, my mum went to get my A-Level results for me and fate took a turn.

I was eighteen, standing in a telephone booth near a tequila-slammer bar in Greece, braced for disaster, peroxided hair, holding a bottle of retsina; my mum was in my old school, William Ellis, reading the results on the wall. My results said, Main papers requiring hard work—mostly fails; much less important oral exams—mostly passes. With fierce maternal love, she read them back to front.

"You've passed!" she told me proudly, and I went back into the Greek tequila-slammer bar for a brief celebration lasting several weeks. I didn't know it at the time, but I'd only succeeded in art and French oral, and I was qualified for nothing but doing pencil drawings of Boy George for tourists outside the Louvre. This was the luckiest break of my life, because on returning home and learning the truth, it was too late to retake the exams and get sensible. Even better, I could blame my mother, who'd done nothing but make me crumpets in the hope that I'd revise one day.

Instead, by a bloody miracle, I met the man who created Alf Garnett (Archie Bunker in his US incarnation), Johnny Speight. He was a patient man who drove a Rolls Royce with the plate "MOO" after Alf Garnett's catchphrase, "You silly moo," which I thought beyond cool. He taught me sitcom writing and I fell for sitcom the way women are supposed to fall for kids. There's probably some IVF/genetically-transmitted-disease/ugly-baby pun here, but I'm tired, for reasons that will become clear. I liked sitcom; good sitcom makes people happy. It says life is OK. Until I started in comedy, the only thing I'd done to make people happy was lose an E at a rave. Again, that's not a joke, although like a joke it comes from pain—it was the greatest E of all time: homemade, a dirty capsule the size of a wood bee, a twenty-first birthday present someone had Sellotaped to a card, which I gave to a bisexual born-again Christian drug dealer friend to look after. She replaced it with a capsule half the size claiming she couldn't tell the difference, but that's bisexual born-again Christian drug dealers for you.

Then, by a second bloody miracle, BBC Radio One was piloting a show set in a nightclub, the only place I'd put any hours in, and I wrote some sketches based on conversations I'd overheard in clubs. I got a job writing spontaneous off-the-cuff quips for DJs. Then Carlton TV approached me because they were looking for young black writers. I got the job. Seven years on the fringes of comedy later, I was an inconsequential writer in development hell, and not exactly cuddling the mainstream by co-writing sitcoms called *The Junkies* and *Put Out More Fags*. However, British comedy in the nineties was fantastic fun; you could rip the shit out of everything, with props. The props were the best part, because they were so goofy, but always said it best. My favorite memory is going through the BBC's legendary props cupboard looking for stupider and stupider sound effects for a short-lived radio show I did with David Quantick, *Bussmann & Quantick Kingsize*. This was the department of the BBC that had provided the props for vintage comedies like the *Goon Show*;

Peter Sellers' jokes had been brought to life by the contents of this room. It felt incredible to watch the Props Girl pick out ancient tiny doors of different sizes that she would slam on stage, their different sounds conjuring anything from castle fortresses to ships' cabins. Then we'd go to the Radio Theatre deep inside the iconic Art Deco Broadcasting House, where the producer would play us the sound effects we'd written into the script. I remember most vividly his shortlist of loud bird farts for a sketch called *Catalogue of the Extinct.*

Somehow I ended up in various rooms where *Veep* creator Armando Iannucci filled an inflatable castle with children in different colored outfits representing different political parties, legendary satirist Chris Morris devised a drug the size of a flan for *Brass Eye*, possibly the best British comedy in history and certainly the most complained about and Graham Norton, the UK's Letterman, persuaded Grace Jones to sing "La Vie en Rose" up the butt of a teddy bear. The BBC's Light Entertainment chief put me on probation for playing a Victorian child sex pest on respectable Radio Four; *Bridget Jones' Diary*'s Sally Phillips stripped down to some gaffer tape and respectable children's TV presenters got heroically messed up on cheap red wine, losing their shoes as they ran giggling between green rooms.

But gradually entertainment was changing. Reality TV struck like a swarm of locusts and the props were the first things destroyed.

One day a posh young producer burst into the writers' room. We were trying to think of something funny to say about Diana's funeral, and failing.

"I've got a really expensive prop downstairs from the reality doc. I'm not throwing it out; write it into the sketch!" he said.

"What's the prop?" I said, optimistic.

"A six-foot rubber vagina," he said, impatient. He was paying us money.

"It's... it's not really... I mean, she's dead..."

"I don't give a fuck! I've got a six-foot rubber vagina and you're using it!" Now any giant twat could get a job in television.

A few months later, another writers' room, this time on one of the first reality shows. "Yeah, it's pretty straightforward, just some jokes, really," said the posh young reality producer.

"Jokes about what?" I said, the first of many unsuspecting TV writers to ask this question to a posh young reality producer.

"It's set in a couples resort... like Sandals... These people are so rough you'll have more jokes than you know what to do with... Let me show you a clip... I mean, look at her stomach, doesn't she know?"

Yes, but she doesn't care, and why should she? She's on her holiday, which she saved up for, you horrible piece of private school poo was not the right answer. Well, that was it. End of an era. TV had become a nasty boss with no mates, and everyone working for it felt dejected, apart from the people who loved coining vast sums from DIY shows. What was I going to do?

I walked back home to Saltram Crescent, W9, also in a hinterland between Kilburn and Maida Vale that smelled of scrambled egg on toast from the Chinese takeaway. This hinterland was known for nothing, just businesses called Davetronics and Vanity Clare and old black guys who sat in their front gardens playing ska to no one. Saltram Crescent was *great*. As my window boxes loomed, I sensed I couldn't call owning some geraniums that weren't dead a personal life, but I didn't care. I knew exactly what I was going to do. I had to knuckle down and write a new comedy that changed the world, about something, something that mattered. About... *Wow, those geraniums are really nice and red. What's that in the letterbox ?*

The estate agent's brochure in the letterbox was telling me that my own reality had shifted. I no longer lived in a hinterland; the Government of Estate Agents had renamed it Queen's Park, or possibly even Maida Vale borders, a desirable neighborhood suited to Upwardly Mobile Young Couples hoping to raise families and take advantage of the Many New Businesses about to open, such as yoga studios. Now I knew exactly what I had to do. I had to sell my flat and get the hell out of there.

I came up with an escape plan incorporating all of the above, and it was foolproof: all I had to do was get a job writing the next great comedy—in Hollywood. A Piece of Cake. A Simple Plan. A Midnight Run. I didn't know a single person there apart from Jackie Brambles, but it didn't seem important. So I took on a load of journalism, did up my flat, put it on the market and boarded a plane with nothing but Jackie Brambles's phone number. I never liked geraniums anyway; they smell of arse.

7

A NICE WARM BATH

LA was so full of energy I drove round for days, staring at streets with names like Wonderland Avenue and Bob Hope Drive. The sun made everything spectacular, and it was spectacular to start with. A three-story Homer Simpson mural, Luke Skywalker, Julie Andrews spinning on a mountain in *The Sound of Music*—that must be 20th Century Fox! Everyone in LA beamed at me. LA people were so damn friendly that just walking to buy a newspaper felt like a warm bath.

"How much do I tip?" I asked the waiter.

"We prefer to call it, 'love,'" he said. "Fifteen to twenty percent."

I joined a gym. This was not the Archway Road bodybuilders' basement. Crunch had actresses I recognized reading scripts on treadmills, goddess classes (no, me neither) and an oxygen deprivation booth for people who thought breathing normal air was too easy. I dipped fat-free chips in fat-free sour-cream dip. I could eat what I ate in London and lose weight. This was unbelievable.

Even people in television were nice to me. Everybody I called wanted to meet as soon as possible in case I happened to be the Next Big Thing. In Hollywood, entertainment is an industry. They are professionals making hours of TV, not sitting around flicking through property sections and making clever-clever remarks about the genitals of Celine Dion and people less posh than them who never did any harm to anyone. I know, I've worked in British television. In LA, they work like stink. A 48-hour shift is nothing in LA. Productions hire mobile espresso bars that rock up at 10 p.m. to keep the demented energy going with caramel syrup. It's 2 a.m.? So what? We've got to have it ready for the network in New York at 6 a.m. In British television, working late meant you hadn't left the office yet because your secretary had tasks outstanding ("Jerry, I'm sorry, it's just too bloody early, I'm not getting your coke till 6 p.m." That's a production assistant I knew, London, 1998).

I thought I'd probably better get an agent. The first Hollywood agent was a manic bald man who boinged in his chair.

"What do you think is good money?" he said. *Wow... maybe like, 750?*

"Maybe a thousand a week," I said.

"A thousand? What are you, British? I have people making fourteen thousand dollars a week. A thousand. Bupkiss. You know bupkiss? It means poopah. Now don't call anyone else..."

The second agency was like a branch of the Pentagon. There was a reception security guard to walk me twenty feet to the elevator and an elevator security guard to watch me in it, in case I'd spent the last decade creating a fake identity as a foreign comedy writer in order to assassinate one of their clients. And if I'd succeeded, believe me, those clients would have got more column inches than Benazir Bhutto. The second agent watched twenty seconds of my showreel.

"What is this, animation?"

"No, it's a sketch about—"

"Don't talk to any other agents. Who else are you meeting?"

I told him.

"Do you *hate* yourself? His list is hacky. Hacky, hacky, hacky. Are you a hack? Who else?"

I told him.

"What are you, Tina Turner? Because that man is Ike. Ike Turner. I am not going to tell you what his reputation is like in this town," he said. "His reputation is horrible in this town. Who else?"

I told him.

"He's got cancer. Who else?"

At this point an elderly black man in an apron got up from under the desk: during our conversation, he'd been polishing the agent's shoes while they were on his feet. He'd probably been down there since the Depression.

The third agency had been described to me as a "small boutique agency"; it was a monolith occupying a whole corner of Beverly Hills. These agents ran Hollywood, they had the use of private Gulfstream jets, their assistants wore headsets and knew my name and CV, in case the Next Big Thing was British girls in Topshop dresses who wrote sitcoms about heroin.

It was dress-down Friday, which meant the agent facing me wore brown Hush Puppies like weapons. He watched eight seconds of my showreel.

"What is this? A documentary?"

"Er... no, it's a sketch about—"

"Don't talk to any other agents." By now I realized this was more for the other agents' protection than headhunting me, but I didn't care. "You have Adam Sandler in your country? I'm sending this to Adam Sandler." This was too silly for words. But still not bad for a Friday.

On the way home I stopped at the last agency, an old-world office in the stable university quarter of Westwood, with an older, reassuring agent who watched the tape while chuckling quietly. I quickly signed with him and went home to write, or rather sit in a hammock with a strange American beer, watching hummingbirds in the sunset. This town was so warm, so fat-free, so full of hardworking people all being so nice to me.

I became a classic LA newbie, off my head on spin classes at dawn, losing ten pounds, planning which hilltop house with a retracting roof and indoor/outdoor swimming pool I'd buy, then going for a bizarre facial. (One celebrity spa actually has a Cradler, a mum-like woman who cradles you in her arms as she walks you to the treatment room—don't touch me!) I'd escaped to the Magic Kingdom, and once I'd finished the script, my reassuring agent would take me into the castle keep to meet the king and queen. Then something jumped up and bit me on the arse.

8

A LONG COLD SHOWER

Getting a job in British TV works like this: you ring the show's producer; they say, "Send in something you've written"; if they like it, you go in. Blundering along in this manner, I'd written bits for around fifty shows, from *Loose Ends* to *The Fast Show*, and hung around green rooms all over Television Center, eating bad sandwiches with Britain's comedians after they'd performed better versions of jokes I'd written. You can get an agent if you like, and I did eventually, but if you can convince a BBC producer that your sample script won't be covered in loose hair and anthrax, they'll take a look at it. Now, however, I was in America, and in American TV, your *agent* sends your sample script to the show's producers. Not a problem; I'd hired an agent and he had a real track record. But—and here comes the life-changing, stupid mistake—I had also hired a contractor to refurbish my place, and he didn't. He was a cowboy who had shown me fake references. After I let his guys stay in my house while I was away, he did $70,000 worth of damage.

Suffice it to say I did not spend the summer taking meetings with 20th Century Fox. I spent it lying spread-eagled in west London staring at the rubble of my flat, ice-cream in one hand, plastic spoon in the other, plastic bladder from the inside of a wine box on my chest, plastic tap in my gob. When I finally returned to LA, thirty pounds heavier and seventy grand lighter, I called the reassuring agent. He'd decided to close his business, which meant I had no agent. Now none of the other agents would take my call. In fact, the assistants who'd learned my name wouldn't take my call. The unthinkable had happened. I was an "unrepresented"—inside the Magic Kingdom, but outside the keep, and no one would send my scripts over the wall.

"Send them yourself!" you say sensibly. But Los Angeles is not a sensible city. Producers literally won't open an envelope containing the dreaded "unsolicited submission" from an "unrepresented" in case you turn out to be a crazy person who sues them for stealing your idea for an episode of *Will & Grace* in which a couch is mistaken for Barbra Streisand and wakes up with Tom Jones's willy caught in its springs. Represented scripts are hand-delivered with watermarks for legal protection. Everyone else? Return to sender.

I told myself I'd be fine. I'd still do journalism for the people I'd worked for in Britain, and I did get to interview Brits occasionally. It was reassuring to hear Ozzy Osbourne describing his British home life.

"How do you discipline your kids, Oz?" I asked.

"It's not easy when they've come home to find you over an ice bucket with a bottle of bubbly up your arse," he reflected.

In Britain we have three release valves—booze, blasphemy and bad taste jokes—and LA doesn't approve of any of them. The warm bath of Hollywood was really a pressure cooker. I didn't like cops with guns pulling up behind me, demanding to see ID and asking why I was walking. I didn't like executives in BMWs nearly running me over and then shouting at me for messing up their email. I didn't like the man I accidentally cut in front of in traffic driving alongside me for five minutes screaming before he threw a rock at me. His therapist had taught him self-knowledge: always carry a bag of rocks.

Eventually I had to admit it: Hollywood is the worst place in the world. It's boiling hot and full of cunts. By astral design, I had stranded myself in Stupid Town at the dawn of the Golden Age of Stupid. There was only one job I could do and it gave me stomach ache. Then one day, annihilating everything in fat-free chips, I looked at the label. They came with a warning on the packet: "MAY CAUSE ABDOMINAL CRAMPING AND LOOSE STOOLS." I hadn't read the small print. I was the stupidest of them all.

9

I COULDN'T BE WITH A GAY MAN

Now look, you say. There is a well-trodden escape route from a rubbish life. You must meet famous men all the time! Yes, and celebrities don't date civilians, thank God; everyone's famosexual in Hollywood. But come on, you say, LA is the land of the beautiful people, people who star in, direct and produce romantic comedies. Couldn't you go out and get pissed, meet some random bloke and everything would be okay forever, as Kate Hudson and Matthew McConaughey have demonstrated time and time again on the silver screen? Firstly, it's true that LA is 70 percent flawless beauty. But if you've ever dated anyone extremely beautiful, you'll know what a pain in the ass they are, forever having crying fits because it *just isn't enough*. Or worse, it's *plenty* enough and they have no sense of humor. Secondly, Americans are very, very different from the British: the United States was formed by a colony of Puritans who left Europe because Puritan Europe wasn't Puritan enough for them. Americans like to get things done, have productive lives. They don't revel in incompetence of any kind and therefore don't differentiate "being drunk" from "being a drunk"—and I insist there is a difference—so what we call waking up triumphantly hungover with no bloody clue how you got home, cause for a bacon sandwich, they call "blacking out" and cause for an intervention. Thirdly, people in LA are just weird. Humans that end up in Hollywood believe they should be entertaining their fellow man and are therefore likely to be suffering from high-functioning mental illness, able to perform simple tasks like being CEO of NBS Television Studios, but unable to hold down a personal relationship. I'm not high-functioning enough for either, but at least I drink.

British men are self-effacing and charming. Take this young gentleman and his wing man, opposite me on the Silverlink train from Kilburn to Euston at about two in the afternoon.

"Go on, talk to 'er."

"I can't talk to 'er. Whamagunna say?"

"I dunno! Jus' talk to 'er, guy!"

Pause. Second bloke offers me some tinfoil with a sunny smile.

"Scuse me, love. Do you wanna smoke some heroin?"

"Oh! She's not gonna go out with you now, you *wanker*!"

Compare their Hollywood equivalent. Men don't bother with pick-up lines in LA, they have exit lines. There was the Actor, stopping to gaze at a very gay neighbor climbing out of a very gay truck.

"I couldn't be with a gay man," he sighed. "I'm too big, I'd hurt him." A heavy pause. "I think about this a lot."

Or the Director, an angry young man from a brutalized country—born and raised in Canada, but that wasn't the point—his people had been raped because of... the issues, man. As he left, after directing himself in a dramatic performance so bad he stroked his *own* hair, he turned to me.

"We're incompatible. I like to fuck like an animal," he said, pointing at me and adding sternly, "Remember, I did that for you. Don't ask me to do that again."

Or the Agent. We got on brilliantly. We had such a good time and he was so fantastically not full of shit. One evening, I seem to recall he had no clothes on when a terrible thought crossed his mind: "You do *know* I'm happily married?" he said. Outside, the pressure to run was building. Life in Hollywood didn't feel like a romantic comedy, it felt like a zombie movie in which no one believes you when you say civilization is about to be destroyed. We were spiralling towards war, and the strange thing was that Armageddon seemed to be masterminded by Britney and Nicole's publicists.

I could have learned a lot from George W. Bush. He'd cottoned on to something only the publicists used to know about— Reverse Logic. Never waste time in defense of your actions, when you can use the new and all-purpose offence: You're the One That's Mad.

Bear in mind that I was no better. I was making a breakfast smoothie when my mum called me from London to ask what Americans thought about Guantanamo.

I told her there was no such place, *don't you think we'd have heard if there was a jail on an island; that's the silliest thing I've ever heard*, while packing a blender with chocolate-flavored eggwhite powder and seaweed.

"Mum, a *jail* on an *island*? Where did you see this?"

"It's just been on TV—"

"Fuck's sake, Mum, that's *Survivor.*"

By the time it all went tits-up, we were none the wiser. I watched as the bodies of four American Blackwater employees were set alight and dragged through the streets of Fallujah. The news reporter called them contractors, never mentioning that they'd been contracted as mercenaries; "contractors" usually means builders out here in Britain. I genuinely thought Blackwater was a firm of painter-decorators. *That's rotten. You go out there to rebuild some schools and someone does that to you. Maybe they painted over the light switches. Remind me never to get Blackwater to decorate my house.*

10

WE'VE GOT TO HAVE A TOP TEN WITH FEWER NUMBERS IN IT

LA had bigger problems.

"Our clients have been violated," said Papilloma[3] the publicist.

"Violated?"

"It means grossly abused. We gave you exclusive access to Danny and Chris and this is how you behave." Danny and Chris Masterson from *That '70s Show* and *Malcolm in the Middle*, talented actor brothers that I'd managed to sneak into the UK's venerable style magazine *The Face*, despite them being unheard of in the UK, and Scientologists to boot.

"Sorry, I'm not sure what—" I said.

Papilloma sighed histrionically. 'We know we're talking about the piece in *The Face*."

"The top-ten list?"

"You didn't say there would be other people in it."

"But .. it's a top-ten list..."

"We know how you operate now." She slammed the phone down and then called back. "Jane. I'm going to be the bigger person here and put this behind me, but we want you to know that we know."

LA was stepping up the ante. Cracks were starting to show in the It Kids' carefree infantilism-more tantrums, more narrow escapes—and the publicists were getting tougher. Not on the kids, but on anyone who pointed it out.

It was war and humanity was losing. I was scared to fall asleep in case I woke with slimy fibres crawling up my body and Britney's head growing on my arse.

---

3. Not her real name.

"We're thinking of going with Geri Halliwell and her breast cancer fears," said the editor on speakerphone.

"She's got breast cancer?"

"No, she just fears it ..."

I scanned the traffic around me for anyone who looked remotely sane and settled on a girl waiting to cross the road. A nice sane size 10. Then she turned round and I saw them, the lipo puncture wounds. They'd got her too. *They could be gnat bites. Like fuck, this is LA. She was probably a size 16 last Friday.*

To up the ante, publicists devised a new weapon more effective than physically standing between you and their clients: ignoring. People would call me up to ignore me. One day, my phone rang and all I could hear was typing. I'm being stalked by a novelist. Thirty seconds later—a full thirty seconds later, and I was counting because it was hilarious—"Jane, this is Campylobacter.[4] You called about Samantha . . ." I did. Several weeks ago.

"Do you still have something you wanted to ask?"

Yes. Does Samantha, who perhaps pays you to do her press, know that you take weeks to reply to a phone call? And where do you get off, phoning someone to type at them? I wouldn't mind if you worked for the Red Cross, and you were typing an inventory of amputation saws after the tsunami (you know the surgeons ran out of saws? How do you break that news? 'You want the bad news or the really bad news?'). No, Campylobacter, I wouldn't mind you typing as you talked if you worked for the Red Cross, but you're a publicist, therefore it's odds-on you're looking for Paris Hilton's piss flaps on Defamer.

LA was getting tougher and I was the rude one. With no way out, I was going to crack up if I didn't find a way to handle confinement. In the end, the solution came from the celebrities themselves.

---

4. Not his real name.

11

TAKE IT ALL, BITCH!

Notice in this paparazzo shot of me and Mischa Barton, I'm the one trying not to be recognized.

I learned from the stars that you don't have to play the game.

"Got any favorite places in LA?" I said.

"I don't like to have opinions," Mischa said, "because I'm young and you never know how it comes across."

"You're absolutely right. So have you seen any good movies lately?"

"I don't watch... *movies*," she said, and sighed. How could I have asked? "I prefer the classics."

"*Absolutely*. Such as...?"

"*The Children's Hour* with Katharine Hepburn... All Katharine

Hepburn's work."

I wasn't about to tell her it was an Audrey Hepburn film; that would have made me the rude one, and I was learning from this mistress. I knew how I was going to handle LA: I was going to behave far, far worse than the people around me.

There was a thrill to being the most terrible employee of all time. Lying, cheating, stealing, raiding minibars, daring them to expel me, I lived by one rule: write nice things. Of course I never read the articles; that would have been like a German in the bathroom, where toilets are built with a shelf for studying your own poo. The ruder the people, the more I would steal. By the time a camel toed publicist loomed and I was sent in to fawn over an actor, my bag would be clanking with hotel forks. I don't even like hotel forks: I stole purely to identify myself as a good person.

When covering fancy parties, publicists would glare if you slowed down near the freebies: "Don't touch the goody bags, they're for the talent." I'd eviscerate the goody bags when no one was looking, leaving a load of old candles for the celebrities. The breast cancer T-shirts I'd give to homeless people. Oh, *talent*. I thought you said Mad Old Woman Living Outside the Gay Church Who Looks Like Nick Nolte.

When I started out in Hollywood, I'd meet the star and order a Diet Coke like them to look friendly. Now I drank margaritas as fast as it's possible to drink without belching and sometimes faster, nodding and agreeing that it is indeed cheaper to co-lease a private Gulfstream jet than fly your entourage First Class. Tequila rocks; if I closed my eyes I could imagine I was working in a Mexican whorehouse instead.

In the early days, when the telltale red light on my tape recorder flashed LOW BATTERY, I'd get flustered and swap the AAs. In the interim years, I'd put a napkin over the recorder. By the Golden Age of Stupid, I'd just stare at the celebrity, daring them to say it.

"I think your tape recorder has... died?" said the celebrity.

"That's just for back-up, I'm recording it on my computer, it's got AudioMix Pro." *There's no such program as AudioMix Pro, you horrible, beautiful moron, I just COULDN'T GIVE A SHIT ABOUT CHIHUAHUAS.*

I noticed that after waking up in a good mood, looking at my calendar and seeing my jobs for the day would make me fed up. So I stopped looking at my calendar. One day I was happily Googling genocide when my phone rang.

"Jane, this is Arooni.[5] I work in Rinky's[6] office."

"Really? Terrific!" I may have been drinking.

"Thank yowwww. I have Chad Michael Murray[7] for you."

"Great!" I had no idea who any of these people were. Chad, Rinky, any of them.

"Are you ready to do the interview now?"

"Sure! Put him on." An interview? I looked in my emails; there was one from a magazine about two years ago—could I interview Chad Michael Murray? Apparently I said yes. As they transferred me to Chad on the set of his movie, I was Googling "Chad" and got a gay travel site.

"Chad. Thanks so much for doing this," I said, desperately scanning the screen. *The Chaps Inn. The greatest clothingoptional Premier Resort for Leathermen and Bears in Palm Springs...* "You wouldn't believe how much we love you in England." *Play in the outdoor sling...* ? "So, it's amazing what you've been up to. How do you think it all happened?

Chad started up, "I've been so lucky..." *No, I want clues, you self-effacing bastard. Give me some names to work with.* It got worse: the briefest Google revealed the young actor was a really nice bloke who'd overcome terrible hardships I knew nothing about. To this day I have no bloody idea who Chad Michael Murray is. I think I wrote something about *The OC*.

The trouble was, there was nothing I could do to get in trouble. In a world where you produced journalism of such

---

5. Not her real name.

6. Not her real name.

7. His real name.

quality as "Who could believe Teri Hatcher is so nice?"[8] and they printed it, no one was listening anyway. Once, I was given an interview that all the magazines were after. Historic, era-defining, a cultural landmark. But as I said, "Thank you, that was brilliant," to the new bloke off *Desperate Housewives*, and stood alone outside his house at the top of Beachwood Canyon, I felt... I can't accurately describe the feeling, but I hoped it might go away if I jogged home. However, Beachwood Canyon was dark, it was raining and as I jogged, I slipped. My iPod skidded along the gravel. I'd been using this iPod as a digital recorder, and the interview of the year? Gone. Could I remember what he said? Of course not, I wasn't listening. I couldn't recall a single word: not who he was dating, what film he was doing next, whether he was the product of an anal birth, zip. Did I go back and interview him again? Of course not, I wasn't mental. Instead I went home and made the whole thing up. Nobody noticed. Not the magazine and certainly not the actor.

Because the first sentence I wrote was, "(Bloke off *Desperate Housewives*) is twenty-six but looks younger. Up close he has very twinkly eyes, gleaming white teeth and is well-built... something of a rock god... quietly macho." It was lauded as one of the most accurate pieces ever written about him.

I just couldn't get into trouble. Worse, I got a reputation for being able to turn a sow's ear into a silk purse. "If anyone can handle her, you can..." was all I heard. When Anna Nicole Smith was only able to speak two words in four hours, one of them being "ugh," we got a fourteen-page feature out of it. One night, when I was up late writing a piece for a serious newspaper, I nodded off and woke up to find I'd finished it. Since I don't own any elves, I must have written it in my sleep. I didn't bother reading it in case it was all a wonderful dream and hit SEND. They published it. *Dawson's Creek*. It was *Dawson's Creek*, not *The OC*.

---

8. She is, but that's *not the point.*

I devised a way to have even less to do with my job. Feeling nauseous one morning while trying to find another way to write "X is so refreshingly *likeable*," I stopped and calculated the perfect celebrity interview: the surprise at meeting them, how they were so much more human than their image, yet radiated true star quality, how their recent emotional upheaval had made them just like you and me, but they'd come through it wiser, happier and in better shape than ever before, thanks to the love of their family/ dog/fans, and how, now it was over, they've been experimenting with something a bit naughty on weekends. I then used this "interview" over and over again for different celebrities. The quotes changed, but the hyperbole was basically the same.

Every few weeks, I sandblasted the jerry-built piece of bastard with a thesaurus, but soon even this was too much work, and worse, implied I had something to do with the end product. I found a way to clock on, go back home and still get paid some of my wages: I started flagrantly not writing the articles at all, instead handing over the tapes to a series of very, very young writers claiming to be me. They were so young they had hopes.

"Jane, I can't work today: I got through to the last round of new-talent night at the Comedy Store and these agents are coming..."

"*What? No!* You don't want to do that! You're an intellectual! Please write eight hundred words on how "X" categorically doesn't have a drug problem," I'd plead, "and they sometimes syndicate to the *Mail*, so don't use the bit about 'Up Her Gary.' Gary Glitter. It's rhyming slang for shitter. Just don't write it..." In fact, my apprentices were American and far too nice to write smut, so I still had to add a greasy sheen of innuendo about the star's sex life, even though the star had made no comment, but other than that I had bugger all to do with my job now, which meant I could concentrate on the screenplay. It was now the most bittersweet romantic comedy ever written and I was ready to start. Heavy study of McKee had explained how to do it: a story is in essence "there is a hero and he has a problem." But every time I tried to write, the phone would ring.

"This is for the summer body issue, so we're only using diet quotes," said the editor. "The peg is 'My Weight Struggle.'"

"Has anyone told her?"

"No. Actually her publicist says she specifically isn't going to talk about the weight thing. We told them that the peg is the TV series coming out in the UK. We had to, you know what her publicist's like..."

"Oh, I know..." I'd drawn a picture of a giant rat in a tuxedo and the editor was still talking.

"... So, she's probably going to want to talk about the reality show, but if you could just steer her on to how amazing she looks, is she enjoying wearing anything she likes on the show now that she's not so big..." *Imagine this is not your job and you are somewhere better. I'm at a rat's funeral. The rat has been shot by a mugger and I'm its brave rat girlfriend and all the rats are being nice to me...*

"Actually, ask her how sexy she feels. Someone at *Elle* reckons she's pregnant..." *They're playing the rat's favorite song, "I Will Always Love You" by Whitney Houston. Everyone's crying. God, his poor rat mum. Perhaps I'll cop off with his rat brother after the service...* I was now humming Whitney Houston down the phone in a grieving rat voice and no one at the magazine had noticed. *BitterSWEEEEEEEET... Memoriiiiiiiies... Look on the bright side: they could have asked to you to write "Kate Winslet Sheds Her Baby Weight" instead when she was never even bloody fat.*

"Kate, about the movie—how did you get in shape for the role of Iris Murdoch?"

In between bollocking the children I paid in toffee to write my celebrity interviews for me, I came up with a tear-jerking second act to my screenplay, the greatest sci-fi epic ever, and almost wrote it down. Meanwhile, the journalism work continued apace, despite my incompetence and aura of death. Nothing I could do was too awful for this awful kingdom; I was cruising for a bruising, but it wouldn't come. However, I didn't expect what did happen.

12

WE REALLY LOVE IT, BUT …

The Ashton story came out in *The Face* and everyone was happy. So happy that the London *Evening Standard* called. Ashton had started dating someone even more famous than himself. It transpired that after he'd left our interview to host *Saturday Night Live* in New York, he'd met his future wife, Demi Moore. Demi was hot news again and the rumors were deafening: $400,000 worth of plastic surgery said one rumor, on the grounds that Demi had nice legs and a man fancied her. It was pointed out that there was no plastic surgery that could cost $400,000. Well, it's obvious, said the rumor, spitting frappuccino, that Demi must have had an experimental operation no one has ever heard of which involves severing the flesh of one's legs at the groin and pulling it up like a pair of tights. Obviously. This was massive news and the *Evening Standard* wanted me to update the Ashton interview so they could re-run it.

"We really love it," said the *Evening Standard*, which always precedes a But. "But... he didn't mention Demi?"

"He wasn't going out with her when I interviewed him." "Yes, but the readers don't know that. Can you maybe go back and get some quotes?"

"Sure." *Sure I'll have lunch with him again: we never made it to the New Testament.* Things were so hot that Ashton could have got a million bucks off a proper news outlet to open his heart about Demi, let alone a kebab off a British daily, but he didn't, which meant they were in love. There was no bloody way I was calling him. But when I looked in the papers, all the "source" quotes about the couple's feelings for each other, which I'd intended to steal, were obviously fabricated. Takes one to know one. In the end I fudged the original piece into non-litigious waffle, like "Demi would be mad not to date him," and such exclusives as where Ashton and Demi went on holiday. The *Standard* were understandably not delighted and called back to ask if I was sure Ashton hadn't said anything about dating Demi, what with her being hideously old at forty and all. I said I was still sure, because they still hadn't been dating back then.

"Oh... It's... Oh... What do you think he thinks about dating Demi?"

"What do I think he thinks? I think he thinks it's great."

I'd had a million of these conversations by now. I fled to the frozen yogurt parlor to stuff my face with cold whey before my English teacher's face started hovering in my mind's eye.

It took several trips to the yogurt parlor to get rid of the apparition, and once there I was served by a teenager who'd gone to all the trouble of becoming a transvestite only to end up looking like Sarah Palin winking. I geared up to ask her for a medium, but I couldn't spit the word out, because I knew what the transvestite would say.

"Baby, mama or papa?" said the transvestite.

"Medium," I said.

"Mama?" said the transvestite.

"Medium," I said. I wasn't backing down. If America brought back the word "large," obesity would end overnight. I paid the tranny for a fat swirl of Carbolite—yogurt sweetened with Maltitol (causes crippling farts, but no sugar)—and, calm at last, I sat staring blankly down Santa Monica Boulevard. Thanks to frozen yogurt, I'd reached a kind of peace with my place in the world.

Endless Santa Monica Boulevard wasn't Old Hollywood, it was Hollywood 2050. The architecture was perfect, the people polite with great muscle tone, the dogs, lawns and fingernails had no poo on them and there was a recreational area named after a queer-bashing. Santa Monica Boulevard was, of course, as gay as a French trombone. Strolling through the hate-crime-themed Matthew Shepard Human Rights Triangle Park, it made me wonder if all civic duties should be handed over to gay men. There was even an open dogging spot called Vaseline Alley, so depravities were confined to a pre-ordained, suitably zoned shag pit.

A police car cruised past, with the City of West Hollywood logo in Gay Pride rainbow colors down the side. I once saw a pair of cops holding hands on Santa Monica, and neither of them was in the Village People. Perhaps I could write a gay cop movie. Aren't all cop movies gay? "They were cops. And they were men. And they were coming to protect and serve up the bum..."

At least I haven't accepted the situation, I thought, peering into a bucket of frozen yogurt with chocolate chips. I think they were chocolate chips. I'd taken to wearing extra-thick black sunglasses so I could barely see. There were people around but I couldn't hear them. I'd taken to wearing earplugs all day so I could barely hear LA phone conversations or lapdog fights. *Maybe Kevin Spacey will be mauled by Chihuahuas and the Lords of WeHo will be forced to reduce their numbers with baseball bats. I've got civic pride, I could help. A pint of ice-cream substitute with zero-impact carbs, it's not that bad here...* I was proudly digging chocolate chips out of the cup with my pinky when the phone rang.

A disinterested-sounding man's voice said, "Is that Jane Bussmann?" *Oh fuck, whoever he is.* "My name is Marty Singer. I'm a lawyer representing Ashton Kutcher. Ashton just wants you to know he is very upset that someone who seemed as nice as you could do... something like *this*."

A pause. He'd made a rough opener, even by LA conversational standards.

"No, I'm sorry, you're going to have to give me more to go on." *I knew it. I should have said I loved priests. Any priests—fat ones, thin ones, I can't get enough cassock. Ow, my farty guts—*

"I'm talking about the quote in the London *Evening Standard*?" The *Standard*? What did I write? Demi would be mad not to date him... Oh Jesus. What did the *Evening Standard* print?

Marty continued, "Let me read it to you. 'Ashton says, "She was the hottest actress in Hollywood when I was growing up... Now it's great, I'm fucking her." By Jane Bussmann.'" My frozen yogurt was now a cup of brown puke. Mama.

13

WE DIDN'T USE ANY QUOTES THAT WERE IN ANY WAY NEGATIVE

Back home, the email frenzy started. My editor, who shall remain nameless,

Liz.Jones@standard.co.uk[9]

explained to me that, while a "couple of small snippets" were added in, which was "not ideal," it did happen in the media when pieces needed updating. She went on to stress that they didn't use any quotes that were in any way negative.

She ended it:

Best,

Liz

I got together with my friends to panic. Maybe Marty Singer was just one of those lawyers who advertised on the back of a bus, "If you got your willy caught in a combine harvester at the workplace, call me." Then we asked Señor Google. "'MAD DOG' SINGER of Lavely & Singer the all-around bad cop for stars like Arnold Schwarzenegger..." Marty represented Rick Salomon, who filmed Paris Hilton noshing him. Rick, instead of being sued to within a whisker of his ballsack by the Hiltons, was a millionaire, thanks to Marty Singer. Marty was the biggest litigation lawyer in Hollywood. Oh my hairy aunt, this was not ideal.

---

9. She doesn't work there any more.

I had known the unnamed *Evening Standard* editor when she was editor of *Marie Claire* and I thought she was very nice, if a little into animal rights, always commissioning articles about the tragic whore elephants of Sri Lanka forced to masturbate German tourists for a rupee.

I thought she was merely crazy for animals. I didn't know she was crazy for lawsuits. British newspapers don't understand America. In Britain, lawyers are old men in long, curly white wigs and black capes like senile gay bats and they're largely harmless. In America, they have lawyers who can end your life. And Marty was Ashton's lawyer, which meant he was probably Demi's lawyer, which meant he was probably Bruce's lawyer, which meant I was dead.

I couldn't afford to be sued for a third time, and the first two were merely damage involving car crashes, not damage to a movie star's reputation. I'd go straight to jail, and not figuratively. *I'm going to be one of the new fat homeless: 300 pounds with bingo wings, collecting coins on the off-ramp in a Coke cup ... A 64 oz. Coke cup...* Why hadn't I just stolen my quotes like a real journalist?

But Marty Singer's office called again, and this time it was Good Cop: a maternal-sounding woman.

She said she was so sorry for what I'd been through, adding that if I would just put it in writing that Ashton never said that, they would never have to bother me again. *Yes, please! I choose NOT being sued! Thank Christ, they must have decided to settle out of court. Celebrities want these kinds of episodes to end quietly.* I quickly emailed Marty's office: "In fourteen years of interviewing people I have never had utterly fabricated quotes put in my work before. I'm particularly furious... I've never had an editor behave like this... I appreciated the time Ashton gave me and the intelligent interview..." Translation: I own nothing of value. I sealed the deal by sending Ashton a sample of my usual sycophantic drivel, accompanied by a letter telling him how fabulous he was, which I expect got piled with the rest of his fan mail, and walked the streets as penance. Everywhere I walked, the newsstands were a patchwork of photos of Ashton and Demi. I felt like I'd blasphemed.

I came home feeling a lot better with a quart of frozen yogurt to stash and eat over the week ahead. Two hours later I was staring into the empty Styrofoam pot when my friend, a BBC correspondent, gave me a private news update that changed everything. "The story's out, love! What you said about the *Evening Standard!*" Marty had released the sniveling email as my official public statement. I wasn't supposed to be a part of celebrity culture; I was supposed to be taking the piss out of it from a foxhole while I plotted its demise. I sat helpless as media networks across America quoted me insulting my employer. The next day, I considered it prudent to look for a new career.

14

I BET I COULDN'T EVEN GET FUCKED BY A DOLPHIN—THE IMPORTANCE OF EPIPHANY

Where the hell could I run? To Germany, and write *Der Naked Guys Gerfarten* for the rest of my life? My family said there'd be no shame in running home and telling my former employers in TV I was no good after all. My dissident friend Michael said there'd be no difficulty in getting the birth certificate of someone my age who had died in childhood and using it to apply for a new driver's license. "Then you say you—the real you—died in a plane crash. A small plane crash that didn't make the papers, obviously..."

I decided to dig in. I moved house again, into a shared condo owned by an elderly man who was the son of a famous person, and also the cheapest man I'd ever met. Never mind being too cheap to replace his old carpets just because we could see black fungus growing through them, he was too cheap to replace his old swimming trunks, and let me tell you, when they got wet, you sure could see through them. Every morning, I would take a break from writing to watch him swim the backstroke, his old-man nads bobbing after him like curious seagulls. The nads helped you think. I had to entirely change my life. I didn't regret anything, except not stealing more from fashion shoots—I could at least have got an iBook—but the trouble with doing a crappy job while you daydream is that if you take away the crappy job, you start to see that the daydream was barely formed, or worse, was just a way to clock on to the crappy job as the years dissolved away. Horribly, the odd interview still came in, but it was too late, I decided I'd a) work on the screenplay, b) stay calm and c) not spend the rest of my savings. I failed at a) and b), waking up in the night sweating with tunnel vision. I kept dreaming about a run-in I'd had with the US Immigration

Department at Dallas/Fort Worth Airport. You don't mess with these people, let alone in Texas.

"You're lucky I don't tear up your passport right now and send you upstairs to Secondary Immigration," the man in Texas had said. "You do NOT work here. You do NOT LIVE here. You will report to the Immigration and Naturalization Service before you attempt to leave this country." John Taylor told me that he once got pulled at US customs, and Duran Duran contributed more to the US economy than the House of Saud. No, if one of these men sent me up to Secondary, I'd be living at my mum's in twelve hours flat.

"Not good," said the doctor at Cedars Sinai. I still had my savings, so I went to cure my tunnel vision and general physical meltdown at the Stupidest Hospital in the Golden Age of Stupid.

"Not... good?"

"There's a significant chance of cancer of the adrenal glands. Urine tests show you are producing huge quantities of cortisol. That's the fight-or-flight hormone."

"Well, there's a bigger chance I'm an indecisive belligerent coward—"

"It's not a laughing matter," said the doctor, adding that if I paid several hundred dollars he'd tell me if I had cancer. I said that didn't sound like a deal.

"Then make lifestyle changes," he said, diagnosing Not Enough Cash and sending bills for thousands of dollars, which took care of c) and indeed resulted in lifestyle changes. I learned a valuable lesson: only ever piss in a toilet.

This couldn't go on; the screenplay had callously refused to write itself and I had to get a plan. There must be something I could do. Then one evening I was job-hunting, in the sense of watching TV, when I had an epiphany. I was staring at the foreign news: endless reports of happy Iraqis welcoming their American liberators. Reality was slipping fast; the American government had been caught red-handed distributing these news broadcasts of happy Iraqis—they were fake, filmed by the government, but the networks still broadcast them. Nobody cared.

But then a bloke appeared on TV, a bloke who wasn't looting, bombing or claiming a reconstruction contract: a Doctors Without Borders neurosurgeon picking his way through the war zone, with nothing to protect him except his walkie-talkie. When I switched channels, I saw someone else on a walkie-talkie: a publicist, shouting into a radio as Tom Cruise got into a limo; shouting as though they were in command of a field hospital, not a tiny Scientologist whose greatest achievement in my eyes was a rack of teeth that made him look mental.[10]

This horrible sight triggered my epiphany: there are two kinds of people in the world, Useful People and Useless People, and I had worked my entire adult life to be absolutely useless. Not like that Doctors Without Borders guy. I bet that Doctors Without Borders neurosurgeon could fuck any refugee he likes.

I looked around the condo. I bet I couldn't even get fucked by a dolphin. My life wasn't supposed to end up like this. I shouldn't be full of Sweet'N Low, in a shared flat, staring at a wobbly IKEA desk, not at my age.

You can't run from yourself. But you can hide. I made a plan: I was going to defect. I would run away from Hollywood and join the Useful People. I emailed my CV straight to Doctors Without Borders.

---

10. This is not the opinion of Nortia Press or any of its agents.

15

HE ENDS WAR

Doctors Without Borders were not currently recruiting celebrity journalists. I was hurt, but I noticed on their website a list titled "Professions MSF Does Not Currently Recruit." Second down was aromatherapists. I didn't know what international incident led to this ruling, but it made me feel better.

MSF Does NOT Currently Recruit Any of the Following

• Acupuncturists	• Naturopaths (ND)
• Aromatherapists	• Neurosurgeons
• Body Workers	• Occupational Therapists
• Chiropractors	• Ophthalmologists
• Dentists	• Paramedics
• Dieticians	• Physician Assistants
• Electrologists	• Podiatrists
• EMTs	• Reike Specialists
• Licensed Practical Nurses	• Veterinarians
• Massage Therapists	

The Internet was stacked with job vacancies for Useful People: Amnesty International, the United Nations, even a refugee camp for children kicked out of their villages for witchcraft. I could see myself in an African dawn, banging the breakfast gong: "Right! Which one of you little shits curdled the milk?" However, the world of selflessness was highly competitive; I sent twenty CVs and got one reply, from Save the Children, asking what skills I had. I told them. That was the last I heard. Apparently pediatric surgery ranks higher than a Radio 4 sketch about a magazine called *The Wrong 'Un*, for the man who likes it where he shouldn't.[11] Well, that was it. I was useless. I could die tomorrow and no one would

---

11. Special supplement: *The Wrong 'Un Pour Femme*, for the girl who didn't know she had it in her.

suffer, apart from the underwear department and my mum.

I lay in bed going insane in a puddle of chocolate covered raisins. *Let me defect. I'll do anything. Reality's almost gone here now.* It was the run-up to the 2004 American general election and experts were predicting George Bush would win again. Once again, they explained, he would fix the election results, but this time in Ohio, not Florida; once again, no one was doing anything to stop it.

Then the election came, the president fixed the election results,[12] but this time in Ohio; once again, nobody did anything to stop it. We were all going to hell, and my contribution to society was the procurement of chocolate covered fruit.

I was still in bed, flipping through an obscure political journal—I think it was *Vanity Fair* —when I came across a photo of a man. He was looking at me from a page called "Hall of Fame," profiling people who were trying to end a war in Africa. That's him on the right. I tore out the page, got up from bed and showed it to my friend Pauline, a journalist for the *New York Times* with wide, innocent blue eyes.

"This is it, Pauline," I said. "This bloke's day job is to end war. In Africa."

He was John Prendergast, forty-one, a hero. A renegade White House Director of African Affairs under Clinton, he was one of the world's most respected "conflict resolution experts."

---

12. This is the author's opinion based on circumstantial evidence and personal prejudice. But look, I haven't got time for this, here are some other people who did more work:

http://www.rollingstone.com/music/pictures/was-the-2004-election-stolen-20060601/ohio-gallery-16543658

www.harpers.org/archive/2005/08/0080696

Photograph by Mark Schafer, text by Jacques Mensch, © Condé Nast Publications

HALL OF FAME

WORKING AGAINST TIME Journalists Nicholas Kristof and Julie Flint, photographed in New York City on July 27, 2004. Representative Donald M. Payne and key policy point man John Prendergast, photographed in Washington, D.C., on July 23, 2004.

VANITY FAIR NOMINATES   DARFUR MOBILIZERS

BECAUSE they gathered the evidence, then sounded the alarm, alerting the world to the humanitarian crisis in Sudan's remote Darfur region, where a nomadic Arab militia, the Janjaweed, has reportedly killed some 30,000 black African villagers and driven more than 1.2 million from their homes, with the alleged sanction and assistance of the country's rulers. BECAUSE New York Times columnist Nicholas Kristof made two trips to the Sudan-Chad border to interview survivors of the onslaught, then relayed their tales of mass murder and rape in more than a dozen impassioned op-ed pieces. BECAUSE Julie Flint, a British journalist and researcher for Human Rights Watch, traveled through the region's burned-out villages and was among the first to reveal what many now contend is an ethnic-cleansing campaign, documenting the crimes and accusing the Sudanese government of complicity. BECAUSE John Prendergast, a specialist in African affairs at the International Crisis Group, held scores of meetings with U.S. policymakers, tirelessly lobbied for intervention, and earned the epithet "enemy of the state" in the corridors of Khartoum for suggesting that Sudanese officials be held accountable by a war-crimes tribunal. BECAUSE U.S. congressman Donald M. Payne, ranking Democrat on the International Relations Subcommittee on Africa, introduced legislation, unanimously adopted, that labeled the atrocities in Darfur "genocide," thereby employing a term more likely to muster an urgent international response. BECAUSE, 10 years after the world failed in the face of the Rwanda genocide, they have served as moral watchdogs, pricking the global conscience in an attempt, as Prendergast puts it, "to shame the world bodies into action." BECAUSE as the international community begins to move in fits and starts, they continue to press for swift response. BECAUSE as a thousand die each week and hundreds of thousands more remain in imminent danger, these four have given us the facts and the opportunity to do something about it. —JACQUES MENSCH

PHOTOGRAPHS BY MARK SCHÄFER

It had occurred to me he was also extremely attractive. For purely journalistic reasons, I spent about forty-eight hours straight Googling him, cursing John Prendergast Wedding Photographer of Liverpool for clogging my search results.

The real John was a mystery. Where he came from? How he ended up in Africa? If he was single? All terrible unknowns. The fanciest newspapers published John's editorials about foreign-policy fuck-ups, but angry as his words were, they revealed nothing about the man writing them. But when I found him on CNN and heard him talk, I knew I was on to something. I read transcripts (women are horribly thorough). He was the wild card at every pompous debate, and I could understand what he was talking about.

This man had boiled war into a simple argument: while old-fashioned poverty and injustice set the scene, war is bad guys committing classic bad-guy crimes like murder, theft and rape, and we let them get away with it by pretending it's more complicated than it is. Staggeringly, he said these problems actually have solutions.

Over 800,000 got filleted in Rwanda and 4 million died in the Congo while the superpowers sat on their hands. More than that, the superpowers deliberately belittled these crimes as ancient tribal/sectarian/ethnic squabbles too complex for us to get involved in. Imagine if the boot was on the other foot and Europe had been colonized by Africans who couldn't be shagged to get involved in that tricky tribal squabble between Hitler and the Jews. Damn, I had to meet John Prendergast. He wasn't just hot; he was wise. I wondered how wrong it would be to sit on his knee during the interview.

But the obstacles were massive. John specialized in conflict resolution. I'm English middle class; we specialize in conflict avoidance. My parents didn't speak to each other between 1976 and 1990 because they were trying to avoid a scene. So how could I persuade a man who used to work at the White House to let me, who still freelanced for *Glamour* magazine, follow him round Africa? I knew I was an A-Level failure from Muswell Hill Adjacent; there was no way I'd ever get to meet a former White House director. Until, from nowhere, the highly prestigious *Independent* newspaper called.

"We wondered if you'd like to write something for us!" *Me? Christ!*

"I'd love to!" *Be politics. Please be politics.*

"Now don't take this the wrong way," said the *Independent*. "But we think you'd be perfect to write a story about dating out of your league."

Pause.

Before you read the next sentence, bear in mind that I have no sense of irony.

"There's this guy in Washington," I said. "I'd like to interview him instead."

"What does he do?"

"He ends war!"

"Is he attractive?"

Jesus fucking Christ. "Well, yeah, I mean classically... but his day job is to put an end to war!"

"I'm not sure he's right for the *Indy*..."

"He's perfect for the *Indy*. He's on a one-man mission to save the world, but he's normal..."

"Right..."

"Imagine if Bob Geldof wasn't a ██. OK, never mind. Imagine if there was someone who gave a shit about the rest of humanity, but who wasn't an 80s pop star."

"Dating out of your league... do you know anyone that could do it?" *Yeah. Lisa Snowdon. How the shite she did George Clooney I'll never know. Maybe he thought she was a waitress.* But the *Indy* was the only chance I'd get; John wouldn't meet me for *InStyle*. The *Independent* was about to hang up when I remembered that truth had got me nowhere.

"You have to run it—John's a celebrity!"

They told me to get on a plane to meet John immediately.

16

CRAZED ON ESTROGEN PATCHES

Washington, D.C.: I was so into politics by now I'd bought a trench coat. I wore it with sunglasses and looked ridiculous. The doors slid open at Ronald Reagan International Airport— RonaldGetthefuckoutofhereReagan Airport—and I was in a snowstorm. Snow! This was the cleverest weather I'd experienced in months, and I was on my way to interview the most attractive serious person in the world. He'd never guess the most serious thing I'd written until now was a piece comparing spa hotels for dogs, give or take a sketch about the Virgin Mary driving a car for *Brass Eye*.

I rode through snow in the back of a Washington cab. Everyone we passed was walking fast, off to do something for the common good; everyone looked like they ran the world instead of doing its hair. LA is a city of the self, which by its very nature gets depressing. Spend your day gazing over the precipice of your own navel and you'll want to jump. In LA, whole office blocks on Wilshire Boulevard are secret cosmetic surgery clinics with clandestine back entrances, where celebrities shuffle out in bandages having been cut to pieces in order to be more themselves. Here in D.C., every building looked as if decisions that affected others were made inside.

My interview with John was scheduled for 3 p.m. in his office at the International Crisis Group, but I was going to introduce myself at his first appointment, where he was debating with George Bush's Ambassador for War Crimes. Subject: Sudanese genocide. Location: legendary think tank, the Brookings Institution. Holy crap, this man began his day with mass death, and this town had places where people got together to think. In LA, they got together to hold hands and pray for the strength not to have a drink like a normal person, before chugging a pint of GHB and doing a U-turn in front of the cops on the Pacific Coast Highway.

I arrived in a shambles, late because I'd forgotten the name Brookings, and telling a taxi driver "the think tank" didn't narrow it down in Washington, D.C. Coming from LA, I had low blood sugar and a giant venti coffee to make it worse. Brookings was an elegant building crawling with septuagenarian geeks, wizened and crippled by years of thinking. The atmosphere was giddy, waiting for the main act; it could have been the Apollo if the crowd hadn't been aged 75 and clutching coffee instead of Budweiser. John was transparently the rock star of human rights violations.

The septuagenarians' perky spokesman introduced himself.

"We think better than the other think tanks," he said. "Can I take your coat?"

"No!... thanks." I'd gone out of my way to blend in—black polo neck, trench coat, fishnets—and it wasn't working. Worse, when I read the blurb, I realized I'd spent so long messing up my lip-plumping gel and nude lip liner—ah, the natural look— that I'd swotted the whole genocide wrong: Sudanese Peoples' Liberation Army = good guys; National Congress Party = genocidal maniacs. *OK, whatever, fine.* But where was John? No one had a clue. *Call yourselves a think tank, how—*

And then I saw him. He was charging out of a cab, late and rushing in a big coat. As he walked through the door he seemed to become unnaturally huge, or maybe I was shrinking; I certainly felt five years old by the time he stood in front of me. *He looks like a fire god.* He was better-looking than in his photo because he was older and his hair had gray streaks, therefore making him more available in my imagination. Gray streaks were now the coolest thing I'd ever seen. He shook my hand before anyone else's, because I shoved it at him before anyone could get a look in.

"Hello, Jane Bussmann, *Independent.*" That was one lie, right there.

"Hi! Hi! Pleased to meet you." *Hi. Wow. He said hi.*

I tried to appear professionally neutral, like the BBC's Kate Adie, while getting as good a glance at his eyes as I dared. *I knew it: his eyes are red, from saving the world.*

I watched him smile at everyone. This to me was the essence of being a grown-up, not cowed into being reserved, thinking you're being mature when really you're guarding yourself like a smarting teenager. I watched the women watching him. So that was how women talked to him, with their heads tilted. The younger ones tilted towards him with wide shining eyes, biting back inappropriate requests, "Do you wanna... ? Our class is having, like, this party and would you... ?" before settling on "How do I apply for an internship?" The older ones tilted their heads away from him, their eyes half-closed in maternal amusement at this human work of art, but coquettish in spite of themselves. And I considered myself the ultimate grown-up for watching his suitors from the sidelines. Or was it my desperate self-defense, pretending I had power in the face of this tidal wave of love that the world swept him up on? Yes, I'd lost it.

I parked myself at the front of the audience; I wasn't wasting fishnets. Then I spotted cameras and realized the thing was being televised by the C-Span network, the Open University of thrilling live coverage. We were in for a long haul. Worse, tiredness from the flight was settling on me like the snow. Worse, the debate was about the savage butchery, firebombing and gang rape of civilians who'd had the misfortune to live around oilfields... I think; things were getting a little hazy. When a woman academic (that's two strikes, right there) started listing the crimes of the Sudanese government against the Darfurian tribes, I could feel my head starting to drop. I actually fell asleep during a description of unbearable human suffering. I'd done a red-eye flight in economy for crying out loud.

I came to when John took the chair. My interest in him—I mean Sudanese villagers—got deeper. He was the golden boy of the debate.

"If the President of the United States called and you had one minute to tell him what to do about Darfur, what would you tell him?" said the moderator. John grinned, his crinkly Clooney smile warming up all the coffee in Washington. *Oh my God, he's smiling at me.* I smiled back. Then I looked behind me. I knew it. All the old-lady boffins were making goo-goo eyes at him.

"I did have my minute with the president," John said. *Fuck, he's describing his audience with George Bush and he still sounds like a good guy.* I had to get a grip: I was live on C-Span; six people were watching me. "I somehow snuck into the White House when he was in office, at some bill-signing deal. Our eyes met and he rushed over. He was chatting like I was his best friend; seemed to know in great detail what was going on in Africa, had no trace of the Texas accent you always hear. He said he looked forward to working with me, which really creeped me out," John said. "Later one of his aides told me he'd thought I was Bono." A room full of professors exploded into laughter. I think I fell on the floor.

John explained what he was trying to do in Africa: get everyone to quit waffling and stop the bad guys. Women weren't randomly getting raped, he said. Everyone knew the Sudanese government had rape squads, but rather than send international troops, we left it to 2,000 local soldiers to protect an area the size of France. "In other words, every day, when women go out, we have chosen—*chosen*—not to protect them." Even I could see this was messed up, and I wrote "Nicole Looks Amazing" for a living.

Likewise, we knew who the bad guys were, and we knew that they were rich. Hit 'em where it hurts: freeze their bank accounts. Like most rich guys, they were vain, so ban them from traveling. Highly embarrassing at airports. It had worked before; when we banned these same guys from traveling in the nineties because they harbored al-Qaeda, rather than leave the jet set, "They booted Osama bin Laden out of the country." My God. This was brilliant. I felt an odd sensation. I think it was hope.

I flashed forward to my future useful life. I'd be making cocktails in a twenties safari tent on the Serengeti, with Arabian carpets on the floor and a surprisingly well-stocked portable bar. For some reason I'd be dressed as Doris Day. I would take the cocktails outside, where John would be talking with a guerrilla leader, a big game hunter and a member of MI6. Oh, and a pygmy. I went back inside to get snacks, which I wouldn't touch, because I'd be too happy to ever eat again.

The debate finished and I fought my way through the HRT-crazed elderly professors mobbing John. He talked to all of them. As good as he was with people, he was endearingly hopeless with technology, dropping his phone, fumbling with his BlackBerry, losing business cards as soon as they were pressed on him.

"Hi, just checking on the interview. Could I get one hour?" I said. I was way gone by now, I wanted to spend the rest of my life with him—fifty years of war crime, political discourse and filth. The feelings weren't mutual. I sensed this because he laughed in my face.

"No way! You can have thirty minutes max or I ain't doing it!"

But... I've done so much preparation... I bought a $15 lip plumping gel...

I was wincing now, literally, from some unnamed $15 irritant designed to inflame mucus membranes, something only a woman would use to help their mental state. Meanwhile John turned and walked away with George Bush's Ambassador for War Crimes instead.

I operate from the Fuck You No Surrender camp. I still had the interview booked, so I jumped in a cab and sped across town to research. I had hope.

17

TOFFEE CAKE

I conducted my research from the Starbucks opposite his office, focusing on Horn of Africa-based genocide and other matters.

"Caramel macchiato and a toffee cake, please." The lip-plumping gel was nothing. I had cut out sugar until now in preparation. Oh, to be a man. You could have the girlish figure of Harvey Weinstein and people would still be nice to you.

Outside, the new world of Washington came out for lunch: men and women in suits, sexy and real. I was so over the freedom to dress how you liked, because in LA everyone from ten to fifty likes to dress as Xtina Aguilera revenging herself on the Mickey Mouse Club. This was a town of grown-ups wearing shirts with backs, not a butterfly tattoo on display anywhere.

At 3 p.m. sharp I marched into the offices of the International Crisis Group. It reminded me of Floor 7½ from *Being John Malkovich*; a gray and navy-blue tunnel stacked with reports on wars around the world. Young female interns carried documents back and forth; I tried to kill a redhead by staring at her, but it didn't work. No sign of John, so I read his CV: under Areas of Expertise, it said, "counterterrorism." Still no sign. I found a stack of reports written by John and his colleagues. The Islamic Liberation Front was fighting in the Philippines. Twelve dead in Pakistan. A king in Nepal disbanded his own government. Wads of photocopied paper detailing limbs hacked, grudges fermented, opportunities bungled. As far as I could understand, John and his colleagues clocked in every morning to work out where the next war was about to kick off, then emailed international governments telling them how to stop it. Foreign offices around the world subscribed to John's team's emails; 40

percent of their advice became law. It was surprisingly common sense advice too. I read that in areas of Pakistan, the only free schools available to parents are run by Islamic extremists. So if you want to stop the spread of Islamic extremism among young Pakistanis, the report suggested, don't bomb them and annoy them even more, start by building some normal schools. *The redhead's back; what's her game? Does she—*

John came out. *Oh dear God, he's wearing an Aran sweater. That's not fair. That's like a woman coming out of her office in a bikini.* I kept it together and ignored him, opening my laptop instead. He looked confused.

"You checking your emails?" he said.

"No," I said, not looking up. "I'm going over the questions I'm going to ask you so I don't fuck up."

Swearing in a posh British accent: it worked for Hugh Grant, and it worked for me.

"Can I take your coat?" John said, wrong-footed. I handed the trench coat over. Its work was done: the romance was on, at least in my mind. I was no longer a Hollywood showbiz hack, drunk on glucose and coffee. I was Kate Adie up the Matterhorn, if that's the tallest mountain in Africa. All I had to do was write a history-changing front page article about the most evil war of the century, and not let John find out my horrible past at *She* magazine.

"Are you cold?" he said. "I'm cold. Let me turn up the heater. Hang on, I'll get you a chair." *No, that's OK. I'll sit on your knee.* After years spent around celebrities, I was so touched anyone would be polite to me that these small gestures seemed like a proposal. The interview was phenomenal. (Thirty-two minutes. Hah, I won.) He talked about war crimes, human rights violations, counterterrorism, didn't mention a wife. You could tell he negotiates for a living, because as we talked, he mapped complex wars into simple patterns in the air with his hands. I was embarrassed to realize I was swinging my legs under the table like a kid eating Sugar Puffs.

He told me about one of his missions in Uganda, East Africa, which was to talk a renegade madman called Joseph Kony into a ceasefire. I asked him if he was going to meet Kony.

"You can't go and meet the rebel leader now," he said. "No Westerner who's gone to meet him has come out alive."

"Doesn't it occur to you that you might not come out alive?"

"Nope."

That's so fucking hot. My brain froze.

"Why not?"

"Because when you walk around northern Uganda at night, there are all these kids, and all they want is a chance to go home, and not to be stolen in the night and made to work as soldiers or sex slaves," he said, his voice dropping. "So it's very easy to have motivation to do this kind of work when..." I wasn't listening, because after the word "kids," it was all I could do not to chew my knuckle, and I don't even want kids. John said he would go to Uganda and work with a local peacemaker to establish Kony's demands, a local peacemaker who sounded like a truly brave and wonderful person. Hopefully they'd be the one who got killed.

John didn't want to talk about his personal life, but I had fifteen years of experience as a stealth rapist. "You've got rather long hair for a peacemaker," I said. Soon he told me about growing up as the son of a traveling salesman. He told me he slept barely four hours a night and got 500 emails a day.

"You can't just not reply to them, they're from people who maybe saw you speak, maybe wanna help..." He'd never met Campylobacter.

His father sold corn dogs from the back of their car.

"Never staying in one place for more than three years, moving on to find people who hadn't gotten sick of corn dogs," he said. Then he laughed. I suspected it was less funny as a kid. It could explain how he became the person he was, a man who got up exhausted every morning to try to save people he'd never met. I bet he even knew what it was like growing up in Muswell Hill borders. Maybe if he liked the article I wrote, he'd invade with NATO and burn it down for me.

If all this was written in the stars, it was written in brackets that John should have some women friends. And of all of the women out there, it wasn't enough that she was the world's most famous humanitarian and gave millions to charity. She had to be the Sexiest Woman in the World 2002, 3,4 and 5.

"If you asked me who was the strongest advocate for these issues, it would have to be Angelina Jolie," he said. "I met her at World Refugee Day." *Rats, if I'd known WRD was still the happening rave, I'd have been there to cock block.* "She came over and we got to talking," he recounted. "I told her I was going to the Congo, and she said she'd been planning a trip there too..." *John, you are remarkably naïve for a counterterrorism expert.* "We ended up going together. Her main area of interest is refugees, particularly the rights of female refugees. She's highly motivated by violence against women." *I bet: spanking.* "We built a rehab center for child soldiers in the Congo."

"Did she fund it?"

"She paid for the whole thing." Oh well, perhaps I'd build an impressive origami crane.

And then something strange happened. I asked John to describe the worst atrocities he'd ever seen, and this man who could put any horror into words stopped talking. His eyes visibly glazed. I realized I'd just seen my first 1,000-yard stare. Now we were in a world far from Washington and Hollywood. I had no idea what he saw, but it shut him up for a full minute. Finally he came back and thumped the table.

"I didn't... I choose... It's best I don't have memories," he said. "I prefer to channel them into policy advice... trying to change things..."

Oh my God. He was fighting back blind fury, emotions thundering across his face. I had an idea, and it was a bad one.

"Have you ever thought about being in a documentary?" I said to a man who's always on CNN or CBS news. "I know... knew... some TV people in England."

"Why not?" He gave me his mobile phone number as the redhead swung past. "Hey, Lindsay."

"Got time for a beer later?" I said. I couldn't help it. Lindsay, the name of a goer.

"I don't drink beer..." he said. *Oh, why did I make such a rubbish pass? Of course you don't; you've got to end war; you can't go and get wasted.* "But I sure love orange juice." *You sure love—oh. Orange juice, that's easy, I could drink pints of the sickly stuff...*

There was no time for orange juice that day, but John said he was sure we'd meet again. He shook my hand. This time I looked down. No ring.

18

BACK DOOR

I spun home in bright sunshine, puddles flaring under the taxi wheels. Tarmac hadn't looked this full of promise since the acid house days. I'd worked on fifty shows; in all the years stumbling between green rooms, I must have met someone who'd do a documentary about John. That was my new job: documentary broker. Sod Bob Geldof; this guy ended war, hadn't tried to relaunch a pop career and he smelled nice.

I cold called the head of the BBC's documentary division, BBC Factual. He said John sounded really cool. "Get some footage." An opportunist slut at Channel 4 said John sounded really sexy. "Get some footage." *Me? I'd hoped you'd call Bob Documentary, who'd shoot it professionally, and I could turn up on set like a completely neutral patron, with orange juice.* I had no idea how to actually make a documentary... but... how hard could it be to shoot a searing, multi-award-winning factual feature?

Both networks warned me not to spend any money. I immediately spent $10,000 of my savings renting camera equipment and a crew. What could I film? How could you make ending war in foreign lands look exciting when you couldn't afford to visit one? I sat on this while I was guest hosting a radio show from a comedy station on Sunset Strip, high above the lake of city lights. The Strip is where the rock clubs live: the Viper Room, the Rainbow and the Whisky a Go Go, pisshead sister to London's WAG club. This was Led Zeppelin's Los Angeles; they trawled the Strip hunting pussy. They didn't hunt far. In fact, they'd usually sit down at the Rainbow and realize some bird was giving them a blowjob under the table. Imagine that, you're sat there with a vodka and pineapple, and suddenly someone you can't see is taking your drawers off.

Guest hosting means creating a crazy party on the radio, with loads of crazies calling in to leave dedications. The dedications were coming in like crazy because I was making them up. No one calls radio stations. Ever. No one ever did. It's all an enormous fabrication. That is, I fabricated them, because the few times I spoke to the real people who call radio stations it made me so depressed I never answered a phone with a flashing light again. At One FM, as BBC Radio One was known during its dismal trendy phase, our champion prize winner was usually Carol in Staines. Carol won a lot of fax machines, most of which I gave to friends. It was a terrible job, but worth it for the daily parade of Mangina among Radio One DJs. One came to the studio every day with his plums on either side of his flies. I used to pretend to be stacking sound effects under the desk, racking up blue plastic cartridges marked "BOING" and "UH-OH" so I could stare rapt and wonder how far apart a couple could drift that his wife let her husband go to work like that, or if she hated him so much that watching him leave, nuts akimbo, was the highlight of her day. Sorry, that's completely irrelevant.

Back on Sunset Strip, I was fumbling for time, playing a long Chris Rock routine while I trawled my laptop for tired jokes about pornography (delete: Pamela; replace: Paris) when my phone rang. It was John Prendergast. I turned the mic off. John asked if I had time to go over the interview. I'd mentioned I needed to do some fact-checking with him. I could hear banging and screams in the background. Perhaps he'd really pissed a warlord off.

"Um, I'm a bit busy... Oh, why not," I said.

"Great, great, 'cos this is the only free time I got," said John. "So would you mind if we did it in the gym?" God bless America for its lack of double entendres.

"Er, sure, John..."

"Great! I'll work out, you go ahead!" A pile of weights crashed in the background.

"Right, so, what were you doing in Sudan?"

"GAAAA-gatherin' evidence of war crimes by the Bashir regime against the non-Arab population to justify a definition of genocide... AARGH!" CLANG.

"Because if it's defined as genocide... ?"

"Because under the Geneva Convention, if a country commits... NYAAAAARGH!... genocide, then the rest of the world is obliged to respond."

"Is that why they keep calling it ethnic cleansing?"

"You betcha... Hh...hh..." He was panting. Oh...

Long pause.

"You still there?"

"Sorry, John, what genocide stuff... forms of evidence did you get?"

"Women will show me knife scars where Bashir's men slashed their leg; it's a sign to their families that they've been gang raped by the Arab militia. They call them "you blacks," "you slaves"—you know, mass rape is very political, a weapon of war..."

"Wow, that's mad. Hang on, John, one minute. You're listening to Comedy FM, live from the Sunset Strip! So we hear Paris Hilton's opened a nightclub here in Hollywood. Very strict entry policy. But don't worry, guys, just try the *back* door, she'll let anyone in... Here's Bill Hicks." *God, I hate myself.* "Sorry, John, gang rape, where were we...?" *Ask him, ask him, ask him.* "Ah! Listen, the BBC and Channel 4 want to see some footage. Are you doing anything we could film?"

"Well... I'm going to New York for a meeting with Kofi Annan." He shrugged, audibly. "That be any good?"

The Secretary General of the United Nations. I turned off the mic at Comedy FM because I couldn't stop laughing. This was so wrong.

19

A SPY MOVIE

John was hitting New York at 7 a.m. Monday, because at 3 p.m. Tuesday the superpowers were voting on whether to stop the Sudanese president Omar al-Bashir from buying weapons... or let him carry on. Kofi Annan had called John in together with the heads of all the Useful People—Amnesty International, Human Rights Watch, Save the Children—to tell him what to do. I did some research—I was a documentary filmmaker now—and established that Bashir was a lookalike for Chef from *South Park*.

I flew to Newark with my director of photography, Guy, an Israeli with a face built of circles: round cheeks, curly hair, half-moon smile. DPs are often grumpy, because "the light is shit" and they know exactly how to make your movie look like *Titanic* if only you had $200 million. But the more fed up Guy got, the more he laughed. I wondered if it was because he'd got out of Tel Aviv without being car-bombed, or whether he was just a sick bastard.

Our plane from LAX landed in sheets of rain.

"This will look bloody awful, you know that?" Guy said. "Ha ha ha ha. A total fucking disaster. Ha ha ha. *God*." I didn't care: I was incinerating the money I'd made by interviewing celebrities on a documentary about hate crime and a hot guy. It seemed symbolic.

We had no permits to film, so after a bollocking from security, we hid behind Newark Airport's Starbucks with our camera, waiting for John's plane to arrive from Miami. He'd just done Uganda and Chad before tearing across American universities from San Francisco to Boston rallying student protest against President Bashir, who was wiping out the black population.

From what I'd read about the chaos in the Horn of Africa, Bashir was a throwback, a less faggy Hitler. To me, Sudan had echoes of 1938, when Hitler swept through the ghettoes, sending the Gestapo to smash windows and set fire to Jewish shops. It was Kristallnacht again, the night of broken glass, and once again, no one was doing anything. I've always wondered why nobody stopped Hitler after Kristallnacht, because plenty of smart people lived in Europe in the thirties. Like my grandmother, a young medical student who'd run away from home aged sixteen to Berlin, where she cut her hair short and got a day job shifting props at the State Theater. Looking around her, she must have suspected that several hundred Nazis in a Jewish ghetto never ends well.

It could be that genocide is seen as a disease of the poor; many rich Jews thought the war wouldn't touch them, a belief that failed to secure them a Club Class holocaust when the Gestapo arrived. Rich, you say? Well, sit at the front of the train and leave your art collections on the kitchen table, they'll be there when you come back. My grandmother wasn't Jewish, but her mother had money, and she'd married a Jewish chocolatier to protect him.

I don't know whether my great-grandparents were captured the evening of Kristallnacht or whether they presented themselves the next morning for that regrettable train ride. I don't know what happened next either, but I should imagine it wasn't an all-night dance party. My aunt showed me their Third Reich identity papers, with a big eagle stamped at the top; on it my great grandparents had been renamed Moses and Sara Israelisch. The Third Reich had a thing for comedy Jewish names, apparently, and as German comedy goes, this rates funnier to Germans than *Schindler's List.* The rest of my family got out somehow; my great uncle Hermann, having style, put on a fur coat and escaped from the Nazis by running over the Alps. Or he fought for the Nazis on the Russian front until he got sick from being very cold, having no fur coat. I have no idea what did and didn't happen. All I know is that every Christmas, I think about my great grandfather and all the free chocolates I'm not getting, and it upsets me more than anyone can know.

If this was 1938 and Bashir was Hitler, then John was a whistleblower, trying to get anyone to listen. *Villages; he's burning whole villages, you have to believe me...* John's problem, of course, was that his genocide was taking place in Africa, and on international give-a-shit provisos, Africans are Jews without the money, bagels or *Seinfeld*. As John came through the gate, I said, "Look, I got you an orange juice," like a social worker in a nuthouse.

John was charming, as before, and red-eye knackered, as before. He looked ill, but he was charging on. Now that he wasn't in the White House, he couldn't *make* the law, he could only advise people who did. This trip was a big chance for him to influence the people changing history. Soon New Jersey was a smudge in the steamed windows of a taxi as we passed over into Manhattan.

I sucked chocolate buttons and asked John if he'd ever been in fear of his life.

"I've been shot at, particularly in Somalia. I've had missiles fired at the plane I was in. Guns, you know, in the forehead..."

"Yeah." You know.

"Had a landmine blow up in the car right in front of me... but when you do this kind of thing a lot, it ceases to have an impact. My pulse rate doesn't go up."

"Chocolate button?"

"Ah, no, thanks, I'm lactose intolerant."

"What's the worst thing you ever saw in the field?" I said. He got the 1,000-yard stare again.

"I don't like to talk about it," he said. "What about you?"

I remembered Ashton counting priests. "I don't like to talk about it," I muttered.

"I hear you," he said. Clearly this man had not Googled me. Good, good. His BlackBerry kept buzzing.

"Mia Farrow," John said. "She says, 'When shall we organize the fundraiser at Sting's house?'" He looked quite proud. Clearly he'd never Googled Sting.

Kofi was waiting for John at UN Headquarters, a towering green plinth overlooking the East River, a backdrop from a Cold War spy movie. I was still determined to blend in—black polo neck, miniskirt, but I'd lost the fishnets now—and it was starting to work. Stunning steel-eyed women headed toward HQ in black polo necks: perfect. The place was staffed by Bond girls, and not the yours-for-a-nickel 80s ones either.

Security was of Cold War intensity, and I didn't have enough forms of ID. John called his old buddy Fred, boss of half the UN or something, and we were ushered straight in. There are no rules, there are just passwords, and you are either one of us or one of them.

We walked under forty-foot windows into *Doctor No*: pale green circular corridors ringed with disappearing runway lights. As soon as people saw John, they came up to him as though he were indeed Bono. A short, terrier-like man pumped his hand.

"I just want you to know that what you're doing... keep it up." He carried on gushing. "Keep it up." John looked slightly stunned.

"That's Bush's acting ambassador to the UN," he said. "That's him." All the red eyes, all the speeches, all so this yappy little man could go to his boss and say, "No matter what we want, the public is calling for action." John's eyes looked optimistic, but he checked himself.

Bernardo, a giant Italian with a round red head who did something for the UN involving security, told me to wait in his cubicle. I spotted pictures of a tiny red faced granddaughter on the cubicle walls. He came back, and while I don't remember telling Bernardo he was in amazing shape for a UN official, I may have congratulated him on his beautiful daughter, and expressed amazement that he was old enough to have a grandchild, because instead of asking me what the fuck I was doing in UN HQ, he told me about his days as a young soldier on the banks of the Black Sea.

"You can't trust an Arab, they'll stab their classmate," he said paternally.

"You're absolutely right," I said, a celebrity journalist reflex.

Annan's wood-paneled boardroom was on the billionth floor and guarded by goons, a secret summit of the Elders in the world of the Useful People. John parked himself under a huge golden UN logo, right opposite Kofi's throne, and I waited at the back with real political journalists. This was getting wronger. In came Nicholas Kristof, a crusading *New York Times* correspondent. He looked cynical but excited; this was a glittering event in the genocide calendar. In came Samantha Power, a tall, 34-year-old Harvard professor with long red hair and vast blue eyes that had John's 1,000-yard stare. Instead of eating Kit-Kats for two years, Samantha had passed her exams and become a champion athlete. When I was writing jokes about Lenny Henry buying a lucky pig, Samantha had covered the Srebrenica Massacre. By thirty-two she'd won a Pulitzer for a book on genocide and gone unearthing mass graves with John for the eight o'clock news. But Kit-Kats are really nice if you dip them in hot chocolate.

In came a cordon of suited men. The cordon parted and there was Kofi. Bernardo swept all the journalists outside, but left me hidden among UN staff. *Because I agreed with a giant Italian that Arabs stabbed their schoolfriends, I'm locked in a closed meeting with Kofi Annan. If Kofi Annan reads* Grazia *I'm screwed.* The goon next to me was a scary FBI-looking guy with cowboy boots under his suit, and he'd clocked something was up, if only because I was frantically scribbling everything everyone said on the back of a Starbucks' napkin, then turning it 45 degrees when I ran out of space.

"Four aid workers have been killed in December. A USAID

girl has just been shot in the face in broad daylight," said one of the Elders, who had a Santa Claus beard and was therefore probably the wisest.

"I will look into this," said Kofi, whose voice never rose from a monotone. You could tell people brought him shit all day long. His number two, Jan Egeland, however, a fiery Norseman I'd peg for six foot four, rubbed his face when people reported that Sudanese gang rape survivors who'd made it from their burned out villages to the refugee camps were being guarded by the same mercenaries who'd gang raped them. Camps, I later learned, that were paid for by you and me.

"We can do something," said Samantha Power. "We could look into the radio communications, like we should have done in Rwanda… if we'd blocked Radio Mille Collines…" Mille Collines was the propaganda radio station that had urged the Hutus to exterminate the Tutsi "cockroaches."

Kofi agreed that the local African Union troops were failing and he was preparing to send peacekeepers to help Darfur. The Useful People asked him when that would be. Kofi said he didn't know; he hadn't got any at the moment as they were in Iraq and Afghanistan.

"It's as if the world has been in labor for two years only to give birth to a mouse!" raged Egeland incomprehensibly. Meanwhile, I observed that John Prendergast reminded me of Harrison Ford in *Blade Runner*. The FBI cowboy looked round. I may have said that out loud.

After the meeting, Kofi went downstairs to tell the five superpowers what John and the Elders had told him. We had thirty-six hours before America, Russia, China, the UK and France voted on whether Bashir should be banned from buying weapons. The trouble was, four of the five were selling him weapons or helping other people sell him weapons: Russia, China, the UK and France.

"Do you think it'll work?" I asked John.

"I learned early on never to get optimistic or pessimistic in this job," he said. We both knew he was lying.

John spent those thirty-six hours charging round New York talking to anyone who could influence the vote. I tail-gunned him with the camera, asking questions and trying not to fancy him. I sat on the end of his bed as he told me about his last visit to Bashir's capital city, Khartoum.

"I went on Al Jazeera, saying something like, 'The president of Sudan should be prosecuted for crimes against humanity,' which he should. The next day there was this story in the local paper: there's a particular guest staying in a particular hotel—my hotel—under a particular room number—my room number—who should cease and desist his destabilizing activities... Marines had to come and get me from my room, before... y'know."

You know. I felt more at ease with John's goofy side— hopelessly lost in his sentences around 4 p.m. when the no-sleep kicked in; wearing shirts that looked like they'd been forced at gunpoint to go with ties, and as for technology, well, he was its bitch. The hotel staff fell over themselves to offer him DSL.

"DSL? What is that?" he said, scared. "Is that something that will blow up the computer? 'Cos it's not mine. Mine blew up..." I wanted to film him being normal and asked him if he ever did anything other than work, ever.

"Well... you could film me in the gym." An hour later he was lifting weights in a tank top. I didn't know which way to look. Look, this wasn't my idea, it was his.

"My mother has a rosary club—women saying prayers in a circle —which has to be the charm that's gotten me out of some of these situations," he said. I think. I wasn't listening. How could I have been?

"Was it Bashir's guys that put a gun in your face?"

"No, that was some kid on the Rwandan border. Figured he was taking something: that kid was highly agitated."

"Why didn't he pull the trigger?"

"The rosary club, right?"

"John, when you wake up, do you know what city you're in?"

"At least fifty percent of the time," he said with great certainty.

We were running out of time. Sleep was a gap in my headache; Alka-Seltzer a way to keep coffee down. John, however, stayed up answering 500 emails a night. On a whim, I asked him what day it was.

"Wednesday," he said. "It's definitely Wednesday." It was Tuesday. I hadn't seen him eat anything other than a Mrs. Fields chocolate chip cookie all week. He crunched a Lactaid tablet with it: "For the migraines. Chocolate. I'm getting one now." I still knew nothing about his home life. He seemed to live on the run, like Special Forces behind enemy lines. I sensed he'd probably married young, and she was a marine biologist, who was now on an Antarctic substation she could never leave because of her loyalty to flightless penguins. I reasoned that this was OK, because there was some fatherly geologist with her who gave her what John never could. I'm a nice person.

With hours to go until the vote, we tore by taxi to a posh Manhattan law school that was hosting an event about the Nuremberg Trials. John was supposed to be giving a speech to rally support from young lawyers, but we were seriously late, and the taxi turned onto 5th Street instead of Fifth Avenue. I looked at John. It was finally getting to him; his face had changed. I saw a rage arrive on the horizon, rolling in like a storm. He nearly killed the taxi driver as we skidded to the door halfway through John's supposed speech. I was scared. However polite John was, he was also not someone to fuck with.

Inside, two elderly men, judges at the Nuremberg Trials, came over. I asked a stooped and baggy judge if he remembered my grandfather and his foggy eyes shrank back in time. My grandfather was a German/English translator at the trials. My dad said he once described the sound a rope makes when it hanged someone: ting.

"What do you remember from the trials?" I asked the second judge, a small, effervescent man. Without missing a beat, he said, "Nazis saving bullets by shooting mothers through their babies." And they say Jews are cheap. I looked at the foggy judge and wondered if my grandfather was ever tempted to tweak grammar as he translated the testimony of the men who'd gassed his wife's parents; an adjective here, a superlative there. Then I ran off to the buffet because I'd spotted Alec Baldwin and there was free sushi.

Finally the vote went ahead. John's eyes could barely focus by now. He was angry with China, angry with Russia, furious with me. I'd been harassing him with a camera since 7 a.m. Monday. Late that night, still in the law school, he got a call from his colleagues at the International Crisis Group. From the look on his face I thought he was going to kick Kofi Annan's door in.

"For the first time in two years they voted to take action against Bashir," he said, careful not to show any feeling. But then he smiled.

"Are you happy?"

"I wouldn't say happy," he said. "I would say pleased." He was very happy.

20

NADTASTIC

How hard could it be to edit a documentary? While John was rock climbing with his eight-year-old brother Jay-Z (not the result of his mother's affair with the eponymous rapper, but a big brother mentor scheme), I was trying to work Avid, the world's hardest program, running out of disk space at 4 a.m.—*fuck it! Delete my iTunes library. Who needs music?*—before staggering out to meet Teri Hatcher for breakfast so she could Open Her Heart. When Teri asked what I was doing and, too tired to lie, I told her, she said, "I totally get it," bought me a double-shot cappuccino and gave me quotes about her Search for a New Love as fast as she could so I could get home and finish editing. Week two, I paid a real editor.

Maybe it was the patchy sound, maybe it was the lack of clear narrative, maybe it was *I'm Alan Partridge* writer Peter Baynham (Oscar nominated for *Borat*. Nice one, Pete!) playing a publicist for a Janjaweed death squad:

REPORTER (JANE): Your client was seen leading the gang rape of an eight-year-old girl.

JANJAWEED PUBLICIST (BAYNHAM): He was looking for his car keys!

Maybe it was a piece of crap, but the BBC and Channel 4 rejected the documentary.

When you're writing a script, your fictional characters are completely real. You can hear them talk, you can see them flailing, you feel for them when they make terrible decisions. The late John Sullivan, who wrote the British sitcom *Only Fools and Horses*, said his wife wouldn't take him out because he talked to himself in his characters' voices.[13] But when these characters are rejected, after a bitter week of hating yourself and wondering which murderers commissioned this unspeakable shit they're insulting the public with at 8:30 p.m., your characters' faces start to become blurry, their voices harder to hear, and eventually you get some new ideas. But now I'd screwed John over—a real person—and this was a horrible new feeling that didn't have a "but it's okay because..." at the end of it.

Not even writing a new column for *Red* magazine about my glamorous life in Hollywood could take the edge off. I stood on my balcony in LA, glumly realizing that now, after paying for a real editor, I was twenty grand in the hole. Oh, and I'd made no difference to any war crime whatsoever. I looked down at my landlord's testicles. Everything was going wrong.

Then, from nowhere, John emailed. Last I'd heard he'd been at the CIA, giving a seminar on terrorism to a bunch of spooks. Now he'd had some news from some of his own spies—analysts and locals in East Africa—and he had a new mission: Uganda.

Renegade madman Joseph Kony was still as crazy as ever, but suddenly his spin doctor—Sam Kolo, the Karl Rove of Uganda—had defected. Kony had made contact with the brave peacemaker friend of John's, a Ugandan woman called Betty Bigombe. He told her he missed his relatives and was worried about his children's future. He even hinted at a possible life for himself after battle. The monster was tiring.

Now Uganda's president Museveni had started making noises about a ceasefire, and John was going to steam in and seal the deal by drafting a peace treaty with Betty before both sides changed their minds. A twenty-year war could be coming to a

---

13. *Now That's Funny!* by David Bradbury and Joe McGrath. Methuen, 2000.

close, and John and Betty might be the people to close it.

Some words at the bottom of his email caught my attention: "Do you want/need to go to Uganda?"

Argh, you bastard! Yes, but on what excuse? The documentary had just been shitcanned. I couldn't waste this man's time filming him again for nothing. I called him.

"Could I... *write* about what you're doing in Uganda... ?" I said.

Understandably burned by the failed documentary, John growled, "Who for?"

"A newspaper," I snapped, rather foolishly. Because John said, "Yes."

21

THE MOST EVIL MAN IN THE WORLD

It was obvious. My only job skill was turning people into celebrities. If all I could do was make Paris Hilton interesting, why didn't I write about real villains? Warlords, war criminals, bent presidents? I was perfect for this job: I already had a DKNY safari dress. I'd be a foreign correspondent having sexy, dangerous drinks in exotic hotels with sexy, dangerous men. Uganda would be just the start: Kate Adie covered Albania, Sierra Leone, Tiananmen Square, and I could do all of that, once I found out where those places were. All I needed was to make this a really big story, so I went straight to Google.

On a hunch, I Googled "Most Evil Man in the World." *Osama bin Laden, blah. Why didn't that guy get a better photo? You can run a Jihad but you can't get a professional headshot... Bush, in some daft Top Gun jacket. You can destroy Iraq but you can't buy an overcoat...* Then a new face stared back at me: a black guy with dreadlocks, a cowboy hat and mirror shades. I'd done it. The story I'd write would be John going to stop Joseph Kony, the Most Evil Man in the World.

Now, he may look like Dave Chappelle as Rick James, but he is Joseph Kony, leader of the Ugandan guerrilla group the Lord's Resistance Army. I'd heard of the LRA, but couldn't place them. In a civil rights report so boring I had to read it with my finger, I found a tiny footnote that stopped me dead.

"If Kony believes you have said anything bad about him, he cuts your lips off and makes you eat them." That was nothing. If Kony was feeling creative, he punched a padlock through your mouth and threw away the key. "Joseph Kony has spiritual if not magical powers."

*Joseph Kony looking like
Dave Chappelle as Rick James.*

This can't be right. I checked again: the report was written by lawyers and political analysts. Kony was so mindshreddingly evil that people with real jobs blamed the supernatural. So mindshreddingly evil that he could dress like this and people still did what he said. Gumboots!

Joseph Kony talked to God. God was quite chatty, and told him to start an enormous war against a particular man: Uganda's president Yoweri Museveni, one of Britain and America's favorite leaders and highly respected on the world stage.

Here he is with former foreign secretary Jack Straw. Museveni's the black guy.

Yoweri Museveni is the boss of a major African country, but Microsoft Word keeps underlining his name in red: "wrong." Microsoft, for the record, told me I meant Yoda. Bill Gates, down with the third world.

Museveni, the poor bastard, had his fair share of problems, what with poverty and AIDS—6.4 percent of Ugandan women were trotting round full of HIV. Luckily Museveni got budget support from Britain and America, probably as a thank you present for not being Robert Mugabe.

One thing about these two men stumped me, though. How did an obvious loony like Kony manage to gather together an army, let alone an army that held off President Museveni, who had millions from the West? Initially Kony had very few followers; he tried to get more, promising that bullets wouldn't hurt them, but had some difficulty recruiting. Then he hit on a much simpler idea: Joseph Kony kidnapped kids. And not just a few kids. He'd abducted "between 20-30,000 children."

This wasn't a misprint—Kony had been kidnapping children for twenty years and nobody had caught him. Not surprising if things were so slipshod over there that the abductee toll was 25,000, give or take *5,000* children.

That was why the LRA sounded familiar: Kony led an army of children whom he somehow persuaded to work as his soldiers and sex slaves. Britain and America, it seemed, had done little to stop it. We were already involved: our governments had sent tax money to Museveni. Strictly speaking, in my case, they'd sent the tax I pay on underwear, but Kony was still kidnapping, and I have eighty-three pairs of underwear. Mostly from Topshop, so I figure 75 bucks in sales tax.

Meanwhile, in Uganda, such vast numbers of people were being kidnapped that it didn't count as kidnapping for the first twelve weeks. That meant that for the first eleven you were just late for supper. Pretty much the only American who counted as kidnapped by Ugandan standards was the teenager John Paul Getty III, and that was only because his billionaire grandfather was too cheap to pay the ransom until the kidnappers cut off his ear. The Gettys didn't believe in spoiling children. I'd love to have been at the Gettys' Christmas dinner that year.

"More turkey, John Paul III?"

"Sorry, Mother? You may remember I CAN'T HEAR YOU."

Kony the Kidnapper was an incredible story. It was July 10. John was leaving on July 21. Against the clock, I had to scam my way to Africa.

22

THE SCAM

This was the scam: slap bang in the middle of the Golden Age of Stupid, I had to convince an editor that he or she should run a big fat story and buy me plane tickets immediately because kidnapped Ugandan children were cool. Success: unlikely. The scam was made more unlikely by the fact that it wasn't just against the clock, it was against the backdrop of my most surreal time in LA.

I'd fled the floating nads to move house again, this time to the set of the Yellow Submarine. It was a communal hilltop compound filled with big eared coyotes, two-foot-tall owls and citrus trees shedding eight-inch lemons that dented your car as they fell. Below us, the skyscrapers of downtown LA floated on a purple magic carpet of smog. The compound was shared by bohemian journalists, toy specialists and Antipodean musicians who hosted astonishing parties. We'd become friends with Lucha VaVoom, a troupe of masked Mexican wrestlers and burlesque dancers, and their aftershow parties were held in the compound. I'd be preparing my Kate Adie pitch while stepping over Mexican wrestlers who came onstage with matching midgets of themselves (Mascara and Mascarita); the Wau Wau sisters, who came onstage as Catholic schoolgirls and left on trapezes; Roky Roulette, who came onstage on a pogo stick dressed as a cowboy, did a striptease on the pogo stick and left naked apart from gold paint, a blonde wig and a thong; and Karis, who came onstage as a woman and left as a man, via a series of hula hoops and a very long rope. Commanding the whole vision were Liz, a femme fatale who reduced the toughest wrestler to baby talk, and Rita, aka Ursulina, a tiny blonde bombshell who came onstage as a Victorian widow with a horsewhip and left as a horse, and I still have no idea how.

Against this backdrop, I undertook the first part of the scam: make Uganda cool. It occurred to me that before I pitched, I had better be able to answer the question "Where the fuck is Uganda?" So I did some research. Uganda is in the middle of Africa. And there's more! Uganda was one of Britain and America's favorite African success stories, unlike Rwanda or Zimbabwe. For maps and a cursory history, turn to the appendix.

Monday. Here's what I was pitching while covered in gold paint in the shape of a male torso where I'd hugged Roky Roulette. I had conversations like this one with a thong print on my stomach. The names are inaccurate, given the historical conditions, and because I changed them.

"*Telegraph?*"

"Can you put me through to the foreign editor? Wait, wait. What's his name? Emma, hi, my name's Jane Bussmann. I wanted to run something by you about guerrilla insurgency in Uganda—"

"If you're satisfied with your recording, press one."

Now bear in mind that I had no idea about guerrilla insurgency in Uganda and was Googling as I spoke, well aware that the people listening to me were, er, experts. One time I actually dried up completely and had to pretend I'd been cut off.

Tuesday. John was leaving within days and I had a small problem: no one wanted the story I had told him I was doing. The responses had an annoying habit of ending with "Have you tried *Woman's Hour*?"

I called everyone. I even called NPR and they would cover a fart in a cup. Nothing.

I was furious with myself. What was I thinking? Trying to sell a story about 25,000 young black people, none of whom was even getting bummed in the Arsenal Football Club showers? I was sitting on the greatest story in the world and I couldn't think of a way to make anyone run it. Useless. As I pitched, thousands of children were being tortured and forced to live as sex slaves; this was the exchange that tipped me over the edge:

"No," said the editor.

"Why not?"

"We've already had Africa Week." That's word for word. *Newsnight*.

Wednesday. The wrestlers left and the party evolved. I was going mad. I did call *Woman's Hour*.

"And I thought straight off, This is a story for *Woman's Hour*, because half of those children will grow up to be women. Unless they're killed…"

But *Woman's Hour* had their own correspondent, no one needed a Britney Spears eulogizer in Africa, and there was a large man dressed as Santa Claus sitting on my bed claiming to be Keith Richards's dealer. That's not the surreal bit. The surreal bit is that someone had a new prototype pogo stick that let you jump five feet in the air. I'd be on the phone looking out of the window and see someone bounce up into the air completely out of sight and disappear.

I was starting to realize the catch 22 I was in: while the kids were still captive and being tortured there was no story. Now listen to this. This is accurate.

"If Kony decided to release the kids, then we could do something," said the editor. "But we've just had the Bob Geldof series… you know…"

The kids' story was unsexy and old, the two worst words in publishing. I was doomed.

But then my sister called. Kate was features editor of *InStyle* magazine—on purpose. Kate was better at her job than me, not to mention younger, blonder, thinner and infinitely more attractive. She hated stupid jokes and thought superstars deserved respect. Kate had a job offer for me.

"You're going to love it," she said in her no-crap, peppy voice. "Rachel Weisz has just made *The Constant Gardener,* a film about the drug companies exploiting the slums in Kenya. We want you to ask Rachel, "Who is your favorite designer?""

I told my sister, "No."

And later "Yes," for money.

But it gave me an idea: show business. I looked at the map: Kenya was next to Uganda. I hatched a completely logical plan to get myself to Uganda by writing a piece funded by a travel company about the locations of *The Constant Gardener,* featuring quotes from the famous and lovely Rachel Weisz and a nice big pic of her being sexy. Then once in Kenya, I would take a bus across the border to the capital of Uganda, which was only about... four inches on the map. This was not only completely logical, it was brilliant, because maybe after John had ended the war, he'd have time for a Kenya safari. A safari lodge overlooking the Serengeti, which until now I'd thought only existed in Toto songs.

I stormed to New York's Soho Grand Hotel, where the terrifically nice Rachel Weisz was waiting in a satin skirt that I was probably supposed to write about. For fifty-five minutes I relentlessly quizzed her on the movie's locations, and while confused by the change of editorial policy at *InStyle,* Rachel was, like me, English middle class and therefore wanted to avoid conflict. With five minutes to go, I remembered the interview was supposed to be for a women's mag. Rachel was a pro: we did her Hopes and Dreams in four minutes thirty seconds flat. Shit—nearly forgot—who's your favorite designer? Bob Gay? Never heard of him. Thanks, bye. They printed it. Oh come on, Kate, you said your editor held it up as a textbook example of celebrity journalism.

I ran back to JFK and straight into an obstacle: the travel company I'd persuaded to fund the "Locations of *The Constant Gardener*" piece had realized that *The Constant Gardener* locations I planned on visiting were picturesque Lake Turkana, where Ralph Fiennes gets murdered by contract killers, buzzing Nairobi, where Rachel's autopsy reveals multiple rape bruises, and finally the pastoral Kenyan countryside, where Hubert Koundé's balls are cut off and stuffed in his mouth. They couldn't see a way to package it as a charter tour. Shit. No matter, I'd noticed Uganda had lots of monkeys. A company that did trips to a Ugandan monkey sanctuary was up for funding it. I'd hug monkeys, then cover a war. Done. I started packing. But there was another obstacle.

"Which vaccinations have you had?" said the monkey sanctuary people. "Because there's a small risk of exposure to measles."

"I'll take the risk," I said.

"It's not so much about you," said the monkey sanctuary people. "Chimpanzees are a very vulnerable primate. We don't want to expose them to..."

I was too dirty for a pack of chimps. Fuck the apes, what about *Cosmopolitan...* ?

Thursday. John was getting his trip ready. He was now traveling with Don Cheadle. The *Hotel Rwanda* star had got very deep into Africa after hanging out with the bloke he played, hotelier Paul Rusesabagina, and had taken months off from lucrative acting gigs to work for humanitarian causes. Now he was flying his family to Uganda at his own expense to make a documentary about the kids with John. Wanker. I was still stuck in Hollywood.

Santa Claus upped the ante, producing a bag of magic mushrooms with stalks the size of Silk Cut. The theory at the time in LA was that the fastest way to feel their effects was to turn the mushrooms into powder and mix them with orange juice, so while I was pitching the foreign pages at 6 a.m., the party was still going on and I could hear the whirr of a coffee grinder producing not coffee but a day pass to Pepperland.

I was flagging. Then John sent me an email. He ended it with a smiley. Now I had no choice, I had to succeed: I'd got an emoticon from a former White House director. I sexed up the article, played down the black kids, made it all about John and emailed the Sunday supplements. This was a slam dunk.

"He's a hero, a real life hero..." *What the fuck is that in the orange juice—oh, no...* "And Joseph Kony is a real life villain..." Editors explained to me that it wouldn't feel *real* enough to their audience. This was, after all, the age of reality TV. Could I shape it into something more, you know... ? What? *Against the odds, this war criminal is going to... decorate a lounge. But would IKEA let him return the LACK shelves that looked great in the catalogue but were JUST TOO HEAVY for the plasterboard?*

It was July 17 and the party was finally over. As the sun rose over the cacti, the compound was desolate, give or take a few strippers looking for a bottle opener. No one wanted the story. John was getting ready to leave. There had to be some media outlet I hadn't called. I was absolutely desperate.

Which is how I came to call the *Mail on Sunday,* Britain's somewhat politically right-of-center family newspaper. Headline of its inaugural issue: BLACK PEOPLE—WHOSE FAULT ARE THEY? I contacted the *Mail's* travel editor because he's a nice man with a sense of humor and because I was also a serious travel writer. "Forget the hype, Bangkok's hip again!" That was me.

"Hi, Frank, it's Jane. How about I write a travel piece about volunteering as a teacher in a Ugandan school?"

Frank thought about this, then replied, "Go for it. Altruism is in." *Thank fuck for tsunamis! And now I'd get proper right-wing money, not that* Independent *crap.* I went on the Internet and found a Ugandan school. *Can I come and be a teacher? Thanks, bye*. OK, there was more to my request, but not much; there was a charity that ran volunteer programs, there was a school in Uganda, and they would be happy for me to volunteer there.

So, to recap: I was now flying to Africa to teach, with zero teaching qualifications, because what I really wanted was to write a serious piece about 25,000 kidnapped children and a peacemaker, and the only way I could achieve that in today's media climate was by sending *Mail on Sunday* readers on holiday to a war zone. A war zone full of black people.

I discussed this with the remains of the party. While I had doubts, they were terrifically positive.

"So? You're Kate Adie!" said one of my friends.

"No, I'm a travel writer," I said.

"It'll be fine!" said another of my friends.

"But... John's a peacemaker," I said. "What if he ends up next to 'Top Ten Beaches for Seniors' with a picture of Clint Eastwood in Speedos... ?"

"He'll think it's great!" said a third friend.

"If you don't go, do you know where you'll be?" said the first. "Still here."

"Shit, you're right... and I mean, if he wants to take a holiday afterwards, the *Mail on Sunday* must need a piece on safari lodges..." I said.

"Nobody don't like lions," said Santa Claus.

Fuck it! I'm going to Africa! Then something occurred to me.

"You're on ecstasy, aren't you?" I said.

"Yes. Yes, we are," they said.

23

DRAGGED INTO THE BUSHES AND MACHETED

I couldn't have asked John if he minded being on the travel pages even if I'd wanted to, because John was AWOL. He'd gone off radar, deep in the Congo, land of gold, silver and coltan (the mineral in mobile phones, video games and computer chips). Everyone wanted coltan, and gangs of men with guns were grabbing land from local villages in pursuit of it. I met up with John recently in Los Angeles and he explained exactly why he'd gone AWOL.

We had lunch in a hotel bar, one of those mausoleum business hotels where the staff flirt in order to stave off suicide. But not with me. The waiter, a straight man, was giving John the eye.

"The boss of the main militia in the Congo is a guy called Laurent Nkunda," said John, pouring a cup of ketchup on plain chicken. Africa had ruined his guts. "No country will negotiate with Nkunda because he's a warlord, but my thinking is, if you're not going to send in the 82nd Airborne and kill him, find a way to make him stop. So I got a local Congolese guy to lead me and my colleagues to Nkunda's hideout up in the hills."

"Literally a hideout? Behind guys with guns?"

"Can I get you guys some more ketch—"

"We're fine. Carry on, John."

"Rings and rings of guys with guns. He's living on a hilltop in a former Belgian church, heavily fortified, but he talked to us all day. They say he's a rebel without a cause, but we got him to outline exactly what he wanted to calm down his militia..." The waiter was now at the next table, folding the same napkin six times.

"Why do they need calming down?" I said.

"They take over the villages by killing lots of the residents, and then—"

"Are we all okay for—" The waiter again.

"Yes."

"They've come up with all these forms of brutal rape so that everyone talks about it and never comes back," John said.

"Such as?"

"Weeell…"

I won't go into what came after that, but take it from me, that's the last time I say, "Such as?" to a human rights investigator.

Anyhow, I didn't know all this at the time. I bought a ticket to London. This was my plan: LAX-LHR. LHR-EBB. Los Angeles International to London Heathrow; wait at my mum's house till John came back on radar; fix a rendezvous; leave for Entebbe, Uganda. I bought new luggage, perfectly suited to a war report from Africa: a $100 Gucci suitcase from eBay with a torn zip, no wheels and no lock to protect my kit. As I packed I told myself, "Listen, Jane, there is no shame in this; Kate Adie probably paid for her Tiananmen Square trip with some hostess work in Shanghai." We don't know that she didn't. My sister was less equivocal. I believe she may have said, "You can't be a war reporter, you're scared of Paris Hilton. And John isn't going to marry you."

I believe I may have answered, "Kate, it's not about him, it's about twenty thousand kidnapped children." I believe I may have been packing high heels at the time.

I made it to the gate at LAX, triumphant. Final boarding, I had time for a drink. I thumped down cash for a margarita just as my phone rang.

"Paul… ? Oh, hi, Paul." It was a friend of a friend who made documentaries. He'd been to Uganda; he'd give me some reassurance. "Yes, Steve told me about your Uganda documentary; it's a *brilliant* documentary—I haven't seen it— I'm thinking of going to Uganda and I wondered if you had any advice?"

Paul said, "Not Uganda. No! You can't take a taxi without getting mugged. You can't photograph government buildings. You can't even make eye contact—it angers them. You'll get dragged into the bushes and macheted and I am not joking."

Pause.

"I'm sort of already committed..." I said.

"Oh. OK, you'll probably be fine," he said. I stared at my wrong shoes and my fishbowl of margarita.

Paging passenger Bussmann. If you do not present yourself for boarding immediately your baggage will be removed from the plane.

I started typing an email to the *Mail on Sunday*: "I'm sorry, Frank, I can't do it. I lied: there's no such place as Uganda." Before I sent it, I noticed one new message. It was from the *Sunday Times* of Britain, the greatest newspaper in the world, and it was from Sean dot Ryan, foreign editor.

"Jane, we really want this story about John Prendergast. How soon can you do it?"

I was a foreign correspondent. FUCK! I didn't waste another minute. I ran straight to duty-free and bought new sunglasses.

24

TOFF IN A WU-TANG CLAN SWEATSHIRT

Wait in London for John to call, then go and be... a foreign correspondent? For the Sunday Times? *Are you sure this is sensible?* I began to have serious doubts on the runway. My knees were wedged into my fellow passenger's kidneys because it was a Virgin flight, which used to be fun until they nailed all the economy seats so close together that every flight was a circle jerk, and a pissy Virgin stewardess was telling me I wasn't allowed to read a newspaper while they were playing a safety video I already knew by heart, instead I should be grateful to be lectured by a cartoon character in the voice of slatternly children's TV host Dani Behr. *Dani Behr. I bet if Sting chatted you up in a green room you'd give him serious consideration.*

The serious doubts drowned out Dani's foghorn. *Jane, it's you, there'll be a horrible celebrity journalism fuck-up and 25,000 kids will be left to die... Go back to Hollywood and be a celebrity journalist: writing about wankers is a job for life...* I didn't feel sensible, but everything would make sense when I got home to Britain, a common sense country. I didn't have time to get any proper journalistic ID as I wasn't a proper journalist, but I got a letter of introduction from the *Sunday Times*, explaining that I was writing the story for them. Once I heard from John I'd be out of here.

I hadn't reckoned on my mother, however. Mum didn't like this idea one bit. She ironed my socks to make it all stop. But I was already on the phone to all my credit card companies, lifting the phone cable so she wouldn't garrotte herself as she carried washing back and forth. My mother is five foot one.

"I'm holding for the lending department... Mum, you don't need to iron pajamas..."

"Yes, but it's nicer, though, isn't it. I bet you didn't get vaccinations," she said, a surprise opening salvo.

"I'm staying in Kampala; it's a capital city, it's not Baghdad. I'm joking," I said, opting for diplomacy.

"Isn't Uganda Entebbe Airport? The raid on Entebbe, where the Israeli Air Force shot all those planes... Oh, those hostages... Oh, it was an awful mess," she said, spraying water everywhere.

"Yes, I'm holding for the lending department..." I said, packing badly in the hope she'd take over. My mother charged.

"Oh, let me do that, you'll get creases. And you can't afford the flights," she said.

"Eight credit cards," I said.

"Credit cards?! How are you going to pay them?"

"I took cash out on a credit card. That's how you trick them."

"Credit cards. I didn't have my own bedroom till I was sixteen. I had three skirts all through college and one of them was yellow."

"I've got malaria tablets," I counter-blasted.

"Bread and milk, that was Friday night. Bread and milk and sugar sandwiches," she said, turning away.

"I'll be back in a week," I said, sensing victory receding.

"Why don't you come to Italy?" she said, advancing left, then regrouping. "I don't think this man sounds like—"

"It's not about that! It's about twenty thousand kidnapped children! Look, please don't iron those, that's my best underwear. Mum—"

"You always had new shoes. My mother bought shoes from the market. Oh, the chilblains. I'll never forget that time I stood on a moth. I can still hear it crunch," my mother concluded. She'd won. I went to my room.

Then John emailed. He'd made it to Uganda, where he was writing the peace proposal in some hotel suite. Alone. He sounded down. A friend of his, Dr. John, had just been found dead. Helicopter crash. "He was a genuine friend," John wrote. "Although he once had me thrown in jail in southern Sudan, tough son of a bitch." *The medical code of conduct must be a little freer in Eastern Africa...* "Blood up to his elbows..." *Get a new doctor, I would.* "But a brilliant strategist, and he fought his whole life for peace and justice..." *Huh, another rebel.*

"How are you now?" I emailed.

Shortly after, he told me, "I am so sad."

There should be some moral proviso against sad emails from tough blokes alone in hotel rooms. I took Mum's phone while she was salting eggplants.

"Reservations, please. Entebbe, Uganda." And with that, I was on my way to Africa.

25

SHE'S KEEPING HERSELF FOR MARRIAGE

Africa. I looked down over clouds. We were passing over the forests of the Congo, thick with gold and diamonds, a feeding frenzy, kings, mercenaries and colonels elbowing each other out of the way. Kenya, Tanzania, Rwanda... further research in a fellow passenger's Ugandan tabloid revealed that Uganda's slang term for a penis was "whopper." This was Africa, baby.

On the plane I started to feel strange. Drunk, obviously, but also strange. *My God. For the first time in my career I don't feel like an arsehole, I feel... useful.* I had long suspected my life was a horrible dream, but now I'd woken up and my future had started at last. *I am with my people...*

I gazed benignly at the Useful Woman next to me, admiring her undyed gray hair, her unbleached teeth, the simple T-shirt that she and all her friends seemed to be wearing, printed with—baggy white T-shirts are cool in Africa; it's the heat or something—"Ashford Parish Church Outreach Group." No... Surely... Something's not right; they're too quiet. What... ? What are they reading?

Bibles! This was Ashton Kutcher's doing. I was flying to Africa with a planeload of missionaries, come to save the dark man from all faintly interesting sexual positions.

I fled to the toilet for a make-up break to feel superior, and promptly dropped my lip-plumping gel in the airplane toilet. This was a warning, a bad omen in any language, and I should have grabbed it out of the blue bog-juice but it was rudely sucked into the clouds before I had a chance.

"Bastards!" Off it went, my lucky charm, spinning down toward some North African Islamist hellhole, where a young woman would find it and get stoned to death.

I went back to my seat to sleep away the Christians. I closed my eyes until Robert Redford washed Meryl Streep's hair, Bryan Brown took a bath with Sigourney Weaver and Virginia McKenna romped with big cats and whatever that bloke with the beard in *Born Free* was called. Then missionaries appeared in the background, tutting. But eventually I drifted off among lion cubs that hugged you.

The plane door opened at Entebbe Airport and we were on the side of Lake Victoria, a bowl filled with morning mist, so vast it looked like the sea. I saw tooled-up soldiers and flanks of white odd-shaped UN planes. This was properly exciting, planes that actually did things, ejecting squads of Useful People all over the world.

The customs line was endless, not because of African timekeeping, but because of two dozen buck-toothed missionaries bullshitting their way through. What do missionaries write under "Purpose of Visit"? "Cleanse your filthy people of their inferior moral code"? Why did anyone let them in? Did they bring cookies?

While I was stuck in line, I stole an old newspaper from a soldier. Ugandan tabloids became essential reading, full of stories of opposition leaders killed in mysterious circumstances, prison inmates who had "no idea that men could use their arses for such wrong purposes" and a government minister stating sternly for the record, "I am not a homosexual. I am not. I have a wife and the capacity to marry fifty women." Wow. And this was after more than a hundred years of missionaries.

I was interviewing John in the capital city, Kampala. There was no way to get there except by taxi and I'd already been told that I'd get mugged. Shifty-looking cabbies made a beeline toward me. I scanned the ground transport desk: deserted. Some kind of information office: deserted. Police booth: empty. One of the cabbies looked nice, and he had a badge with a photo.

It was a photo of a cat. But I still got in his cab.

"Is Uganda... safe?" I said.

The driver, Harry, chuckled. "Ohhh, yes," he said. Then he clicked the doors locked.

As we left the airport, Africa welcomed us with a statue of two rhinos that from behind looked unfortunately like they were mating. The landscape was fresh and green—fertile. I'd read that 39 percent of Ugandan children were stunted by lack of food, but that didn't make sense. This was a country that could, theoretically, feed itself, and every building seemed to have a slogan about hard work. "ACHIEVE! EFFORT!" said a school sign. Something had gone wrong.

Through my tiredness, the African sun had melted a hole in the sky. I asked Harry to keep me awake and he rose to the challenge, driving right up the bum of any trucks in front until they pulled over and flipping on the radio. Actors in adverts literally shouted over jangling music, as if they knew the roads would be noisy. "When you have a choice, Sleeping Baby is the RIGHT CHOICE!"

The first billboard I saw advertised abstinence, with a picture of a smiling woman, just so happy not to be having sex. "She's keeping herself for marriage," the billboard shouted. "What about you?" Well, I was trying to give it away at cost, but thanks for reminding me.

Harry told me abstinence was the official government policy for beating AIDS. All you had to do was stay a virgin till you married, because your husband would be a virgin too, and married people never sleep with anyone else ever again. I was curious to see where this wise advice came from, so I asked Harry to pull over while I took a closer look at the billboard. On it was the logo of the United States Government: George Bush Senior's US Agency for International Development. Don't have sex, African people, said GB Sr. A bit rich coming from a man whose own shagging produced GB Jr. And even if both sides were totally inexperienced, it surely made for disastrous wedding nights. Like a drowning person trying to climb on a raft, next day they'd still be there, paddling.

Abstinence had been a big hit for Museveni in the nineties, but humans denying primal urges hadn't lasted, and now the policy was doing more harm than good because it was taught by Christian fundamentalists who also denounced condoms. But the US was still pumping money into billboards saying good Africans didn't like sex. Surely someone could explain the dieting parallel: at first it's "Just one quick bunk-up, then I'll go straight back to abstinence..." Next thing you're Eddie Murphy, cruising crack town giving lifts to transvestite prostitutes, or, in his words, "Being a good Samaritan."

Shacks gave way to modern buildings; harsh, boxy 70s cubes, thrown up in a hurry, then left to get filthy. We were pulling into Kampala, the capital, a rough-and-ready place where shop fronts flashed unconvincing slogans apparently dumped in the third world like out-of-date medicine. *It's the taste you taste!*

Kampala was the stomping ground of Idi Amin. You could tell this city had been home to a dictator not too long ago; someone had apparently removed all money and rule of law for years. Horrendous acts of political violence aside, it was somehow brilliant. Here was a country that cut the crap. In LA, people bang on about their Toyota Hybrid like it vacuums the dirty countryside. In Africa, the cars laughed: *We're cars, we pollute, that's what we do!* Old Chinese lorries smothered me with black pillows of smoke on the Kyagwe road. Even the men's clothing stores cut the crap. *We're going to wear denim safari suits with leopard skin elbow patches, and we're going to wear them with pink high heeled boots made of boa constrictors because we're MEN, baby!*

The wildlife knew no rules. As I stared out of the taxi window I met the eyes of a four foot tall bird, idling on a city center pavement, scratching itself and staring me down, a horrific thing with a sickening beak and a sack of pinkish gray wattle hanging off its face like a giant scrotum. The marabou stork—a fluffy name for an obvious child molester. If this stork delivered your baby, Baby would arrive with both eyes missing.

So this was where the It Girls' feather boas came from. Overhead, more storks were circling. Harry saw me looking and beamed.

"They know there's a slaughterhouse nearby," he said. "They eat the cows' heads. So why are you in Uganda?"

"I'm writing about Joseph Kony," I said. This name didn't register with Harry. *But... I thought we were in all-out civil war.* "Kony ..?"

"Oh, the Kony. That one. He would rob girls from school and use them as wives. Big problem," said Harry and whistled through his teeth. Then, as an afterthought: "I think he is dead."

I was wide awake now. Harry showed me an old tabloid. There was President Museveni talking about Kony. Kony is defeated, President Museveni said. Down to a handful of troops. *But... balls, give me a chance; I haven't even got to the hotel yet.* If the Most Evil Man in the World was already beaten, my foreign correspondent career was dead in the water.

Suddenly Harry swerved to avoid a pile-up. Another truck was sailing towards us. Harry leaned in his seat as he pulled the steering wheel down and we cleared the truck. BANG! The truck smacked into something. I looked round.

"Was anyone hurt?" I said.

Harry chuckled again. "Ohhh, no," he said. Then he looked back to check. "No."

The area got posher. I knew there would be white people somewhere because there were men on the doors with guns. I saw a hand painted sign: the Red Chilli Hideaway, where I'd booked. A youth hostel. I hadn't picked a youth hostel because I hoped to give Prince Harry a hand job in the communal showers, but because this whole mission to meet John and save the world was being conducted on my credit cards.

"This is my hotel. The Red Chilli," I said.

Harry was concerned. "You're not staying at the Sheraton?"

"No, this is my hotel."

"That's not a hotel, that's a youth hostel."

"I know," I said.

"The Sheraton is much better," he said.

"I know," I said.

Harry gave up and affably slammed the taxi into the curb. Behind us the crash was getting bigger. It looked like it had been going a while, and a telegraph pole had come down to join it. I have been known to furtively slow down by a crash. Here, a car pulled over and four people got out to watch. I wasn't sure if they'd made the journey specially, but if they had, from their expressions, this crash wasn't all it had been cracked up to be.

26

IT DOESN'T MAKE YOU GAY IF YOU'RE A TOFF

I pushed open the red iron gates of the Red Chilli and sailed up to the guard, a skinny man in an overcoat and gumboots.

"How are you?" I said, smiling.

"Fine," he said.

"Oh, only fine? What's the matter?" I said.

"Malaria." *Shit.*

"You shouldn't be working," I observed helpfully. "You should be in the hospital."

"I have no money," he said. I'd only been in Africa two hours and I was making things worse. I fumbled in my bag and gave him everything that seemed relevant to malaria: a dismal two pill sachet of paracetamol and a banana. "I can't take this from you!" he said, holding up the paracetamol. "I have no money!"

"No, really, take it, I got it free..."

"You got *this*? *Free?*" he said.

"Yeah, I ran the San Diego half-marathon..."

"You ran a marathon? But... why?"

"Half-marathon. To... to... you know... lose weight..." *Leave now. Leave now.* It's a lifetime mantra, along with "He doesn't fancy you," and "Find the door."

I hurried through reception as I had to spend two hours putting my make-up on to call John. I'd also better remember to call the school where I'd ostensibly planned to teach... Then I stopped: this didn't look like a youth hostel.

I was in a romantic equatorial travelers' bar. Rays of morning sun were climbing the hot-red paint, warming the air that drifted in from a lush garden. There was the familiar smell of mosquito coils. Shattered spirals of ash lay at my feet. Women's flip-flops slapped the floor as they hung out washing. The traffic of Kampala was far away and I could hear beer bottles clanking as the barman racked the fridge with stumpy brown bottles of African beer. Nile Special, it was called, and on the labels, cartoon lions roared. The Red Chilli was perfect. Nothing about it said, "You must be broke and rubbish."

The receptionist was reading two newspapers at once. No receptionist does that in LA.

"Hi, I'm checking in. Any messages for me? Jane Bussmann." Adding casually, "*Sunday Times* foreign desk."

"Yes!" said the receptionist and went into a back office. I smiled at no one. The sun's rays came to rest on my shoulder with the heat of a hand. Outside in the garden, monkeys squawked.

The receptionist came back with a message and unwrapped it slowly, playing me like a violin.

"But this is for Jane Bussmann, *Mail on Sunday*, travel dep—"

"No other messages?"

"Are you a teacher? Because it's from a school. It says, 'Miss Bussmann, could you call us? It's urgent.'" *No, it isn't, you're a school.* I crumpled the message. That day John had a meeting with Uganda's President Museveni. That day John was going to end the war, and I was covering it. Then perhaps cocktails. I called him.

A treacly Ugandan lady operator told me the person I was trying to reach was not available. The sun was hitting my eyes now. Time was slipping, I needed to check my emails as John would be going out for the day, but the computer was being hogged by a young white girl who had flown to Uganda to reshuffle her iTunes playlist. *Oh, she's not. Is she?* And then the Red Chilli's other guests arrived. I couldn't believe it. *She is. They all are. What the fuck do trust fund babies want with Uganda?*

The bar had been taken over by world-weary nineteen-year-olds, sunkissed on the high cheekbones they'd inherited from generations of rich men diluting their murky gene pool with supermodels. They smelled, and not just of money. I was the only white female in there without a bandana and sarong. White people: the second they arrive in Africa, they start dressing like

Mammy from *Gone with the Wind*. Even Mammy from *Gone with the Wind* knew black people don't dress like that.

"Babes, wanna do the AIDS orphanage or whitewater rafting?" said one.

"Both," she said, and sighed. "It's so hard to tell AIDS people in this country because they're all, like, really buff." I wouldn't mind, but she'll go home to a semi-senior position at Coutts Bank, which will somehow qualify her for Minister of Health, charged with destroying the British National Health Service.

Their menfolk were doing what male trustafarians always do abroad, grow an unusual beard and wear Velcro sandals with ethnic 'loons. King Trusty was wearing his hair up in two pink elastic bands as he swaggered through the reception area shirtless. *You couldn't look hard, you Jamiroquai fuckwit, you've got pigtails.* He tried to barter Marlboro for beer. *I wonder if he's shagged Prince Harry. Probably. That doesn't make you gay if you're a toff.*

It got worse. Germans started appearing. Not even the rich beach Germans with their gold belchers and pork-crackling tans, these were the scraggly hip Germans, wearing torn vests but still braying orders. They were on an overland bus journey across Africa. Why? They've mastered racism. *Fuck it, my credit card is just going to have to suck up two nights at the Sheraton. Then on safari.*

John will be leaving and Toff is still on the computer. Jesus Christ, could she type any slower? Don't they teach words at prep school? Some of us have got work to do—he'll be gone...

"Are you a teacher?" she said.

"No. Could I just—expecting an email—thank you." I logged on. *No, Toffo, I'm not a teacher, I'm a foreign correspondent now. And I have an email from John Prendergast.* I opened it smugly. It said, "Sorry, Jane, I've gone back to Washington."

27

THE SELFISH BASTARD

I lay in my room studying the splotches of blood on the walls. Some were small with dried slivers of mosquito still attached. Others were disconcertingly large. I'd spent four grand on airfares and ludicrously expensive sunglasses, and I stunk of missionary farts.

I wiped my miserable make-up off. John wouldn't be back in Uganda for a month because President Museveni had been forced to postpone their meeting. The receptionist's interest in newspapers had been another warning I'd ignored—I'd arrived the day after Africa's JFK was killed: Dr. John, it seemed, was not just another one of John's dissident friends. John Garang was Sudan's best-loved rebel leader, who'd died violently in a helicopter crash, the selfish bastard.

Joseph Kony was possibly dead, John Prendergast was gone and I couldn't afford to nip home and come back. I was staring at the textured plaster above my head, thinking, "A cottage cheese ceiling, could it get any worse?" when I realized I wasn't lying under plaster bumps, but what appeared to be thousands of cocoons. I jumped up and moved the bed, only to find it was hiding a huge smear along the wall that looked like... fat, chunky poo. So Prince Harry had woken up in the middle of the night and thought, "I really need a poo, but it's half a mile to the toilet. I can't just leave an enormous crap in the middle of the floor, that would be wrong. But if I spread it out..." Half an hour ago, I'd been in a fantastic imaginary relationship. Now I was in a wartorn African country, alone, in the poo room.

Then, after a while, I remembered I was supposed to be a foreign correspondent for the *Sunday Times*, investigating the Most Evil Man in the World, not waiting for John to catch him.

God had obviously decided I'd be a real reporter despite my best efforts not to. John's email had mentioned a friend I could talk to, a Kony expert who'd been in the field for years. I got off my backside and went to find him.

28

YOU CAN WRITE IT DOWN

I was beginning my foreign correspondent career with nothing but a phone number, but that was all I'd had when I emigrated to LA, and Jackie Brambles let me crash on her couch despite the terrible jokes I'd written for her at Radio One.

"I'll meet you at the Sheraton," said John's friend in low, precise tones. "In an hour and thirty minutes." It was on.

I staggered out of the Red Chilli. I'd decided to preserve my sanity by dressing as little like a trustafarian as possible, even if this meant hopping potholes in a ridiculous Grace Kelly wrap dress and stilettos, and Grace Kelly never had to get it together in a communal shower with toff-pube tumbleweed caught between her toes. I asked the guard with malaria—still alive, that's paracetamol for you—for directions to town. "*Boda boda!*" he answered. I smiled and waved; he was probably hallucinating.

Down on the Yusuf Lule Road the accident was still going strong. It really was a magnificent crash; it had lasted four hours at least. A motorbike with a live pig lashed on the back pelted at the mess of cars and I covered my eyes. The pig thrashed, presumably trying to cover its eyes too, but the bike missed the cars. Two men tried to push a wreck off the road. This seemed at best symbolic, and they gave up. A taxi slid inexorably towards the collision. I wondered why he didn't use his brakes. Maybe he'd got the cab cheap without any.

A moped skidded to my feet. "*Boda boda!*" said the little driver. His voice was high-pitched because it hadn't broken yet. "You go to town?" *Boda boda*, scooter taxi.

"But you haven't got any helmets," I said. He shook his head soothingly at this nervous grown-up.

"The police won't catch me," he said.

We rode so fast that the girls crossing the road with baskets of green oranges on their heads shrieked. I cringed on the back, holding my dress down and trying not to whimper out loud, but this kid half my size knew no fear: when we got stuck in traffic, he kicked cars out of the way. At a traffic light, we pulled up alongside another boda boda boy with eyeballs like orange gobstoppers. I hadn't thought to check my child's pupils. Resourcefully, the boda boda boys had taken steps to make the roads less dangerous: they were off their faces.

John's friend, the Kony expert, was waiting somewhere in the garden of the Sheraton's Rhino Pub, which hadn't quite worked out whether it was a sports bar or an African theme pub. In the meantime, someone had nailed number plates randomly across the wall. A large cartoon rhino that looked like Jack Black after a few rounds of special reserve MDMA gave me the eye.

I knew John's friend was called Joshua and that he kept his ear to the ground for information about the war, a sort of right-minded spy. I knew nothing else. I looked across the chairs but could only make out some kind of business meeting in the corner. Then I saw him, directly in front of me; a longfaced man sitting alone with a generic laptop, his orange juice separating in the sun.

Joshua was a quiet observer of his fellow man—I think. I hadn't met any in Hollywood, so I had little to base this on. I beamed and loaded my tape recorder.

"OK to tape?"

"You can write it down," he said, muted.

"So it's okay if I tape it?"

"You can write it down," he said, more muted. Gradually it dawned on me that this was different from interviewing a girl from *Buffy the Vampire Slayer* in the garden of the Chateau Marmont. The business meeting looked harmless to me—two white European types talking in self-help lectures to an African man—but Joshua wouldn't relax, so I amped up the interview persona that had worked for years in Hollywood: harmless, deferring to my host for an opinion.

"So what are all these black magic stories, then?" I said. Joshua winced.

"Unless you've done a lot of research it's hard to understand," he said. For the first time in years I dropped the persona and felt a weight lift off both of us.

"I don't understand how Kony has got away with it for nearly twenty years," I said. "I've read about his magic powers, but surely no one really believes that?"

"They all believe it, and he believes it, too," Joshua said. "It cuts across all ranks. I talk to soldiers, I talk to commanders, everyone says, 'He takes a rock, it sparkles and explodes like a bomb.'"

"They say that because they're scared of him?"

"Perhaps. Certainly the children are disorientated at first. One day you're an eight-year-old at school, the next you're firing an anti-aircraft missile. But they all say, 'When you are with Kony he's so kind, he's so very polite.'"

"Joshua... this is the same Kony that kidnapped them at gunpoint, that cuts people's lips off..."

"That's how he works: his enigma. I've never heard anyone say he is a bad person."

This story was too good to be true: Joseph Kony wasn't some two-bit war criminal, he was an antagonist worthy of the Bond girls at UN Headquarters.

"There is a group of families in Gulu you should speak to. Ask for the Concerned Parents' Association."

"What's their story?"

"Their children were taken," he said, "but they didn't keep quiet." Concerned was something of an understatement.

"Someone told me Kony's dead," I said.

"That's Kampala. People have no idea what's going on up there. Go north, people are living under army guard there, you'll see. Go north to the protected villages."

"Can you give me a couple of names of people who live in protected villages?" Joshua rocked back with a small laugh.

"There are one point six million living in them," he said.

Then Joshua answered one riddle: "This is a country of

farmers," he said, "farming fertile land. Uganda's nickname is the bread basket of Africa. But the farmers aren't on their farms, they've been in the protected villages for years; their farms go untended and now they're living off food aid."

"So you've got perfectly good land and farmers who want to work on it, and they're shipping in food from abroad?"

"Exactly." I got the impression he was trying to tell me something else, but he stopped talking while some people walked past. A land with a fake famine where parents had their kids stolen and kept quiet. What was this place? Black magic or no black magic, 1.6 million people running from one man made no sense.

Joshua leaned in. "I believe very, very strong forces got Kony when he was young, nurtured him and his ideas."

This was more than a news item on page 23. I was fired up now. I rummaged for my phone, ready to bleed Joshua for numbers.

"If Kony's kids have anti-aircraft missiles, do you think they could have shot down Garang?" I said, just killing time, still rummaging.

"Well, his kids shot down a government helicopter in 2002," he said. "But you can't write that or they'll send you to jail like the other journalist." I stopped rummaging.

"What other journalist?"

29

HOT FRANK

Two boda bodas tried to hail me outside the Sheraton. I went with the one who was cheaper.

"You didn't know where the newspaper is, did you?" I said as we did a U-turn in somewhere that looked disconcertingly like Wood Green Shopping City.

"Right!" he said.

"You just repeated what I'd said in a convincing voice, right?"

"Right!" he said, and smiled. I paid double.

By the time we pulled up in an industrial district outside the offices of the *Monitor* newspaper, I was convinced I was being followed.

"Frank Nyakairu, please. I'm from the *Sunday Times*. Of Britain." Nobody questioned me.

Frank was a star investigative reporter, tall and hot with a fiery gaze. As he looked at me steadily from under eyelashes as thick as Ashton Kutcher's, I'd never seen a man with less doubt in his eyes. Why was Frank so certain? And so certain of what?

He picked up a copy of the *Monitor* and walked me to the outdoor cafeteria, where he bought me a cup of tea.

"I read that President Museveni says Kony is down to a few remnants of troops," I said.

Frank smiled and wrote something on his newspaper. He passed it to me. It was a phone number: Betty Bigombe. John's friend the peacemaker.

"I went to the bush with Betty. She was trying to negotiate with the rebels," Frank said. "I saw thirty, which meant fifty more were hiding. Last year, a member of parliament said there were four thousand in one area of Sudan alone." Frank said this almost offhand, as if it were a thread he'd brushed off a bigger confidence.

"How did you end up in jail?" I said.

"I was up in Gulu, trying to find the crash site of the helicopter that went down in 2002. The police took me in. When I came out, the government had taken my computer and shut down the paper for a week."

"Do you think Kony's kids could have shot down John Garang too?"

"I don't know. All I know is that my friend told me they've found too many arms and legs. Some say possibly a hijacker, some say possibly a whore," said Frank. "It was Museveni's helicopter; he gave Garang his personal pilot."

"They're blaming pilot error," I said.

"The pilot had thirty years' experience."

"But if conditions were bad..."

"He would never have flown," said Frank.

"Are you sure?"

"Yes. He was my father." It was the certainty of a marked man. Any doubt in Frank Nyakairu was gone now. And his father had just died in a helicopter crash with a rebel leader on board... *No, don't you DARE ask Frank if he's single...*

"I'm so sorry," I said, sitting up. "Will you go to Sudan straight away?"

"No, have to move house this weekend," he said.

"Moving. Yikes. What does your wife think?"

"She's glad. We'll need more space for kids." I promptly wrapped up the interview, and Frank walked me out. At least I'd learned that if the Ugandan president thought Kony was down to a few remnants, he was at best out of the loop.

"Frank, it's a stupid question, but why would the government lock you in jail for writing about Kony shooting down a helicopter?"

"Because Kony is officially defeated," he said.

As we reached the door, Frank turned to me. "When my father was alive, he would say, 'I worry about you criticizing the government.' Now I have nothing to fear." Frank almost smiled.

I sat on my bunk in the Red Chilli for days dialing Betty Bigombe's number. I wondered if Betty was still in the bush, negotiating with Kony. Ugandan phones had no voicemail, so it rang endlessly until a treacle-voiced lady said, "The telephone number you have called is not available at the moment. Please try again later." *Fuck. What if Betty's dead? I can't take these sunglasses back.*

It was a shared dormitory, and even when I thought I'd closed the door the trusties would crawl in at the end of a long day's sighing, dump their wretched ethnic bags, paw at their wretched blonde hair and start their wretched talking.

"You know that guy Ben?"

"Who, Marcus?"

"No, his name's Ben. Anyway, right, my sister went to France with him..."

I wouldn't mind, but in ten years she'll be foreign secretary, her friend will be head of marketing for the Sheraton Hotel Group and they'll laugh about the day they roughed it in Uganda.

I ran to the bar. I wouldn't call John Prendergast, I was a foreign correspondent now, I didn't need to make feeble phone calls.

"This is John," said the deep bass growl. He apologized profusely for having to leave. It wasn't profusely enough.

"Where are you now?" I said, with a silent *How could you do this to me?*

"Los Angeles," he said.

Oh, for Pete's sake. "Yeah? What have you been doing?"

"I've been going round some of these movie companies. They're talking about doin' some kinda story about my, er, y'know, the stuff I do. They saw the *Vanity Fair* thing, wanted to see if we could come up with an idea..."

"Wow! That's fantastic," I said. *Scarlett Johansson's already found his hotel. She's in the elevator on the way up, practicing her sexy face in the mirror and accidentally exposing her bra strap.* "Get anywhere?"

"Nope. Johnny Depp's guy was the most keen. We were talking about whether a human rights investigator could pal up with a Darfurian refugee and go on a journey..."

"What was their take on that?" *Don't open the door. It's not room service.*

"He said, 'I'm starting to see a *Brokeback Mountain* scenario,'" said John. "He was a funny guy. I got to go back for more meetings..." *She'll find him. It's just a matter of time.*

There was no sign of John coming back to Uganda in the near future. We said goodbye and I picked at the roaring lion on my beer label. It was evident from the little investigation I'd done so far that the Most Evil Man in the World was a real story, bigger than I could have hoped. I would stay in Kampala, diligently collecting facts. My new independent life as a foreign correspondent.

Kampala was going home for the night. The beer held an equatorial sunset in its pink and orange bubbles. The bubbles popped and I walked across the garden to the dormitory. A pair of scarlet-breasted sunbirds flew across the burning clouds to their nest. Below them, a couple held hands in silhouette. My eyes adjusted: the woman was King Trusty in his sarong and bunches; the man his girlfriend, wearing his crusty 'loons.

They came into the dorm. He ripped off his sarong—no pants, balls swooping—and pulled on some jeans. What was *that*? A private school thing? Do the teachers do it in class to toughen them up for the adult world, where men flap their clanks at each other in meetings?

I turned away, only to come face-to-face with the poo. *OK, that's it; I need to get out of here.* I remembered something about a school. *Shit! The* Mail on Sunday—*holiday journalism, I had a travel gig.*

I called some poor headmaster who'd probably been marking books since dawn, muttering something along the lines of "I could probably come and be a teacher now." He sounded quite pleased. That was the solution. I would teach the children of Uganda, then save them from war.

30

THE SECOND MOST FUNNY THING

St Luke's Primary and Secondary School was 40 kilometers from Queenstown, a three-hour journey northeast of Kampala towards the Kenyan border. The school sent a coordinator to help me, a blonde called Ruth with the pragmatic calm of an era in British history that probably never existed. Two boda bodas rushed to her side, eager to bathe in her love. Watching Ruth riding through Kampala with her hair flying, she looked like she'd woken up one rural English morning, milked a pig and decided to decamp to a war zone to make peanut butter and jelly sandwiches for orphans. Then she saw my newspaper and stopped the bikes.

"*The New Vision*? Rubbish! Propaganda!" Ruth said, glaring at the headline as though it had smacked her. "Government newspaper. State owned.[14] The *Monitor* has the real stuff." She sprung on a boy newspaper vendor and gave him a filthy banknote for a paper that looked exactly the same as the other one, with out-of-focus photos and florid headlines. There was Frank's byline. "When Museveni abolished his own term limits so he could stand in a third election, there were riots," said Ruth.

"I read that the election was a big success, first democratic vote," I said.

"The election was a *joke*. The ballot papers just showed a tree and a house. Nobody knew what it meant. My friend went to vote, they asked her who she was voting for, and when she said the government, they gave her seven ballots."

---

14. *The New Vision*, 11 August 2005, letters page. Headline: THANKS, PRESIDENT MUSEVENI. "Sir—I thank President Museveni for giving us a first-class tarmac road..."

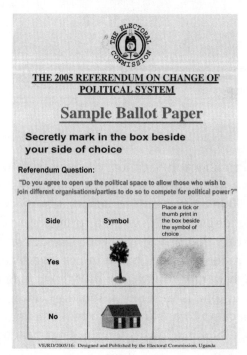

Somehow an openly corrupt country felt comforting. Talking about government plots back home made you a kook; they wouldn't invent weapons of mass destruction, that would be silly. Here it was expected. Expected and challenged. Ruth unlocked my SIM card, wedged my Gucci suitcase under the boda boda kid's chin and told him to take me to the bus park. When I looked back, she was waving me goodbye, an earth mother again.

I rode across the grubby town, past a sign for Didi's Amusement Park.

"Seventeen acres of real amusement!" Nearby, the Namirembe Parents' School was presenting a play, *The Wooden Umbilical Cord of Mbele*. My boda driver lurched to a stop.

"Taxi park!" announced the ten-year-old. We were looking down on a town square filled with hundreds of white minibuses. From above, the buses were a swarm of steel bees. Engines buzzing, they were leaving for different provinces.

"MBALE! MBALE!" someone shouted.

"TSCHOOM! TSCHOOM!" yelled someone else. I scrabbled for coins to pay the boda boda boy, then looked up. He'd grabbed my suitcase and was disappearing into the crowd. The stoned little fucker was selling my Gucci case for meth. I stumbled after him on stilettos, asking for the Queenstown bus, hopelessly confused by buses with big painted names like ARSENAL! GOD IS GOOD! BISMILLAH! A nice man led me to a fucked-up husk of a Toyota where I found the boda boda boy lashing my suitcase to the roof and reserving me the best seat. I gave him a million-shilling tip. The currency was running about 1,800 shillings to the dollar; third world countries try to keep their very poorest citizens in the game by making sure everybody has a wad of cash, even one that's only worth a nickel.

Inside the New Bus Park everyone was selling. Pants. Mobile phones. Balls of groundnuts and sesame seeds held together with sugar. Oval-faced Somali women folded banana leaves into cubes and stuffed them with green khat leaves. They were doing a good trade despite their glassy eyes. Never get high on your own supply, unless you're a two-woman khat operation from a country so fucked it doesn't even have a government; in which case, wanker yourself into the middle of next week, because odds are you won't get to see it anyway. A teenager held out children's coloring pens, fanned out in his fist like a pastel-pink nail bomb. There was a man selling water bottles refilled with yellow liquid.

I was nervous. *Was* this man selling his own piss? Was this a business plan he'd had for a while? Or did he just wake up one morning and think, "What *am* I going to do with this record-breaking collection of piss?"

The bus was alarming, so old it had no dashboard, with deafening reggae coming from a giant speaker hanging from fuse wire. My feet were nice and warm despite the holes in the floor. I looked down and saw my toes were stuffed up a live chicken. What's worse than wearing a hen as a slipper is the indignity of the creature; to stop it pecking, they'd tied the poor bird with its beak fair up its own front butt. These Ugandans are very practical people. The chicken didn't seem to mind, though; in fact, I think it farted. As I looked down it turned away quickly, staring into space.

As I sat there trying to tell chicken farts from human farts, a woman walked down the bus selling three-course meals on plates wrapped in cling film, omelets with cucumber slices and rice. The man next to me, an extremely tall fellow with a recklessly happy outlook, bought us both biscuits called *Maximum Glucose!* The labels showed a picture of a sumo wrestler to prove how fat and powerful they would make you. Wow. A country where sugar still gave you energy.

People pushed stuff at me through the windows. A man shoved his arm in, wearing watches up to his armpits:

"Watches, watches, watches!"

"Er... No, thank you, I've got one."

Horror gripped him. "Only *one*?"

Another held a red comb through the minibus window, with necklaces strung between each tooth. A boy silently presented me with a cardboard box cut down into a tray, displaying over a hundred knick-knacks meticulously tacked on with pins. I ask him how much for some hoop earrings.

"One thousand five hundred," he said.

"A thousand?" I offered.

"I don't discount," the boy said.

"Good man," I told him and paid. The boy's eyes tilted back in a slightly hurt expression. *Shit. Not only did I just haggle with a Ugandan child, I asked him for change.*

The bus driver said we'd be off in a minute. The extremely tall man found this amusing.

"We leave when the bus is full," he said. It looked pretty full to me, with thirteen people on fourteen seats.

Two hours later we still hadn't left; we had twenty-three passengers in fourteen seats and the extremely tall man was sitting in my lap and had started sweating heavily. He was a nice extremely tall, sweaty man, but this wasn't the holiday I had planned. I was swooning in the heat as the three-course-dinner lady came by with dessert, bottles of Coke, and I knew the question I was going to ask her no matter how hard I fought it.

"Have you got any Diet Coke?" An awkward pause.

I found myself holding the first full-fat Coke I'd had since moving to Los Angeles, scared to open it. The bus engine fired up. The three-course-dinner lady panicked. "She wants the bottle back for the deposit," said the man in my lap. And sure enough the bus finally started to leave. I drank the whole thing in one go, handed the bottle back and went into head spins, whimpering about sugar rush. That was it; I'd read the Internet, I knew from several authoritative diet blogs that I'd gain fifty pounds.

We plunged out of Kampala at 50 miles per hour. After waiting two hours to leave, the driver was now trying to cram an extra run into his day. We sliced across a dam over a vast river. Looking back, it must have been the Nile; I really should start reading travel guides before I leave. I looked down and saw a bird floating on a log. The log opened its mouth: an alligator! Or a crocodile, one of the two. I looked up to see another bus tearing headlong towards us. I clutched the ceiling.

"Do the buses ever crash?" I asked the man in my lap.

He ignored his cue to laugh reassuringly and say, "Of course not, young traveler," as we swerved, almost hurtling into the river below. "All the time!" he yelled, delirious with happiness. "I saw the most funny thing here. A bus fell off the dam. Ha ha ha! Then a man on a bicycle saw the crash and he was so distressed that he jumped off the dam. Wooh! Ha ha ha! Then a thief stole his bicycle. Ha ha!" A pause. He frowned. "Actually, that was not the most funny thing."

"What was the most funny thing?" I said.

"The newspaper. It said, 'Military Coup Tuesday.'"

Once you adjusted to the constant terror, Uganda was beautiful. Everything was more acute: red-soil pathways slashed electric-green fields under royal blue mountains. No hedgehogs in the road; plenty of baboons. Somewhere in the mountains of Uganda there were gorillas, and I imagined myself as Sigourney Weaver, or whatever the monkey lady was called.

It was a touching daydream, until I started thinking about ticks jumping off the gorillas, and whether or not gorillas fart, or grope your bum with their stumpy gorilla thumbs.

At one stop, an earnest man got up in the aisle and started ranting.

"I am very serious! Who are the people that will help you?" he said. "The Chinese people!" He whipped on mirror shades and held up a small bottle of green liquid. "This is the best new medicine! Sore throat? Can't sleep? Paining of the stomach?" He rubbed it on his arms. The women passengers hooted with laughter. "I am very serious!" he insisted, peeved. He walked the aisle showing a salesman's briefcase full of the stuff, but nobody bought any, so he sat down again in a sulk.

There was only one way to identify a bus stop: adolescent boys sitting on a log holding sticks. When the bus slowed down, they pelted towards us waving their sticks; the sticks were kebabs. Then another posse arrived with plastic trays of chapattis, followed by their little brothers, who ran up with heavy black carrier bags bulging with green oranges. Third-world practicality: make the little ones carry the big weights before they know any better. Finally mums came up with pudding, roasted bananas in cups. For the sugar junkie, thin men with very big biceps dragged ten-foot lengths of sugar cane, macheted them to the exact width of the minibus floor and clattered them in through the window. I wanted the sugar cane so I bought a bag of green oranges. They weren't just bitter; they got worse after I'd eaten them.

Queenstown was unspoilt Uganda. Verdant, beautiful, stretched out under Mount Elgon. We passed coffee plantations, children farming, a lone woman at the side of the road with one tit out and a hoe on her head. She looked like she'd come out from the photocopy room for a sly cigarette, torn her shirt and thought, "Ah, fuck it."

The journey ended in Queenstown Town, a small dusty place with a few Indian shops spilling cheap Chinese suitcases onto the pavement and stalls repairing watches on the roundabouts. Having bought all these watches, keeping them running was a big responsibility. We came to a stop at a grim station. "Please allow passengers to get off first" didn't apply here. Filthy and exhausted from clenching the bus's ceiling, I missed my chance to get off and the incoming passengers crushed me backwards as though this were the last bus before the Apocalypse. For a moment I thought I'd never get out from under the bums and bags, but a hand grabbed my wrist and I was shot out like a pea from a peashooter. It was the local detachment of the volunteering charity: Roddy, a smiley young man who'd been receiving the cream of American student volunteers all summer.

"Thank you so much for giving me the chance to teach," I said. "I've always wanted to work in education."

"Wonderful," said Roddy. "Will you be staying for the whole summer term?"

"No, a month will be fine," I said. "Can I get a receipt?"

"Of course. You start teaching on Monday, so you have the weekend to get used to life in a village. I'll take you to your new family." I didn't mean to look confused. "Did you not know you were staying as the child of a Ugandan family?" said Roddy. Of course I didn't, that would have meant I'd read the research. *I only came to doss for a month; teaching was pushing it, I'm not going to be someone's kid too.* This wasn't fair. I pouted in silence and got in the car.

31

AN 80s PRINCE ANDREW

We drove away from the grime and pressure of the bus station into farmland, past Guinness and Omo ads. The road sign only had two options: Queenstown and "Sugar Factory: Twice As Sweet As Normal Sugar." We passed small huts and into a neighborhood with large fancy houses set back from the road, one flanked with white ready-made statues. It faintly recalled North Hollywood. We parked outside a walled house and honked. A maid in a pale blue uniform opened a spike-tipped gate and kids came running out—seventeen of them.

"This is your father, Wallace," said Roddy.

I turned to see a tall elderly man with a nice smile and halfclosed eyes. Roddy presented me as the new daughter, a daughter covered in dust and several different people's sweat. Despite this, Wallace gave me a three-way handshake with his soft hands. I'd known him six seconds and he hugged me. Already he was the best father I'd ever had.

"Oh, you are most welcome," said his wife, Rebecca, so embarrassed not to have heard the guests arrive that she started making popcorn. Inside, their house had no ceiling, so you could hear everything in the adjacent room, but it was posh, with more sofas than Graceland. Graduation portraits looked down from the walls. Rebecca and Wallace had seven children—the national average—despite the lack of ceilings.

Rebecca's seventeen grandkids took turns to line up in front of me and smile. No sign of their parents, but everyone called Rebecca Mummy. Bleating and clucking outside were chickens, goats and a turkey that almost came up to my waist—no pets you couldn't eat. I heard what sounded like a dog barking, but turned to see a raddled old mother hen sitting next to me on the sofa. Rebecca shooed her out and brought me some passion fruit juice, and I sunk into the couch, listening to the voices around the house, speaking a soft, sing-song local language that sounded like pigeons on the chimney.

Over the next few days, I completely forgot about the Kony mission. Betty's phone still wasn't picking up, so I told myself this was background research, color, planting the *Sunday Times* readers in the setting. That, and the food was great.

Life in the village was slow and friendly with nothing to be scared of, apart from death. After a while, I realized why I felt so good here: everywhere I went, people were pleased to see me. In Hollywood, no one is pleased to see you unless you're casting *Ocean's 14*. Ugandans can't even begin to relax until the guest is settled, and I felt wary, as if I'd accidentally gone on a date with a nice person. I know that liberals always say local people are nice, "poor but kindly," "sad but proud," etc., but I've travelled a lot and it's not true. Romania: sulky. Morocco: arrogant. Sumatra: history of cannibalism, which is just rude. In Uganda, however, the niceness was out of control. I stood blinking as people hugged me relentlessly. They brought me bowls of warm groundnuts. Choirs serenaded me. I felt like an 80s Prince Andrew, minus the porn star and sailors.

One by one I met my new family. A girl of about fourteen ran in first, slim and poised, with a scarf tied at her neck like Audrey Hepburn.

"This is your sister, Lucy," said Rebecca. Lucy knelt in a curtsey to me and stayed kneeling. These people were evidently very polite. She held out my old Evian bottle.

"We found your water bottle—in the rubbish!"

"It must have... fallen," I said. I felt bad, however I did get charged three quid at Heathrow so it was obviously a priceless heirloom.

"Do you have any brothers and sisters?" said Wallace.

"Two brothers and my sister, Kate," I said.

"Where is she?"

I looked at my watch. "Probably at Elton John's party," I said. "Do you have any brothers or sisters?"

"A brother," Wallace replied.

"Where's he?" I said amicably. I converse easily.

"He was taken by Idi Amin's soldiers; they chopped his feet off and killed him. Lucy, it's OK, you can get up," said Wallace. Lucy staggered to her feet. It had obviously been my job to release her from the curtsey.

"Right," I said. "Could I have a bath?"

"Now?" said Rebecca. Too late, I realized this was a loaded question.

"Sybil!" called Rebecca. The maid left her goat-wrangling duties and shuffled inside. "It's no problem. If you would like a bath, Sybil will chop some firewood—the trees are only very close, as you can see—she can easily build a fire. We have a tap in the yard so she can fetch water and boil it and when she has enough to fill a churn she will carry it to the bathroom for you," said Rebecca. "So do you want to wash now?" Sybil locked eyes with me.

An hour later, I learned that to have a bath in an African village, you got your own bowl and jug like a Jane Austen novel, the difference being you actually took your clothes off to wash. Jane Austen probably died of cystitis.

As Ugandan children went, I had a lot to learn. All the girls wore long skirts and sensible shoes and told me I was "most welcome." Formal British, a hangover from the colonial times. Uganda was a British colony until 1962 and the British kept their hand in, with MI6 helping to install the president's army chief, a bright young thing called Idi Amin.

Wallace and Rebecca noticed that the new child refused to use the toilet. But inevitably, and I'd been dreading it, I finally had no option. Going to the loo in the third world usually means a latrine: Ugandans called it "going for a short/long call." I'd call it a hole in the ground in a shed. I found it very confusing. You could argue, "It's a hole in the ground you piss into, how is that confusing?" Because the hole is a keyhole shape. I approached it differently every day, but always managed to pee on my feet. Then there was the problem of whether to leave the door open or closed. When you walked in, black flies roared out of the hole. If you closed the door you were in total darkness with the flies, so I left it open a crack for the light, and just as I got my trousers down, baby chicks ran in, *eek eek eek*, straight towards the hole. I stumbled around in the dark with my trousers round my ankles, swatting baby chicks. I gave up and peed in the bath, i.e., in the drain on the bathroom floor. *Only ever piss in a toilet*: I came out to find it trickling across the courtyard to an old lady cross-legged in a puddle of my pee. The senior citizen sat impassively in the urine, assuming the new daughter would grow out of this behavior eventually.

I decided to take Lucy under my wing. Having her as a sister was a result, as she was the anti-Kate, washing my clothes, laughing at my jokes and generally accepting that I was older and wiser and therefore to be served. Lucy was so well raised it was difficult to teach her to mock people and swear. We would sit and listen to the radio together, giggling at the announcer. From Lucy's hesitation, I think it was probably the first time she had taken the piss out of anyone.

"Ten thousand have fled from Burundi, where attacks by the National Liberation Front... the Burundi Liberation Front... the... I beg your pardon... the... have continued," the newsreader stated. "The Ministry of Agriculture is promoting the cultivation of yellow sweet potatoes and a powerful new strain of cholera." RUSTLE OF PAPER. "Has killed eighty people. That was the news." This latest cholera was called Super Cholera, or, as Lucy and I called it, Smashing.

At our first dinner, I had my fork almost in my face when I heard Rebecca say, "Thank you, oh Lord, for the gift of this food. May it make us strong." I'd been curious about the staple diet of Uganda—posho, runny corn porridge made with water—and I remembered that 39 percent of Ugandan children were stunted by lack of food. This gave me pause for thought: I could lose ten pounds in a month. That first night I got fried chicken.

"Was it nice?" said Rebecca.

"Yes, thank you, it was delicious," I said. Every night from then on I got fried chicken. I got fried chicken when no one else was getting chicken. I tried to put a stop to this, I really tried, but Ugandans just couldn't relax until that guest was settled, and I'd gone and said the chicken made me happy. At breakfast I tried negotiating for bananas and posho like the kids, but Rebecca had spent a fortune buying me white sliced bread and margarine because it was posh and American. I tried giving the Maximum Glucose biscuits she'd bought me to the maid, but with humility taken to African heights, Sybil wouldn't take a biscuit directly from the packet: I had to ration them out into her hand, which made me want to eat them from the contact high. A week later I'd put on four pounds and there were fewer chickens running around outside.

At night, Wallace would turn on their black-and-white 70s TV with chrome trim, and UTV would hiss as the mother hen pecked me hard in the shins. There was only one channel, blithely broadcasting with an apology for the continuing lack of sound. My favorite show was a phone-in about tuberculosis. The host was a fifty-something intellectual who fancied himself; the resident expert a chubby doctor with a stern moustache who gave advice while looking straight down the lens.

"If you know someone with TB, tell them to go to hospital," he said sternly. By now, the host thought he was off camera and started digging his ear out with a pen, but the cameraman was following his own rules, whip-panning and zooming so we got to watch the host yanking wax out of his head for some time.

A hoarse old man rang in to ask if he should avoid people with pink lips.

"I think he is already a victim," Wallace said sadly.

"That is actually not true," said the doctor, pondering on the piece of wax at the end of the host's pen. "And you can only catch it from someone who is currently sick. But ninety percent of Ugandans are infected with the TB bacteria." *Ninety percent? Shit, I was already dead.* "The situation is particularly bad in areas where people are close together..." *Fuck. He's going to say*

the protected villages. Why didn't I have a vaccination at school?
Why did I hide in a cupboard? It would only have been a dent in my
arm; it wasn't a sex crime.

"... And particularly bad in the protected villages to the north."
Great. If Kony didn't get me, I'd die like D.H. Lawrence, hawking
up into envelopes and leaving them around the house for his
wife to teach her a lesson about marrying romantic novelists.

Sometimes the TV didn't work at all, and without WiFi I
went low tech and started reading paper news or, as they used
to call it, newspapers. The tabloids just got better and better:
I got hooked on a column by an angry Spanish missionary
called Father Carlos Rodriguez, who railed about checking his
friend into a government owned hotel, only for the friend to be
offered child prostitutes. The tabloids were full of mugshots
posted by famous Western charities with warnings such as
"Public announcement: the man calling himself Rupert is no
longer employed by the International Red Cross." Meanwhile, in
entertainment news, pop star Chameleon had got into a fracas
with fellow artistes Bebe Cool and Bobi Wine. Chameleon later
presented himself to the police, accompanied by his brother
Weasel and his lawyer, Paul.

In the mornings, I'd go jogging past women skinning ears of
corn, past the old lady in huge Yootha Joyce spectacles who sat
outside her hut reading the Bible all day, past round-bellied kids
at the water pump. As I passed them, I'd hear a voice squeal:
"Muzungu!" Meaning "A white person!" I'd turn and see the kids
pelting towards me. They thought my jogging was hilarious;
they'd never seen an adult running out of choice.

"Come on, then," I said. They whooped and gave chase.
Somehow I made it to the gate first and jumped up and down
punching the air. *Nice one, you've just cheered yourself for beating*
a bunch of barefoot starving children. Come and have a go if you
think you're hard enough, AIDS babies! I'll have the lot of you! I
shook hands with all of them by way of an apology and they ran
back to their mums at three times the speed. The little sods had
been too polite to beat me.

32

STUPID *BLADE RUNNER*

I was sitting outside, locked in a staring contest with the hen, when Rebecca gave me the bad news.

"You go to school tomorrow," she said. I really didn't want to go to school. Rebecca handed me some laundry, specifically my white shirt and my friend Pauline's button-down blue skirt. *Oh crikey, not those, I'll look like a nun...* "I starched your clothes!" she said. "For school!" Wallace also came out.

"So what lessons have you prepared?" said Wallace. They wouldn't let this school thing go.

"Do teachers normally... prepare?" I said. My African mum and dad exchanged glances. But how hard could it be to teach a large class of rural primary school children with English as a second language?

I walked to school with Lucy at 7:30 a.m. the next day. The clothes were starched stiff, my Victoria's Secret underwear not unlike cardboard. If it creaked, Lucy didn't mention it.

"I can teach. I mean, I went to school," I told her. "All I've got to do is not be one of those teachers with sweat patches and their flies undone." Lucy agreed that this was a good place to start. I was confident. The night before, Rebecca had told me a good story about a rat that stole a loaf of bread, so I'd done some lesson preparation after all. I'd drawn this picture of a rat.

On the way I saw some kids in school uniform. They were maybe fifteen, sixteen years old. The rat wasn't going to fly. Shit, I had nothing. Then it hit me: writing scripts. Brilliant! I was going to teach African village children how to tackle an unexpected obstacle at the beginning of Act Two.

As I approached the school, the kids came running out, delighted.

"Hello! Hello! Hello!"

I called back, "Hello!"

"Hello! Hello! It is the teacher!"

This was fantastic; I was useful here. A teacher, that's what I was supposed to be. Then one of them called, "Andrea! You came back!" All the children ran towards the school, cheering, "Andrea has come back!"

I was sulking by the time I reached the principal's office. Outside the school was huge and flat, ringed by low concrete classrooms. On the walls there were lists of the pupils I was expected to teach. Very long lists. There was no sign of the principal, or, for that matter, any teachers. A lone schoolboy sat in the corner, feet chastely tucked under him, waiting for some kind of punishment.

"Where is the headmaster?" I asked finally.

"He is there, Andrea," said the schoolchild, pointing out of the window. A man sprinted past, chasing children out of the school. Some time later he came into his office and leaned on his knees, panting.

"They did not pay their school fees so I am denying them exams!" heaved the principal. "Are you replacing Andrea?"

"Maybe," I said sadly.

"Andrea was most welcome," he said, sadder. "She formed an environmental club. She planted an organic vegetable garden; she got us free seeds... Look, that's her mango tree. Very nutritious..."

He gazed mournfully out of the window. The schoolchild sighed for the good old days. Then the principal perked up.

"Miss Ochana! Come here!" he said. "This girl is replacing Andrea!" A teacher came in, beside herself with joy.

"Oh, how wonderful!" said the insensitive academic. "Andrea was too excellent; she taught math and biology, very effective." Another teacher arrived and boorishly gave me a snapshot of some young, clean, wise-looking tramp. This was Andrea, the volunteer teacher before me. An American, of course, maybe twenty-two, the kind of high achiever who doesn't burn out at forty as a courtesy to normal humans, she just becomes a senator with a charity on the side.

"Andrea got the family planning people to come and do a film show..."

I changed the subject. "How many teachers do you have?" I said with remarkable restraint.

"Twelve," said the principal, surprised at my aggression.

"And how many students?" I said. He knew perfectly well where I was going with this.

"We have nine hundred students," he said.

"The classes must be massive." He can't expect me to teach nine hundred divided by twelve.

"Only in the younger classes. P1 has two hundred students. But S2 is much, much smaller. So will you teach Andrea's class?"

"Maybe," I scowled.

"Oh good, because they loved Andrea's drama lessons. And her girls' football club. She was headmistress for a week and we didn't have any riots. In fact, the school was cleaner." Perhaps it was. But could she teach "Where to Place a Page Ten Moment"?

The head led me out in front of the school. I calmed down. *Remember, Jane, Andrea wasn't these children's fault. Women like that descend on the third world with no warning. Just look at the Spice Girls.*

"Here is Jane," said the principal. "Do you know where she's from? Remember how I was teaching you about World War II? Who were the Allied countries?"

Silence. I couldn't think about the link as fierce sun was

pouring in my eyes and a sea of 900 children were staring at me thinking, "What the FUCK is that?" while I was thinking, "Sun damage! Sun damage!"

A bell rang and all the children started running. Then I noticed they didn't have one flip-flop between two. A tiny girl tripped and fell, dropping a little bag of peas. She howled in agony for her lunch, a handful of peas scattered in the dust. This was biblical.

In the classroom the staring continued. I told myself it would be fine. Just bond with them.

"Hello, my name's Jane. Do you know who the richest woman in the world is?"

Blank faces. I scanned the classroom. Please, someone say "J.K. Rowling, miss. Now tell us your inspiring anecdote about how she was so poor she wrote the Harry Potter books in a café and how, thanks to the ancient art of storytelling, she's more minted than the Queen." Total silence. Shit.

"Hands up who likes Harry Potter!"

Blank faces. Never mind Harry Potter, half these kids hadn't got adult life expectancy. I took a deep breath.

"OK, so I'm going to teach you storytelling, which goes back past the Ancient Greeks to... er... Anyway, there was this young man. Not in Greece, in America, and he was poor. Not like poor, poor..." *They're thinking, "She's rubbish compared to Andrea."* "Er, how this young man got his break was, he used to go on the Universal Studios tour. That's like... er... He would take the tour and he'd sneak away from rest of the tourists and find an empty office and put his sign on the door—I forgot to say he had a sign made, with his own name on, that said he was a movie director—and he'd invite people who worked in the studios to have meetings with him. But secretly he was trying to learn what they did." *OK, they now think I'm clinically insane. Rats, it's too late, there's no moral to the story.* "But the *moral* of the story is, anyone can be a storyteller if you learn the principles, because do you know who that young man was?" *I wish I was dead, I wish I was dead.* "Steven... Spielberg."[15] The children stared at me, baffled.

My mind went blank. *Think of a story, any story.* All I could think was that these nice kids had scraped together a penny to come to school today and I couldn't think of a single thing to teach them. *Find the door.* It was open because they didn't have one. *Just run, they'll never find you... Any shitty bloody story, come on...* A perfect example of a hero's quest came to me in a vision. *How about...? Oh, they are going to love this. I AM brilliant.*

"OK, this is a 'Be Careful What You Wish For' story. There is a hero, his name is Rick and he's a policeman, he has an inciting incident. That's like a thing where he realizes his life is rubbish. He has to catch four escaped criminals. Who've escaped..." I started frantically drawing stick people on the board. "... And then he meets this girl and then he's told he has to kill her and..." *Why am I drawing the plot to* Blade Runner *on a blackboard in Uganda?* But I couldn't stop. Andrea's picture was watching me. I could sense it.

"End of Act Two, his partner arrives on a spinner..." *Tits.* "That's like a hovercraft..." *Shit.* "That's like a car, in space..." *Stupid* Blade Runner*!* "... and at the end, we learn that her *spirit* is more important than the fact that she's a..." *Bollocks!* "... replicant. It's like a robot. Never mind. Just write, 'There Is a Hero and They Have a Problem.' That's a story. Write a story. Can anyone think of a name for this hero?"

A girl at the front took pity on me. She said slowly, "His name. Is Jane."

"Thank you. What's your name? Melanie? Thank you, Melanie." I drew a stick man and named it Jane. "There is a hero. His name is Jane."

I could feel sweat patches. I sat down, and the starch made Pauline's skirt bend open at the buttons. They could see my underwear.

"I'll be back to collect your books..." I said and ran outside.

---

15. This may not be a true story.

A few minutes later a young boy brought me a pile of green exercise books. Here's what the kids wrote:

"There is a hero. Her name is Jane..." *Aw, that's nice.* "... and she has a problem. She has AIDS."

"There is a hero. Her name is Jane. She has a problem. She has poverty, poor nutrition and AIDS."

"There is a hero. Her name is Jane. She has a problem. A man follow her home from school; now she had AIDS."

These kids had copied each other's homework!

They handed me more and more tales of suffering. Jesus, what had I done? By the time I read the last assignment, the hero had been kicked out of her village "for great shame" and died of prostitution in a Kampala slum. I turned over one girl's homework and on the back she had written me a letter. "Dear Madam," she wrote. "I am a complete orphan. Can you help me as I cannot pay my school fees. My mother and my father are dead, both from..." Great, it was 9:20 a.m., and I'd made sixty AIDS orphans realize they were all doomed.

"You can, er, tear this exercise out of your books and let me keep it," I said casually. If the board of education found out about this, I'd be prosecuted.

Mr. Kikuubo, their real teacher, stepped in. He was a real teacher in every sense, his whole body formed by teaching. He walked with his chest out, hands clasped behind his back as though holding a cane, his belt slung low, even though he wasn't a fat man.

"Are you OK? You are enjoying teaching in Africa?"

"I think I've messed up. I wanted to teach them storytelling, but, er... look." I showed him the pages and pages of real-life tragedy.

"The lesson you are teaching is what? A life-skills class!" he said. Thank God, whatever life skills were. Mr. Kikuubo started flicking through a textbook. This standard-issue textbook contained the line "Think about the results of every decision you take and choose decisions which have good results. Bad decisions will affect your future life. During your free time, engage in indoor games, then those that want to teach you bad manners like drugs and alcohol will not find you." My friend paid several grand to be told that at a clinic in Malibu, and she had to share group-hug sessions with the kid from *Terminator.*

Mr. Kikuubo kept flicking through the textbook. I prayed for him not to stop at sex education, but God was off picking his nose somewhere and Mr. Kikuubo thumped the book open at a diagram of an enormous penis, triumphant. Even textbook nobs were bigger in Uganda.

"So here you have what they are taught..."

Which is how I came to learn my African ABC: Abstinence, Be faithful, Condoms, followed by "How Not to Catch AIDS From Your Mum Off a Safety Pin." As I wrote it up on the board, determined to turn the day around, I caught Melanie looking at me, and I recognized the look: betrayal. I was dressed in a white shirt with a blue skirt and I'd flown to Africa to lecture teenagers about abstinence. How did this happen? Never mind Andrea, I was Julie bloody Andrews.

"Right, well, that about wraps it up. Thanks very much." I grabbed my bag and ran out. Pause. The kids sat there, looking at each other. I looked at my watch and casually walked back in.

"OK, so there's forty minutes to go..." Then, from nowhere, came inspiration: "Who wants to play with a digital camera?" Instantly they mobbed me. I was the most popular teacher in years. Andrea was just a name on a list.

When I left the school, I saw a stray priest and instinctively grabbed Melanie's hand. As one, the kids saw it was okay to touch me and I walked home with them all trying to hug me at once. Obviously at that point I was missing the genuine warmth of Christmas at the Gap, and frankly, those kids would make useless guerrillas.

That night Rebecca walked me through her garden to her son's house to witness the miraculous recovery of Faith, the daughter of a family friend. Faith had suddenly dropped to the ground on the way to school. Next thing she was in hospital, paralyzed with a mystery infection of the spinal cord. But now Faith could walk again, and Rebecca was letting her recuperate in their son's house because Faith's mum had spent all their money on hospital bills.

Out of financial respect to Rebecca, Faith and her mum were sitting in the dark to save the cost of a candle. "Blimey, it's dark in here!" I said. Come on, was I supposed to just work it out for myself? Then on the way back through the garden, we passed what looked like statues.

"Oh, they're nice, Rebecca. What are they?" I asked probably expecting the answer, "Tribal deities that have cured Faith of her affliction."

"That is the grave of my daughter, and my other daughter, Lucy's mother," Rebecca said.

I finally understood why everyone called Rebecca Mummy, and why she didn't seem entirely over the moon about this. Rebecca had had her retirement plans shelved by AIDS. I could be wrong, but I'd read that the man George Bush put in charge of foreign aid had the chance to make AIDS drugs affordable in Africa. However, the unfortunately named Andrew Natsios said it would have been irresponsible, because these drugs needed to be taken at the same time every day. He really did mean Africans couldn't tell the time. Which is ironic, because Africans have more fucking watches than anyone I've ever seen.[16]

---

16. "If you say, 'One o'clock in the afternoon,' they do not know what you are talking about... They use the sun." USAID boss Andrew Natsios.

Village life was great. I had nice parents, I was terrifying the priest with my washing line festooned with Topshop diamanté panties, and every morning I'd go jogging with seven kids. Being a foreign correspondent rocked. *I could stay for months. Really try to help these children...*

Then John called.

"Can you..." *Yes. Yes I can.* "... get to Gulu?" John was coming back to Uganda to work on the peace deal with Betty Bigombe. They'd be in Gulu, on the edge of the war zone. I could join them there and cover it.

Now, you are on the outside. I am aware it may look to you as though I abandoned those children, but ask yourself this: would a bad person have shown sixty AIDS orphans how to reduce red eye in their holiday shots?

I called a Gulu hotel I'd read about on the Internet and booked a room. As an afterthought, I asked Rebecca if I'd be safe.

"Can John Prendergast come here instead?" was all she said. I imagined John playing cricket with the grandkids in the garden. It was a lovely image; he was terrific with kids and always let them win. How great of him. But then, when the cricket was over, he left to fit doors on the school classrooms. It was now 10 p.m. and he still wasn't back. I couldn't blame him, even if it was *my* daydream.

So I waved goodbye to my Ugandan family and sixty AIDS orphans and began the journey to Gulu, on the edge of the war zone.

33

COLDPLAY

On the bus a man turned to me. A fellow traveler and affable member of the public.

"Are you a journalist?" he asked. How dare he.

"No, I'm a foreign correspondent."

"Well, be careful. People will be watching you." Another warning, this time in the form of a warning, as I'd evidently had trouble with the previous signs, omens and slaps round the face. I should have been worried. Instead, I thought, "Under surveillance. How cool."

To get to Gulu, Rebecca and Wallace had cautioned, take an early bus and arrive before it gets dark. Some of Kony's rebels were active on the Gulu road at night and the first you'd know about it would be a bunch of kids sweeping out of the grass with guns. Not a problem; it was barely lunchtime. Then the bus broke down.

It was barely teatime as the bus broke down for the millionth time. The driver pulled something that looked like a dead octopus out of the engine, said he knew a man who would give him another one and ran away. Instinctively, every passenger stepped out to hail a different bus, but our ticket collector wouldn't let us leave. A bishop started fighting with the collector. I bought a Coke to watch. This was awesome. At least for the first fifteen minutes, then I started to get nervous. It would be dark soon.

"We'll make it," said Helen, a slim girl in trendy tight jeans. "God willing," she added, breaking to a rousing chorus of everyone's favorite funeral song, "I Will Always Love You." They loved country music here, probably warming to the motif of death.

It was barely dinner time as night fell and we were still waiting. Then, sure enough, the driver came back with a new octopus and the journey began again.

We arrived in Gulu after dark. I could make out ditches that brimmed with rotting banana peel, plastic bottles and empty sachets, which I later learned were cheap gin. There was an edge here.

I went to the hotel I'd booked, the Roma. It looked welcoming. I didn't care about the two annoying white missionaries on the verandah; I was safe.

But the Hotel Roma had no recollection of me calling to book a room. I got a bad feeling. A fat moth sizzled on a light. The receptionist pored over the book.

"I don't have that name," she said. "Are you sure you called?" I told them I'd take any room, smoking, non-smoking. They were full. I looked around. The missionaries had retreated indoors. This was not a place to be stranded.

I went to the next hotel. The receptionist shook his head. I was now the only white person and people were staring.

The next hotel; no rooms. At some speed, I lumped my suitcase back to the bus park, thinking I could get a night bus and wake up somewhere less scary, but they told me I'd missed the last bus out of town.

Now it was night and I was alone. Suddenly Gulu looked like a cartoon hell. Flames shot up from the drains, burning off the rubbish. Shadows crossing the road seemed to be limping, twisted; why had all these amputees come out at night?

I was standing in the street with my suitcase thinking, "Oh shit," when a woman popped up from thin air. A hugely tall woman in a business suit.

"Let me help you find a hotel," she said. "I'm Cleo. I'm Betty Bigombe's niece." John's colleague. Saved. Before I could speak, she'd grabbed my heavy case as though it were full of cornflakes and marched off up the road. I trotted after her. All I could think was, "I am so glad to see you, Cleo, even though you are a giant freak."

Cleo took me to a hotel called Sunset, which was creepy, dark and full of policemen. There were no touristic niceties, no soft edges, just gray painted doors, open showers and plastic chairs round a TV in a mess room that looked like a barracks. It didn't even have the reproduction paintings of roses supplied en masse to motels and cancer wards worldwide. But it was better than a night in a burning ditch and Cleo smiled and unlocked my room.

"This is very kind of you," I said.

"You are most welcome." She smiled. Cleo was relieved that someone from the international press had come to cover the war, and I praised Betty's efforts to lure Kony out of the bush, probably hoping this tall woman would tell her aunt about the really nice girl who should be invited round for dinner along with John. We swapped numbers and Cleo left.

I sat on the hard bed, peeking through the curtains. Right opposite me, a gang of cops were drinking. I told myself, "Don't get paranoid, it's only the war zone." But just in case, I backed up my entire hard drive onto a CD and labeled it "COLDPLAY," so no one would want it.

34

SHE THOUGHT HE WAS STILL SINGLE

The next morning I woke up to the Muslim call to prayer; it turned out that Hotel Sunset was near a mosque. Islam really is the most atmospheric religion.

I'd been told to wait for my interview at the Acholi Inn, the finest hotel in northern Uganda, so I set off, dodging a cow with five-foot horns that was asleep in the middle of the street.

By day I could see the town properly: Gulu had been fucked. I don't know the median number of amputees per capita, but Gulu had too many. Something about this town didn't add up. I'd read that Gulu had Uganda's fastest-growing economy, but there was rubble everywhere. Tailors sat at sewing machines waiting for no one to commission clothing from the blue gingham hung around them; stalls sold tins made into different kinds of tins and oil lamps crafted out of motor oil cans; and the garbage collectors of Gulu had plainly come out on sympathy strike with the bin men of London in 1979 and were still standing on principle. This flummoxed me. If this was Uganda's postwar Never Had It So Good, why were people selling empty water bottles as containers?

I walked through a street market selling marble wash jeans and came to a roundabout with an enormous wall of signs, nearly all of them for charities: War Child of Holland, the American Refugee Committee, the Norwegian Refugee Council, the good Samaritans of every nation and endless local NGOs too. There were white people dotted everywhere; purposeful white people in khaki, driving purposeful white Toyota Land Cruisers, the standard-issue vehicle for Useful People. I was awestruck by how the Useful People had landed and got to work in a country I'd barely heard of. Move over and leave this to us, we'll fix it.

On the way to the Acholi Inn, I stopped for street food, starting with a donut and a chapatti Rolex fried at the side of the road. Chapatti, as good as any curry house, because of the Indian influence in Uganda. Idi Amin kicked all the Asians out in 1972, being mad, but kept the cuisine because, while mad, he wasn't crazy. Rolex was the luxury version, with fried egg and tomato rolled in it.

There are those who say you should be careful with street food. I say yes, but they are the kind of people who have never learned how to operate their own intravenous drip after eating a cheese ball carved in the shape of Dracula's head at a vampire party in a Transylvanian castle, and next time me and those people find ourselves on intravenous drips, I will be an expert, and they won't. Those people are the kind of people who have never woken up with a series of inexplicable bruises in a sea gypsy village overlooking the Andaman Sea after discovering a drink locals claimed was "worse than Red Bull." They are the kind of people who would have worried when the live chicken leaped onto the raw donut buns in Uganda, leaving a big hen print of dirt; people who would have found somewhere else to eat when the vendor flicked the hen off and fried the bun, hen print and all.

The Acholi Inn, the finest hotel in northern Uganda, looked like a rundown YMCA with an armed guard. The bar was full of Westerners come to save the children, documentary makers, charity workers and diplomats, all buying drinks from an impassive aggressive barman, an arrangement that would last as long as Westerners came to save the children. It pained the Acholi Inn greatly to have customers, customers who insisted on returning frequently and pressing large sums of money on the hotel in return for minimal service. But the Acholi Inn bore its displeasure with silent fortitude, trying to ignore customers in the hope they'd go away. And much as Paris Hilton's had done, this ignoring helped me realize that I was the one with the problem for objecting to broken linoleum floor tiles, no cubicle doors in the Ladies', and one toilet that even had half the cistern smashed off, for pity's sake. Speakers strung in the trees played ragga so loud it distorted, but no one asked for it to be turned down. I asked the barman, an expressionless man called Roger, if he could lower the volume. He simply wandered off and never came back. The Useful People took it all in their stride. *I bet if the chef couldn't be arsed to turn up one day, UNICEF would do a food drop.* I'd learn to think like them somehow and not care about toilet paper when I was away with John and Betty.

I waited for John in a plastic chair by the Acholi Inn's incongruous swimming pool. By now, I was so excited I was acting casual as inch-long ants fell out of my hair. I was trying not to plan beyond our silver wedding anniversary. We'd be in a safari lodge at sunset, not a tent this time, probably some kind of grand colonial lodge in Botswana, looking down on a herd of elephants, if they had them. John and I would be old, but only with crow's feet, not all hunchbacked with claws. We'd be drinking gin slings with his cool friends, who'd be diplomats—no, archaeologists. The pygmy would be old but loyal. Holding hands with his pygmy wife. No, that's disgusting. Anyway, we'd have returned after a day in the field trying to... er... talk to some rebels or something... I'd have fallen asleep on their wicker sofa—but not be snoring—and he'd come in... Look, where the fuck is he? I've been here for hours.

Roger the barman brought my tab.

"Wow! That's expensive," I said.

"Yes, but the other hotels are not safe," he said. "Are you staying here?"

"No, it appears you have to work for a charity to afford it—"

"Jane?"

I turned. It wasn't John Prendergast. It was a petite black lady in a bright red and white tracksuit and baseball cap. She said John wasn't in Gulu. Suddenly the ants were really getting on my tits. John was in Washington. John had to stay in Washington and lobby because the international community wouldn't intervene in Darfur.

"You're joking," I said.

"I know, the international community has very been slow to react," she said. I turned to Roger the barman.

"Bloody genocide. It's me, isn't it?"

"I think it *is* genocide," Roger said.

"It's me." I lurched unsteadily out of my chair. The ragga was hurting my ears. "Right, it's 9 a.m. I think I'll go to bed. Could I get some beer to go?"

Just then, the small woman grabbed her chair, stepped up onto it and ripped the cord right out of the speaker. It was indeed Betty Bigombe, the toughest peacemaker in the world.

And get this. Where the government and the ruling elders had failed, this tiny woman went into the bush alone to negotiate with Joseph Kony, the Most Evil Man in the World. Former government minister Betty Bigombe was significantly more important than John in the Ugandan peace process, so I decided to interview her to ask her what John was like. Twenty minutes later, we finally established that she thought he was single.

Betty's story was even more unbelievable. A 50-year-old single mother, she grew up in a local village, one of eleven brothers and sisters raised on one meal a day.

"Oh, I taught in a village," I said. "Where did you go to school?"

Betty had been to Harvard. She became a government minister dispatched to end the war with Kony, was removed in 1994, got a new life in Washington not to mention Harvard honors, but gave it all up for one last shot at bringing Kony in alone. And already I knew the question any magazine would want me to ask her: Does she find it hard to meet men?

So that both sides would trust her, Betty didn't work for anyone. "I was using my own money on satellite phone bills and the rebels expect you to call them morning and night. I spent $1,000 in one week. I couldn't send one of my children back to school because I had exhausted everything. I was thinking of taking a flight back," she said. But she stuck it out.

No Westerner has come out alive... Betty took local elders

and some of the Acholi Religious Leaders Peace Initiative, a group of people from all faiths who'd got together to try and talk peace with Kony's rebels.

"There are very scary moments," she said. "You go into the forest. There are no signs of life. Homes that have been deserted for the last fifteen years. And you know that the rebels are observing you. I've seen one elder pee himself from fear and say, 'I can't go on any more.'"

"Would Kony kill you?" I asked her. Betty looked into the tree above.

"I asked Kony and his number two, Vincent Otti, whether he would kill me and they said, 'No, Kony would not want to hurt you at all.'" As an afterthought, however, they'd mentioned that if Kony's advisers decided to hurt her, "It's non-negotiable." Kony had several advisers, including an extremely old Italian World War I veteran called Lakwena, a Chinese man called Ing Chu, who claimed he could conjure ghost Jeeps to scare Colonel Otema's soldiers, and two Americans: King Bruce, who they say turned rocks into bombs, and a thug called Jim Brickley, also known as Who Are You (short for Who Are You to God). All scary, all unpredictable and all figments of Kony's imagination.

My head was spinning. Who was this man?

"It started when he was a teenager," Betty said. "He got a fever. Where people have hallucinations and talk to themselves. Then he disappeared. One day he came back and didn't talk for days. Finally he asked for some little girls to come and predict what was going to happen to him, and two girls totally independently predicted that he was going to be a leader and cure people. I think Kony had cerebral malaria." Cerebral malaria is the kind that messes with your brain—obviously—and would be a prosaic explanation for Kony's craziness, and probably the Chinese magic dude, too. But the physical manifestations of Kony's supernatural power foxed everyone. "Believe it or not, the rebels make little models of the army helicopters, they set them on fire, and from the way the helicopter burns, Kony can predict how the battle will go. He is always right, his commanders say."

Lakwena was the real problem. The Italian World War I vet was the spirit who started the war in 1986, when Alice Auma, a random peasant, announced to her neighbors that they should do what she said because she was now possessed by the spirit of an Italian military officer. Alice promised her supporters that bullets wouldn't hurt them if they rubbed themselves with shea butter, and despite frequent indicators to the contrary, people went along with her. The people of the north were so fed up with poverty that it seemed a raving crackpot covered in nut butter was their best bet for parliamentary representation. Alice's greasy Holy Spirit Movement even won battles before a standoff in a forest with Museveni's artillery ended in a sheet of bullets. The spirit abandoned Alice, hopped into her brutal dad, Severino, and finally took refuge in one of her followers, Kony. Alice turned up in a refugee camp in Kenya, where she sat hounding Betty by phone.

"She's a nuisance. She just wants money." Betty frowned. "She keeps saying she wants to come back, that she has the more powerful spirit and can exorcize Kony."

On the surface it was an epic circle jerk, but an epic circle jerk from people with machetes. I had no idea how John and Betty were going to talk peace with a man like that. Then Betty told me something that threw my whole story.

She told me that Kony, the child kidnapper, wanted to stop kidnapping. He wanted to talk peace. He'd wanted to talk peace ten years ago.

My head hurt: Kony wanted to stop kidnapping? This was a disaster. If John was trying to stop a man who wanted to be stopped, I had no story. Any celebrity journalist knew that without an angle the story might not run, and I'd already told John it was running. Telling your interviewee that the story won't run is the end of the world. It's one thing when it's, I dunno, Tom Cruise, but when it's John Prendergast... this would totally undermine his faith in me as a professional. I'd have to give up the whole dream and go home.

I asked Betty, "Are you sure Kony wants to talk peace? What if he's the Most Evil Man in the World *and* a liar?"

Betty told me the rebels had been calling her to talk peace for years. They'd carried on trying to talk even as recently as last week, when the army had attacked, captured Kony's wife and another sat phone. *Peace?* I was devastated.

Then, possibly as a favor, Betty told me something else: "It's beginning to look like a pattern: each time I inform the government I'm going to meet the rebels, it looks like the government immediately attacks them. The area where the rebels are going to be is very identifiable because of the network coverage."

Deep in my Sweet'N Low-silted, sun-rusted brain, cogs started turning. The army traces Betty's phone calls and immediately goes in to attack. Attack what? Kony's army was largely made up of kids. The Ugandan government are our friends; we give them a fortune. And are they sabotaging peace talks and bombing kids? This was a massive story. I had to write it. Because if I wrote it, John Prendergast might fancy me.

Just then, everybody stopped because a brand new green Range Rover had pulled up outside the inn. The license plate had no numbers, just four gold stars, and a man got out: a huge barbecue steak of a man in combat clothes and a peaked cap, barking at the receptionist in an impossibly deep voice. His eyes flicked from side to side, as though scanning for someone who had seriously pissed him off. I suspected he always looked like that. But what struck me most about this man was his strange walk: one step forward, half a step back, as though hobbled by a pendulum.

My God. His whopper is so big it's breaking his stride. He was Lieutenant Colonel Charles Otema, boss of the good guys in the war zone. Military intelligence chief of the Uganda People's Defense Force, the official government army. As a foreign correspondent, I knew it was my duty to interview this colonel, but for some reason, possibly a donut with a hen print in it, I needed to go to the toilet. When I came out, no more than an hour later, the colonel had gone.

I saw Betty leaving and ran up to her.

"Betty, the religious leaders, how can I get hold of them?"

"Opposite Mega FM," she said.

"Brilliant. Thank you. Oh, and thank your niece for me."

Betty frowned.

"Say thanks to Cleo," I said, "for finding me the hotel."

"I don't have a niece called Cleo," said Betty, and walked off to her next meeting.

35

TWO GREAT PRIESTS

OK. Betty's got ten brothers and sisters, seven kids each; that's seventy nephews and nieces; there must be one she hasn't heard of. Great uncle Hermann gave me and my brother matching dresses for Christmas, for God's sake... *Jane, Betty went to Harvard, I think she can remember a niece.* Shit. And if Cleo is some random nutter, how would some random nutter find me, and how would that random nutter happen to drop one of only two names that would make me trust her? *And you told Cleo all about John and Betty's presumably secret dealings with Kony.* If Betty's phone is being tapped, that's the secret police, military intelligence... Colonel Otema, the human giant. Shit.

I didn't like priests, and the Acholi Religious Leaders Peace Initiative seemed likely to harbor them, but Betty's description of an elder peeing himself from fright stuck in my head. Perhaps I could persuade one to do it on camera. That wasn't my pitch when I turned up at the Religious Leaders HQ, so they gave me a phone number and told me to call it as soon as possible. The number was for Father Carlos Rodriguez, author of the angry newspaper columns I'd been reading at my African family's home in Queenstown. He sounded very keen to talk and said he'd come and meet me first thing.

At 7:30 a.m., the Hotel Roma smelled of fresh roast coffee and fresh roast goat. I'd wandered up from Hotel Sunset to wait for the missionary, and was sitting on the verandah, vaguely scanning the street for Richard Chamberlain in *The Thorn Birds*. I wasn't paying attention to the white pickup truck that pulled up, or the man in a T-shirt and khakis climbing carefully out; a man in his early forties but with very young eyes blinking behind wire-rimmed glasses. When I turned, Father Carlos could have been a German tourist, except he was nice.

The missionary told me he'd come to Uganda from Madrid seventeen years ago and was still here. The people, he said, were just so nice, it made up for days like one in late August 2002.

It began when a letter arrived from out of the bush.

"Myself and another priest, an elderly man called Father Tarcisio, had developed a relationship with one of Joseph Kony's top men, a commander named Charles Tabuley," he said.

The letter was from the rebels and it contained an offer. Father Carlos and Father Tarcisio went to meet Kony's men in the bush, armed with nothing but a Bible. The rebels brought seventeen children and gave them to the priests.

"They came out in that way," said Father Carlos, pointing at his pickup; no bullets fired. The children were back with their families, he said, and if I wanted to meet some former child soldiers there was a charity in Gulu I could visit.

The priests got permission from the government and military intelligence to meet the rebels again in the bush. But when the priests went back to get more kids—and how often can you say that in a positive context?—a bullet flew past. Father Carlos dropped to the ground: he had walked into a trap.

"There was a terrible barrage of artillery fire for about half an hour," he said. The missionary dragged himself into a hut, where a thought occurred to him—grass roof. He ran out again just as the hut burst into flames.

But it wasn't Tabuley or Kony's men firing at the unarmed missionaries; it was the government army. The army beat up the priests and took them into custody. And there had been another peace talk in 2001 that ended in sabotage when Father Tarcisio and a district chairman were attacked by an army unit. And another, sabotaged in 2003, he said. Was Father Carlos telling the truth? From the newspaper columns I'd read, he was no fan of the government. Then Father Carlos rolled up his baggy T-shirt. His elbow was burned, scarred into shiny pink flesh. Catholic religious leaders don't tend to immolate themselves for a sympathy vote: the Buddhists had already claimed that one. I imagined the army making this decision. I don't like priests, but I've never set one on fire.

It was simple to me: the priests had proved that it was possible to get the kids out safely without anyone getting hurt, but someone didn't want it done that way. And now I had living evidence, in the form of this missionary and his burnt arm. I took a photo of Father Carlos and walked back to the Hotel Sunset.

36

MINGEWATER

I did what anyone would have done to digest this information: I went jogging. Already I could tell this was no 800 words for *Glamour* magazine on Nicole Richie and her poor rescue dog Foxxy Cleopatra.

She's a lovely girl, but Foxxy's not a poor dog, it's a rat that got lucky. There seemed to be some kind of cover-up going on, possibly paid for by the British government out of my underwear tax. Or more scarily, no one could be bothered to cover anything up—and still no one was reporting it. This was appalling news.

It was worse than appalling, it was a disaster. It meant I had to stay in Gulu and do more work. I thought I'd have been fact-checking with John by now, in a safari lodge, over dinner at sunset. But this would impress him.

Then things started getting weird. When I came back from jogging, my room was unlocked. Someone had been in and taken my camera. Not my money, just my camera. I looked around, but the courtyard was deserted. I had the following conversation with the receptionist.

"Hi, my camera's been stolen..."

"No. I don't think so," she said with an aggressive smile.

"It was in my room and it's not there now," I said.

"Perhaps you took it somewhere else. Where did you go today?"

"Look, someone's been in my room! The place is full of cops but the key's in the door and my camera's gone!"

She smiled at me again. "Are you sure you had a camera?"

Implications are a luxury for those with large boyfriends. I didn't expect customer service like LA, where the receptionist would have given me a back rub to stop me suing her for Breach of Happiness.[17] But I changed hotels, to the Hotel St. Jude.

Hotel St. Jude was obliquely pleasant, with flowers blooming in cans intended to hold soya-oil rations for the starving. The rooms were bravely fitted with English toilets that couldn't cope with African plumbing and were subsequently piled with stinking yellow discs of air freshener. I resolved to stop peeing. In the streetfront café, a Dutch student soldiered through piles of conflict research documents—no six months studying art history in Tuscany for this sturdy race—and a disturbingly toothy couple shuffled around in sandals like birdwatchers. I felt bad for them, having accidentally bought a holiday in Gulu, until I overheard them complaining at breakfast. Some epic moral decline had offended the female.

"It's so hard to get well-made Bibles these days," she said. I hit the streets.

---

17. That's nothing. An LA-based real estate agent I interviewed was sued by a client after another buyer got a house he wanted. The lawsuit? Breach of Hope.

I reckoned I was on to something with the religious contingent. Not being a pink-bottomed boy, I hadn't seen a lot of spunk from priests, but vaguely remembered from history lessons that they'd been executed a lot, so they must have been rubbing someone up the wrong way.

Word soon got round among the religious leaders that there was a British journalist who wanted to talk to them, because I went back to the Religious Leaders HQ and took it round.

Over tea, a priest from the frontline town of Kitgum talked with the air of a teacher's pet accused of cheating: flushed, indignant. People were watching him, he said. "They put a bug on my car at the Bomah Hotel!" he claimed. He told me he'd read out one of Father Carlos's columns to his congregation, and next thing he'd found seventy soldiers outside his house. They accused him of collaborating with the rebels and locked him up in cells before releasing him without charge.

A bigwig agreed to talk to me: a senior bishop. I hailed a broad-saddled bike taxi and bounced to the mission.

The bishop was a white-haired man in a purple shirt sitting against a sky-blue wall, an image of Design Within Reach perfection. He greeted me with Uganda's traditional Thermos of boiling tea, piling sugar into my cup. I hadn't eaten that much sugar since the Great Bloke Drought of 1991-97.

"I've heard some claims that people who organize peace talks with Joseph Kony are sabotaged," I said, putting down my cup of tea syrup to make notes. But the bishop had something on his mind.

"Something happened in a camp. A woman did a very, very bad thing. A very bad thing in a camp," he said. Whatever the thing was, it wouldn't let the bishop go. "She did a dirty, dirty, dirty thing. She did a very dirty thing. But if I tell you what she did you wouldn't believe it! Do you want to hear?"

"Of course!" I lied, putting down my pen.

"The man has one arm now," he said, a caution.

"Really?" I said, not listening.

"They say that's because he was charmed."

"How?"

"She washed her private part and gave the water to the man to drink!" said the bishop.

"OK," I said.

"I said to my wife, 'If she did it the way people swim in a swimming pool, she washed it and then washed again, that's fine, that wouldn't make me sick.'"

"No, that wouldn't make you sick," I agreed. He ruminated on the mingewater for a while until his face relaxed. I picked up my pen again.

Then the bishop's brow furrowed. "But if they had sex overnight and then she washed her private part and gave me the water to drink, that one I wouldn't like it."

"No," I said. I was never going to get Father Carlos's story corroborated.

Then I hit pay dirt. The bishop had something else on his mind, because in the years before mingewater, he'd got involved with something big and it had ended badly. Now he was living in fear.

His colleagues had gone to meet some of Kony's commanders, he said. "They were attacked. Another one: presidential leaders were going to meet; they were also attacked," the bishop continued, and now he was in a sticky situation. "The rebels have started to be suspicious of religious leaders. Look at the position we're in now. Very dangerous position. Trapped."

The 2003 peace talks Father Carlos had mentioned were a bigger deal than I'd realized. At last I understood the implications of making trouble in a country waging a guerrilla war. In nearby Pader province, Kony's men isolated twenty-seven people they decided were linked to a "collaborator"; some of the twenty-seven people were cooked. I was glad this hospitable old man had a straightforward case of black-magic vag poisoning to take his mind off things.

I got on another broad-saddled taxi bike to see the Spanish

missionary again, leaving the bishop clutching a cup of glucose and fretting about where the mingewater was going to strike next.

Father Carlos's HQ had the air of a small law firm rather than a religious institution; more about keeping records than keeping barking old ladies out of the library. Father Carlos downloaded a file from his laptop onto a flash drive and gave it to me; it was a journal. Below are extracts from Father Carlos's diary.

6 March 2003

When Salim Saleh [President Museveni's brother and a high-ranking army official] arrived, he told us the president might be a little delayed... In the meantime, Father Tarcisio and Rwot Oywak rang to tell us that the area of the proposed peace talks was full of mobile UPDF [Uganda People's Defense Force] units going on military operations.

In other words, the army had started infiltrating the peace venue before the talks could begin. The diary continued:

To add to the confusion, a major from the UPDF rang me (his phone number is stored in my phone book) and told me that he was a rebel commander. I decided to follow the game. What Salim Saleh told me is true. There are definitely people from the intelligence trying to spoil these peace efforts, for reasons best known to them... We made [the rebels] concentrate in an area for peace talks, and then the government attacked them. We are really upset to be used as a bait...

Even I could understand this: the president's own brother wasn't able to stop the army's intelligence unit sabotaging peace talks. And it wasn't much of an intelligence unit if it didn't occur to them that Father Carlos might store contacts in his phone. Did this mean the president didn't know what was going on, and his army chiefs were running riot à la Idi Amin, or did it mean President Museveni knew full well what was going on and had stayed away so he could crush peace talks while looking like the good guy?

Father Carlos had a point about being used as bait: if I were Kony, I wouldn't trust the priests to organize shit after that.

37

THE FANTA GANG

There was something up in Uganda. A satanic Pied Piper drew the children from their homes and had done for years, yet the army sabotaged the people who tried to stop him. I was now very keen to meet the colonel, so I went to where he hung out—the garden of the Acholi Inn—bought a glass of ants in beer and waited.

Finally a truck crunched onto the red earth outside, the door opened and the colonel wrenched himself out. Instantly I was scared again. He really was a very frightening man, and I hadn't worked out if he was stupid, which would make him even more dangerous. He walked swinging his arms. Maybe it was for balance: if he turned suddenly with something that size flailing around in his trousers, it could lasso him like Swing Ball.

"Colonel, it's a pleasure. I'm from the *Sunday Times* and—"

"Today I am busy. An army spokesman will talk to you. Show him your permit," he said, and walked away, leaving me with the name of an army spokesman who would tell me everything I wanted to know about him, presumably how he was still bigger than Christina Aguilera.

I sat down again, sharing turns with the ants to drink their beer. The Acholi Inn had become even more annoying; the whole place had the sincerity of a supermarket toilet, a grudging afterthought put there to stop you from peeing on the floor. The only people who could get a drink in less than twenty minutes were some bigwigs under the mango tree.

The waiters brought them bottles of orange and yellow Fanta at triple speed, and their plates were heaped with rice three inches high. The Acholi Inn attracted bigwigs, since it had a swimming pool. No one was in it, of course. All over the world, hotel pools attract people who like to use water as a backdrop for looking nonchalant while fully clothed. Hollywood is the exception, as everyone shows off their homework—their bodies—at all opportunities. The last Malibu party I went to[18] was thronged with women who went to the buffet in their bikinis. I don't give a crap how much Pilates you do, I don't want your crochet-covered mons over my guacamole. It's inappropriate.

I couldn't contact the colonel's spokesman: the last thing I needed was a publicist on my case when I was trying to talk to his boss. Permit? I didn't even know you needed a permit to report in Uganda. This was going to be a problem as the official letter from the *Sunday Times* saying I was writing for them had been on holiday in my bag, and now looked like I'd made it myself at Staples.

The barman came over. "Are you waiting for someone?" he said.

Thanks. He's in the States, but yes. Oh, for the age of the lady's companion and the manservant, when you could simply hire someone to follow you around the world so people didn't wonder what was wrong with you. In LA, a single actress usually puts her sister on her payroll and calls the lucky sibling her producer; single actors hire some stoner friend and call them their consultant.

As the barman cleared the table of any sociable crockery, I realized the companion wasn't just to reassure hotel staff you were normal, it was to reassure you. The one thing about being single is the doubt. Do I do this? Do I go there? Do I trust that person? I don't know. In LA, people describe their "life partner" as a place of safety, which is revolting but accurate. Without one, you're spinning in endless doubt. What was I doing in *Uganda*?

And what is that noise? Someone was choosing a ring tone from the same menu of piss-poor bleeps we have all over the world. Futurist? It was coming from the Fanta Gang under the mango tree. It gave me an idea. If you can't get a date, schmooze

---

18. I think that it was Snoop Dogg's manager's, but I have no facts to back this up.

his friends and play the long game. One of them would be mates with the colonel. Fuck doubt; I typed a number in my phone, took out a pen and stalked over to the Fanta Gang.

There were about six of them. At one end was a small man with the features of an aged child, at the other, a hardfaced, lean man who didn't chat, just muttered about ulcers and rubbed his stomach. In the middle was a vast human cone who seemed to have been poured from the skies onto his chair. He looked like a cross between Giant Haystacks and Elvis. Here in the middle of Gulu was a man with big black Elvis sideburns, a quiff and Elvis loungewear, with matching shirt and trousers in a wildly patterned fabric. He was unmistakably an important man, so I wasn't sure whether he'd cultivated the Elvis thing on purpose or no one had dared mention it.

"See, look at this. I take his picture," said Giant Elvis, picking up a camera phone and photographing his friend. "Now I put his picture with his contact, look, and now you call me... Not you, him... no! I said you, not him!" Finally a phone rang. "And now look! It is him that is calling me!"

I homed in on Giant Elvis.

"Excuse me..." I said, "I'm trying to call Kampala, but it won't let me dial..."

"Give it to me. Ah, you see, you have to put a zero..." The great thing about advances in technology is that they give women new ways to pretend to be stupid just as the old ones were starting to look obvious.

"Are you working for an NGO?" he said.

"No, I'm a writer—Jane, sorry, hello. I'm doing a story about the war. It's great that the war seems to be over now—sorry." I dropped my pen on the ground and picked it up, bending down for too long in a shirt that could have been buttoned up better. It's possible Mike Wallace did this to Ayatollah Khomeini.

"Have a seat. I'm Walter," said Giant Elvis. "You wouldn't

recognize Gulu."

"What did it used to be like?"

"Rebels running around everywhere..." Walter turned out to be Chairman of Gulu—the mayor, I guess, a warm guy, and the rest were a mixture of brigadiers, colonels and charity honchos.

"So how did Kony manage to get away for all these years?"

"Sudan," said Walter. "Kony was hiding in Sudan."

"Why couldn't you go and get him?"

"Red line," said the aged child. "Army could not go beyond red line."

"What red line? Who says so?"

"Bashir." The red line, it turned out, marked the border of a lawless stretch of southern Sudan where Kony's hideout was located. In 2002, President Bashir allowed the Ugandan government to enter Sudan to chase Kony. North of the red line, however, the Ugandans were not permitted to look for him. So where did Kony go? North of the red line. Once the heat was off, he went back down to Uganda.

Now he was somewhere in the Congo. That's only next door. Why hadn't they got him? Lack of equipment, they said, but now they had state-of-the-art helicopters to get close to the target: the bombing raid that Betty had mentioned—the one last week when the army got the sat phone and Kony's wife—had been a thumper. Kony's core brigade was destroyed. *But Hot Frank said there were eighty in one group alone...*

When? Months ago? The army had it under control, said the Fanta Gang; Colonel Otema had rescued thousands of kids this way.

But the priests rescued kids peacefully, I started to object. Yes, a handful of kids, came the response.

"But if there's a chance Betty can get Kony to stop without killing loads of people and kids..."

Most of the Fanta Gang called Betty an optimist—never a term of praise. General Joseph Kony led an army that would fight to the death, Colonel Charles Otema was an army man, this was an army matter.

I asked if they knew John Prendergast, and the lean, hardfaced man finally spoke. "The peace man," he said. He smoothed his hands over imaginary long hair and laughed.

OK, that's enough. I muttered something about replacing my stolen camera and got up to leave, only to crash into another man joining the Fanta Gang: a cuddly old granddad type with salt-and-pepper hair and a soft voice. He introduced himself as Brigadier Kenneth Banya, and was very sympathetic about my stolen camera. Could he help? Was there anything he could do? He smiled at me with a beatific expression. *Great, I'm being chatted up by an old perv.*

Of course, Banya turned out to be the boss of a rehab center for child soldiers called Labora Farm, where he busted a gut to help kids who'd escaped from the rebels. Brilliant: I'd even misjudged the Fanta Gang. And Banya told me something else I didn't know. Kony also kidnapped adults. Banya was the perfect person to help the kids because he knew what they'd been through; he'd been in Kony's army until the colonel's men had rescued him.

"In the bush there are snakes, lions, leopards, wild buffalo and elephants," he said.

It got worse. When I asked Banya why no one had caught Kony, this down-to-earth old man said even he couldn't dismiss the spirits out of hand.

"It's a very funny thing," said Banya, "all the children say, 'His spirits can hear what I'm thinking; he is even listening to me now.'"

What did I know, north London wasn't exactly steeped in demonic possession, unless you counted Amy Winehouse, and her demons didn't normally tell her to advance into southern Sudan, they told her to buy more drugs.

Banya invited me to come and visit Labora Farm and talk to the children. Walter said he'd help me with my story any way he could and told me I was welcome to see his fish farm. I don't think it was a euphemism.

Like a proper reporter, I headed back to my hotel to sulk. Maybe there was no plot to let Kony escape. Maybe the colonel didn't want priests interfering because this was between him and Kony, two military men. Maybe the colonel wanted to end the war his way, with a bomb, and the advantage of killing someone like Kony was that afterwards he'd be dead. Bottom line: the Fanta Gang, like Kony, were African soldiers who'd spent decades fighting in the bush. I was a white middle class girl from Muswell Hill-Highgate borders in London who hadn't. The endless doubt was all around me now.

38

A STEPHEN KING NOVEL

Outside it was getting dark, and this time I wasn't tucked up with a bowl of hot Posho, I was alone on the street.

And then I wasn't. I'd stepped into a scene from a Stephen King novel. Children started appearing from nowhere. Literally thousands of them, a human tide of kids. They were streaming into town from every road, every dirt track, children of all sizes, some carrying schoolbooks, some blankets, some wearing white United Nations food aid sacks as fleeces. The children had an otherworldly quality—one little girl in a crispy pink ball gown seemed to float. They knew exactly where they were going and some were singing as they walked. Children's singing is invariably creepy and it made the scene even more sinister. A group broke off to drift across a field and I joined them, struggling to keep up, talking to a serious small boy.

"Where are your parents?"

"In the village."

"Where are you going?"

"The shelter."

"Why are you going to the shelter?"

But the boy ran away, slipping through a gate towards some kind of hangar. On the gate was a security guard with a gun. The children walked here every night to sleep, the guard said, because of the rebels. The next morning they would leave for school and be back again as dusk fell. There didn't seem to be bedrooms inside, or even beds. All I could see were nasty concrete sheds. I tried to peer inside, but the guard leaned on his gun. I wasn't about to be let in.

All around me, children poured in from the countryside, and now I realized there were shelters everywhere. A whole town of children was flowing into them, going to sleep under armed guard so they wouldn't be spirited from their beds in the night by Kony, the bogeyman no one could stop.

The tide of kids became a trickle and one by one the gates slammed. All the town's children had disappeared. A dog barked. I was left alone in a pitch-black night. Nothing. Just darkness.

39

ANGUS DEAYTON'S SHOES

Kony was not dead. Kony was so not dead that parents were sending their children miles away every evening for their own safety. I called Banya to take him up on his invitation and set out for Labora Farm to meet the child soldiers. Maybe Kony was still kidnapping because he was just plain good at his job. There was one way to find out if Kony was good at his job: ask the people who worked for him. No one knows a boss's secrets like his employees.

I hailed the boda with the biggest smile and soon we were in remote fields of sunflowers an hour outside town. The sun threw down heat until it was almost a weight on us. I'd been half expecting some kind of outwardbound center, with kids making self-portraits by gluing macaroni to cardboard. Instead, Labora Farm was just a farm, the kids just farm workers; teenagers sitting on tarp rubbing the kernels off sweetcorn.

There was no sign of Banya, but eventually a bloke hopped up, Achama Jackson, another former captive turned farm manager—a sequence of events that saw him negotiating piles of sweetcorn on his one remaining leg. Achama said Banya had been held up. Like Banya, Achama was no spring chicken, but he too seemed to believe in the spirits; he'd even heard about a young boy who was being groomed as a spirit vessel in case Kony died.

I asked the kids about Kony, but they were subdued, eyes on the tarp, whispering their names in voices that drifted away over the fields of corn. I had no idea if they were scared of Kony's spirits, but I tried giving off the air of someone with a more powerful spirit all the same. It can't have worked.

I said thanks to Achama and got back on the boda, who'd got

noticeably less smiley while I'd been chatting to the kids. As we drove through fields the sun had, against all odds, become even hotter. We passed a child taking a flip-flop for a walk on a string, talking to it. Everything seemed to have the melting edges of a dream. Was Betty right? Was John right? Were the guys under the mango tree right? Had any of this happened at all?

Just then I became aware of the driver talking to me. He wasn't happy.

"Why do you hate Jesus?" he asked. That woke me up. When would I learn to tell a smiley man from a nutcase? Brilliant, I'd failed to convince children I had any spirit, let alone a powerful one, and now I was in a pointless religious war to boot. Who says black taxis are too expensive?

We made it back to Gulu. I was ready for bed but I made the nutcase drop me at the charity Father Carlos had mentioned, a small local organization set up to help former child soldiers. It sounded a bit worthy, but I thought I'd give it a go.

I'd got it wrong: it wasn't a charity for child soldiers, but of child soldiers. Years ago they'd been kidnapped by Kony and had escaped; then once they were grown up, they'd banded together to form their own DIY version of Oxfam. Now I was in business, because unlike the Labora Farm kids, the former child soldiers group couldn't stop talking, and they were hilarious. When I mentioned I was thinking of carrying on the investigation into Sudan (it was, after all, a possibility that Hot Frank might be going up there) but lacked a Sudanese visa, as soldiers, they leaped on the task of facilitating my investigation with a series of planned maneuvers. They all involved me waiting for a man several hundred miles away at seven o'clock the next morning and began with hiding in the back room of a grocer's behind 400 tubs of margarine, studying the delivery guys for signs of collusion with the Sudanese immigration authorities.

"Not him, Jane... not him... *him!* He has a brother. But don't tell anyone he knows where to get it. You meet him seven tomorrow morning in Sudan." I firmly believe if I had, I would have gotten that visa.

Another time there was an awesome standup row between the peace coordinator and the chairman of community reintegration.

Sorry, I'm meant to write that the child soldiers bore their suffering with stoic dignity, but since this implies that people in the third world sit around all day getting kidnapped and waiting for Angus Deayton[19] to come and play football with them during Comic Relief, I won't. I haven't done much for charity, but I was once sick on Angus Deayton's shoes under a table at an office Christmas party, so at least I've done something for a good cause.

The child soldiers group had six members and a stream of other child soldiers popping in to talk, often with babies on their backs, all overseen by Stella and Jessica, former sex slaves who now did health education. The group went from refugee camp to refugee camp, looking for fellow escapees and making sure they were okay and could feed any children they'd brought home from the bush, although the jobs weren't glamorous. "Some are working for a thousand shillings [a few cents] a day, putting cow dung on walls," they said. Poo-smearing wealth aside, the child soldiers group didn't have a backer among the big charities, so the only office they could afford was somewhat inconveniently located in a panel-beating workshop. They shouted about peace over hammering.

Charities love job titles, so all six members were on the committee. Steven was one of Kony's former intelligence experts; he was trained as a spy and couldn't break the habit. He never used people's names—everyone was "that man," apart from Kony, who was "the Man." Whenever Steven wanted to talk to me, he'd look over his shoulder and say, "Not here," and make us move five feet to the right. "OK, Jane. That man say—oh. Not here." And we'd pick up and move five feet back to the left.

Their chairman, Alan, had Wall Street dress sense and was the most upbeat man I'd met in years. If you meet anyone that

---

19. He's a TV presenter. Sort of John Cleese. You don't care.

upbeat in LA, they're generally in the honeymoon cycle of a serotonin reuptake inhibitor, just before they go crazy and hold up a post office.

Alan buoyantly recounted how he'd been kidnapped and handed over to some fat bastard wife beater called Ochen: "Short, brown and very rude, he loved to hit his wives." One of Alan's brothers was killed in front of him; the other got sick and died. "I cannot say anything to bring them back; I cannot do anything. So I formed this group."

We were getting on well, so I asked them to tell me about their former boss. I wasn't a soldier, they were, so I wanted to know just how good a soldier Kony was that the colonel couldn't catch him.

Which is how I came to learn that Joseph Kony wasn't a soldier at all. The man holding off the tanks and helicopters and ten-ton Hampton of Colonel Otema had no military training whatsoever. Joseph Kony talked the talk and that was it. His child soldiers painted a picture of Regis Philbin with access to small arms. A daytime TV personality, someone with charisma and, strangely for a man who I'd assumed lived in a hedge, an endless supply of lurid pant suits.

"The Man used to dress smartly with a suit," according to Alan. He liked boots, "Like the Beatles."

"Oh, come on," I said, "he was living in the bush, where did he get suits?" Everyone pointed at a small chap sitting out on the pavement.

"I sewed for him suits single-breasted, green in color, mixed fiber," he said. Kony, the man they called an outlaw bandit, kept personal tailors in the African bush. Benjamin was one of those tailors, and he was still running up clothes from his sewing machine on Gulu high street.

"Was Kony a hard taskmaster? Did every seam have to be perfect?" I asked, sincerely interested.

"Every seam," said Benjamin.

"Could you copy a shirt?" I got a number for the war criminal's tailor. This was to be a fruitful relationship.

Kony really didn't seem like a serious opponent for any army.

Personality wise, Kony presented himself as a lifestyle guru, a one-stop-shop for tips on relationships and domestic living.

"He said, you need to wash your utensils clean and he keeps on checking on them in the house, monitoring them," said Stella. Beyond Kony's *How Clean Is Your House?* routine, he stuck his nose into relationships, saying a man should only have sex with a woman seven days after her period. Anything else wasn't productive.

"Do animals? Do birds?" he would say. There was huge laughter from the girls when I asked if Kony would go from one wife to the next in an evening. They explained that there was one house in the middle of the compound, with the wives living around it. The sex policy was that every three days a different wife went to the central house until the "husband" had been round the whole circle. Alan said, "When I was still there, Kony had eighty-nine children and fifty wives." Kony had so many wives he didn't know their names. He called them by their home district.

I got talking to a group of former sex slaves. How the conversation came round to my life I have no idea.

"How were you abducted by the rebels?" I asked.

"They ambushed our school truck and shot everybody, but I survived because I lay under the bodies like I was dead. Do you have children?"

"I—no. Were all your schoolfriends killed?"

"Why don't you have children?"

"I'm baby gay. So how did they catch—"

"Where do you live?"

"I—Los Angeles, some pogo stick... I share a place with some—"

"You don't have a house?"

"Er... it's really expensive to buy a house these days..."

"Oh," said the former sex slaves, really worried for me now. "Can your husband not buy a house?" *Oh, please don't start. I've just talked myself into being delighted to be single again.*

"I'm not married."

This was too much for them. One of the former sex slaves looked like she might cry.

Kony's big break as celebrity warlord came in 1994: he got a call from the president of Sudan, Omar al-Bashir. This is where my day with the child soldiers group became utterly surreal. Kony didn't wander into Sudan or cobble together some scrappy rebel camp made of twigs and old anoraks like I'd imagined: Omar al-Bashir, Sudanese president, now creaking with cash from oil, invited him to set up shop. Kony would get a luxury village, and in return Bashir would get a private army of kids. The children were trained to fight Bashir's enemy, the selfish bastard Dr. John Garang.

This was how Joseph Kony, a primary-school-drop-out-peasant-conjuror-malaria-brain-damaged nutter who set fire to toy helicopters in strategy meetings, ended up getting his own mini city in Sudan, complete with the arms cache Hot Frank the journalist had told me about, not to mention certain other luxury items.

"The Sudan government gave each commander a very big cultivation growing food, and jai [opium] rarely," said Steven. "And in Big Man's house, latrine is very nice." Kony, who ordered his followers to gnaw the legs off anyone caught riding a bicycle, had several motorbikes and a jeep.

"Did he have any hobbies?" I said.

"The Man listens to the BBC News all the time," said the child soldiers group.

"Why?" I said stupidly.

"To see if they talk about him!" Of course. He was, after all, a celebrity. I've only spent two evenings off duty with celebrities; in both cases they spent the whole night Googling themselves. I shouldn't write that, not least because it indicts me as duller than a search engine.

News wasn't all Kony liked.

"He watch films," said Alan.

"What films?"

"He like very much that man..."

"What man?"

"Man who fights the Vietnamese..." A beat. Then everyone remembered.

"*Rambo!*"

"And *Missing in Action 2* with Chuck Norris."

"Eddie Murphy—*Coming to America.*"

"He would call all the officers, you see this thing, we have to practice this thing in the film, you have to do the same," said Steven.

"When a mamba comes, how to use RPG..." My head was spinning. Kony took thousands of kids out into the Sudanese wilderness and made them copy *Rambo*.

"How many children were in his army?"

"Let me say ten thousand," said Steven. (I've heard estimates of between 6,000 and 12,000 kids living there at any time.)

"At Christmas we would have a big party and slaughter bulls," said Alan.

This was pure science fiction. Kony was breeding an army of children in the desert. He would raid Uganda, harvesting thousands of kids, and bring them back to Sudan, where he would brainwash them with bogus religious rituals, greasing them like Alice and making them carry eggs, telling them the one who broke it would be killed. While Kony was well fed by the Arabs, the kids often lived off leaves. Then he gave them to commanders like Ochen, the short, fat wife beater, who all had the same routine: kill a relative to keep everyone in line, then get to work impregnating the girls. The child army grew steadily. Kony even had to build a separate camp to hold pregnant girls and their babies. Thousands of children lived like this for years and Kony got away with it.

It didn't make sense. All this painted a picture of Kony as someone with a good grasp of human psychology, a weirdo who'd got lucky. Kony didn't seem to be a Hitler, a Stalin, a Karl Rove. He was so insignificant a presence, in fact, that when Bashir first met the LRA leader, he greeted Kony's deputy, Vincent Otti, by mistake, as Otti was the big charismatic guy. Kony wasn't even a soldier.

"What happened to the place in the desert?"

The visits from the Arabs stopped, Alan said. "They stopped when the Sudan government welcomed Ugandan troops." In other words, some kind of peace deal had been struck, the UPDF waded in and it was time to move on.

Kony picked up and moved to the Congo, where the colonel still couldn't catch him. My guts told me now that I was right: right now, this mess was the colonel's fault. Something was up. Then once again the conversation took an odd turn.

I asked the child soldiers group if Kony had magic powers. They all agreed there was one particular thing about Kony that made him indestructible.

"He's survived many attacks," says Steven. "He used to say government forces are coming in this number at this time with these kind of guns, and it would always come true."

"He's very sharp," said Alan. "He'll say soldiers are surrounding us—he will sense it and escape. You won't even know; his mind is always open."

But when I asked them why nobody had stopped Kony, they clammed up. Only the former spy spoke. "This is top secret, Jane," he said.

I pushed them, but all they would say was, "Look around you."

Steven walked me to the Acholi Inn to see if the colonel had come back in a better mood. On the way, I made us stop to photograph a really cool 60s building.

As soon as I pointed at the building, Steven moved five feet to the left. He didn't want me to photograph it. In fact, he wanted us to get the hell out of there, but what Steven failed to realize was that if my sister and I bought it for five grand, shipped it to West Hollywood and sold it to a gay man, we could make a million bucks. Even better was the sign on the front of the building.

I'm afraid if you can't read it, then you must have the beginnings of a very serious eye condition. It conspicuously says, "LINT MARKETING BOARD." Lint does need a publicist. But when I took the picture, a man came running out, yelling at us, "YOU! GO NOW!"

He meant it. We scarpered. Steven told me the locals said this was a UPDF building now, and not just any army building.

"That's where the colonel interrogates people." Which meant

I'd accidentally photographed the colonel's torture chamber... Wait a minute... They don't market lint! They don't market lint at all!

Back at the hotel, burning my photos onto a CD, I remembered what I'd been told about photographing government buildings and felt lucky not to be in Hot Frank's cell. Let alone discussing the public image of waste cotton with the colonel.

But there was good news. John had emailed. He'd quit the idea of the LA movie stuff.

"I thought the meetings were going well."

"I got uncomfortable being at the center of the story. Too egomaniacal, even for me," he said.

"Oh, no! You'd love it in LA!" *Thank you, God. John will stay in Washington and Scarlett Johansson would never find him there.*

40

AND I WILL MAKE PORRIDGE

I went to the market, bought some nice blue gingham and got fitted by Benjamin the tailor for a dress in which to meet John. I asked for a wrap dress adapted from a Gap office shirt and gave him the fabric. Benjamin seemed a little hesitant about doing a fancy number as opposed to the traditional Ugandan dresses—long sheaths with formal puffy sleeves rising several inches above the shoulders—but the war criminal's tailor's dress fitted perfectly and got a lot of looks. Eventually, someone told me I'd chosen the local school uniform fabric. Benjamin was a very tactful tailor.

I needed a smart dress; there were some people I wanted to talk to and they were gun shy. I'd contacted the Concerned Parents' Association on Joshua's advice. They'd put me in touch with a woman whose teenage daughter had been hit by one of the most notorious school crimes in history, a crime with a heroine so instantly compelling that this random story blew up and shot round the world, stirring everyone from Oprah Winfrey to the Pope. There was even a book written about it, *Aboke Girls* by Els De Temmerman, an excellent book written by a real journalist.

And I had a problem, because the parents were all talked out. Worse, a cack-handed Sunday supplement piece had recently implied they were bad mothers. Unsurprisingly, this mother was unwilling to speak. I guess I must have sounded unprofessional enough to be harmless, or maybe it was the school uniform dress, because in the end Laura agreed to tell me what happened. Her office was close to a market and all the children shopping with their mothers lined up to watch us as we sat under a tree.

Laura was an attractive woman with an open expression. She began talking, stopping from time to time, trying to gauge what she should reveal. She explained that St. Mary's College Aboke was an expensive place to send your kids—a boarding school, the best school around, the Trinity School of Uganda—which is why she chose it for Marilyn. They'd had a series of tragedies, with family members suddenly dying.

"I thought, 'I owe it to Marilyn to give her a good education,' so I sent her to Aboke St. Mary's," said Laura.

Laura had picked the worst place on Earth. On October 9, 1996, 150 of Kony's rebels approached the school with the aim of kidnapping the pupils to use as sex slaves. Luckily some local people had spotted the rebels and warned the deputy head, an Italian nun called Sister Rachele Fassera. The nun rushed straight to the barracks in plenty of time to make sure the army came to protect them. So when Kony's men arrived at 2 a.m. on October 10, they saw the army outside the school, aborted their kidnapping plan and the girls were saved.

Oh, hang on, that's not what happened. The army *didn't* come when the deputy head begged them to. Kony's men smashed through the dormitory windows and kidnapped 139 girls.

To be fair, perhaps the army thought it was a false alarm. Oh, hang on, the school had been attacked before, in 1991. Museveni had apologized to the teachers and promised permanent security would be stepped up. Why? Because it had happened before that, too, in 1989, when Kony's men abducted ten girls including Susan, aged fourteen, who was never seen again.

Sister Rachele suspected Kony's men might rape her pupils. She suspected this because one of them raped a pupil before he'd even finished the kidnapping.

With no army to help in 1996, Sister Rachele herself decided to go into the bush to get the kids back. Unarmed, she went with a young geography teacher, John Bosco Ocen, following a trail of cookie wrappers that the rebels had looted from the school store. She waded through swamps in her nun's habit and finally met the rebels on a hilltop—139 schoolgirls were tied in a rope line, together with 150 rebels and another 60 children they had scooped up on the way.

"Upon seeing the white lady, Kony's men told her, 'Your girls are here,'" said Laura. "Sister Rachele said, 'Can I bring them back?' And they said, 'Yes. But you don't hurry. You tired.' 'No, no, no,' she said, 'I want to leave with the girls.' She was forced to take a bath. She was forced to wait for them to cook food. She was entertained as a visitor. How very strange." In fact, Sister Rachele's bad feeling was spot on as Kony's men were buying time while they sorted through the 139 girls.

"They gave her back a hundred and nine girls, but they decided to keep the ones they liked. Thirty of them." Sister Rachele had to leave the thirty girls behind. She asked the head girl, Judith, to look after them and gave her a rosary. Sister Rachele later learned that Kony's men chose Judith to torture to death.

Word got out and the parents rushed to the school. A nun had brought back a list of the thirty abducted girls.

"The first name I found was the name of my daughter Marilyn," said Laura. "She was fourteen. I just cried and cried. And the headmistress came, because there were so many parents crying."

Laura had no idea if Marilyn was still alive. "When children escaped from the rebels, I would go to the rescue center, asking, 'Do you know my girl?' It took almost three years before a girl said, 'There is a commander and Marilyn was given to him.'"

"What was happening to Marilyn?" I asked.

"The girls were brought to Sudan. She was pregnant. When it was delivered there was no food for her to eat and the government sent the UPDF to attack them so they could not even go to get food. She had no breast milk also. Then the child died. Twice more she conceived. She was taken to—what do they call it? A sick bay."

But it was okay because the President of Uganda agreed to meet the parents to see what could be done to get the girls back.

"Did he offer to help you find the girls?" I asked.

"No," said Laura. "But he said, 'If you go looking for them I will tell my soldiers not to shoot you.'"

Eventually the president helped organize a trip to Sudan for

Sister Rachele and another Concerned Parent, but when they arrived in Sudan, they were unable to get the girls.

Luckily the First Lady of the United States, Hillary Clinton, agreed to meet the Concerned Parents' Association at the White House. Clinton said the girls had been condemned to "a life of unspeakable horrors." So unspeakable she couldn't rescue them. But it was okay, because Sister Rachele and the parents also met the Pope, Kofi Annan, Nelson Mandela, Colonel Gaddafi and Omar al-Bashir. None of them got the girls back. But Sister Rachele and the parents wouldn't let it lie. They travelled the world. The Pope gave a message on the radio. Meanwhile Kony built a city of children in the desert and shipped in his prize, the highly educated St. Mary's girls. The girls were raped, impregnated, given syphilis and watched as babies were smashed against trees. Why hadn't his Holiness John Paul II used the might of the Vatican to save the girls? I bet if there was a nickel taped to Kony the Pope would have found him by now. So what did all these rescuers do about the St. Mary's girls in the end? They effectively left them to the army.

Then Laura got a call from another St. Mary's mother.

"She said, 'Do you know God?' I said yes. 'Do you know Jesus?' I said yes. Yes, he is my savior. 'Then praise him, because Marilyn has come!' I wanted to throw my phone up. I was shouting. They must have thought I was mad," said Laura, still delirious. By now we were surrounded by girls and boys who'd stopped to stare. "Marilyn had been gone for so many years. She had delivered three more children, then she came home and said, "Mum, all I want is to go back to school." I told her, "I'm going to care for the baby, you go to school. Now your baby is not going to die. This one is with me."

As we stood in the market with all the children watching, Laura's eyes spilled over with tears while she listed all the food she was going to cook for her grandson. "And I will make porridge, and groundnuts, and vegetables..."

"And all this time, no one ever came to you and said, 'We will go with you and help you find your children?'" I asked.

"No," said Laura. Finally Sister Rachele was recalled from

Uganda.

The Church decided her mission would be served from Rome. She was traumatized and by her own admission still cries easily. Before I could process all this, Laura said, "And the two girls still out there..."

I couldn't hear what she said after that.

Laura phoned me a couple of days later. I'd mentioned I had a computer and offered to teach Marilyn a bit of Microsoft Word if it would help her catch up. God knows, there was bugger all else I could say. Marilyn was waiting for me the next morning in her mother's small, square backstreet house. She had her mother's attractive face and was smiling very faintly as a baby slept in a shawl wrapped round her back.

I've often wondered about heroines from eras where women didn't talk much; they seem to get attributed with the biggest personalities. This seems as optimistic as those same adjectives applied to whichever young Sloane recently signed up for life with the Windsors.

Marilyn didn't talk much, but she had presence.

"I'm going to be a teacher," she said, a little above a whisper. "I'm going to Kampala while Mum looks after the baby. I thank the almighty God who has given me this chance."

She was making up for lost time. Her eyes burned into the computer screen as though she could see past the pixels. I've only seen focus like that in Madonna's personal trainer, and to the best of my knowledge, Tracy didn't spend nine years with guerrillas in the Sudanese desert. Marilyn had Microsoft down in hours. Where did this focus come from? Born smart, I expect, and focused by nine years walking a tightrope across the valley of death. Never mind memoirs, former child soldiers should write how-to-get-ahead-in-business manuals.

"This lesson has contributed a lot," she said afterwards. "Thanks."

Not long afterwards, the *New Vision* newspaper ran a story. The government's helicopter gunships had found one of Kony's sick bays in the Nyono Hills near Kitgum. The helicopters bombed it, killing six rebels, according to UPDF intelligence coordinator Colonel Charles Otema.

41

CARDBOARD BOX

As I walked though Gulu, the St. Mary's story honked like a goose. Everything about it felt wrong. One hundred and thirty-nine boarding school girls stolen from their dormitory in a random attack, the papers had said. Except it wasn't random. So I went visiting.

Dried meat stew.

Sure enough, nothing was what it seemed. People wouldn't talk on the record, but in the back room of a dark restaurant that smelled of dried meat stew, I met an old man. Soon after, I was sent an old cardboard box. The box was crammed with thin typing paper yellow with age, blurry photographs, handwritten accounts, famous names, warnings, pleas and threats. Here's what was in there.

Since the late 80s, the school had been under attack. The rebels made it crystal clear what they wanted. During a 1991 raid, they had a question for the nuns: "Where are the girls?"

When they only succeeded in looting, they told the nuns, "We'll be back." St. Mary's was the finest school around, the girls were the finest girls and Kony had ordered them like a special edition Porsche. By 1996, the home guard had been stationed at the school.

But ten days before the 1996 attack, the home guard was withdrawn without any prior notice, leaving the school undefended. Their fate was sealed: the girls were spirited away to a wilderness across the Sudanese border. Their location would be a mystery to their parents and to the authorities trying to get them back.

Except it wasn't.

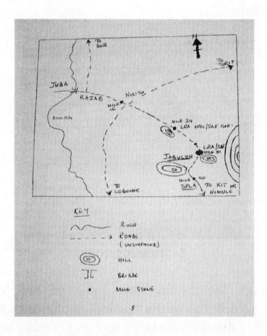

Here is a map showing the three bases of Kony's City of Children in the Sudanese desert, where the girls were kept "hidden" for years.

Come on, you say. This looks like a treasure map. Johnny Depp made this in his sleep; I've seen *Pirates of the Caribbean II*.

But what's this?

SECRET

Annex IV

INTELLIGENCE REPORT PRESENTED TO PRESIDENT EL - BASHIR ON 18th June, 1997.

Date: 15 June 1997

SUBJECT: Plans by LRA High command to shift Aboke School girls from Nsitu and Juba into concealment before the Inspection Team arrives to the area

Summary:

Our Service has obtained with reliable evidence a plan conceived by LRA High Command in Khartoum, a plan to be executed by Okello Matata and Acelam (LRA Officers) in the field, to re-locate the Aboke Girls from Nsitu - Women's camp and Juba. They are to be kept under concealment in LRA HQrs (at mile 34). This is a top secret known ONLY to: Matata, Acelam and Lumumba in the field.

The three LRA Field Officers have already confirmed receiving the instructions and implementing them. They have also been advised not to discuss anything with SAF in Jebelin (Mile 39) and Juba because SAF Khartoum can direct SAF Juba or Jebelin to check all LRA camps for the girls. The LRA field officers have consequently been instructed not to allow any SAF Official in LRA camps except for issues regarding food.

LRA Detailed Plan On Concealment of Aboke Girls 9th - 12th June, 1997.

In anticipation of Uganda's Inspection Team's visit to Juba and Nsitu - women's camp, LRA has made a number of preparations, issued strong directives and undertaken a series of activities aimed at concealing the presence of Aboke girls in order to frustrate the current efforts and commitments of the Governments of Sudan and Uganda to secure their release.

The Following elements constitute the LRA Plan:

1.   All Women/girls married or not married in Juba and Nsitu (mile 15) should be collected and taken to LRA HQ's (at mile 34).

2.   On the directives of Omona and Nyeko in Khartoum, Okello Matata in Jebelin, Acelam in Juba and Lumumba in LRA Hqrs are to ensure that ONLY women with children should remain in the women's camp.

SECRET
28

Ugandan intelligence services were so well informed they were able to produce a detailed Intel report for Captain Chuckles himself, genocidal maniac President Bashir. The report contained information corroborated by two books. As Sister Rachele arrived to get her girls, the report warned that Kony was clearing out the camp and hiding the St. Mary's girls, leaving behind a few young mothers who'd been instructed not to tell anyone where they were. Sure enough, officials took Sister Rachele to Kony's camp, only to find it deserted. Some young mothers turned up and told the officials it wasn't Kony's base, it was a refugee camp and they couldn't tell them where the St. Mary's girls were. The officials said, "Oh, sorry," and left. Sister Rachele demanded to come back the next day. She found the camp heaving with kidnapped kids, and a Sudanese official truck parked nearby. One kid, Monica, aged twelve, told them that yes, the St. Mary's girls were being hidden in Jabulen, the LRA base. No one would help Sister Rachele rescue the girls, and Monica was killed for talking.

"When your child was taken you weren't supposed to complain, you were supposed to stay quiet," Laura had told me. But these parents had the means to complain—they weren't peasant farmers who had to spend their day walking miles to pump water. They were middle class, doctors and teachers with access to phones, faxes and email accounts—and they used them. They raised a stink despite threatening letters from the LRA decorated with symbols that named the parents personally.

The St. Mary's case became one of history's most famous kidnappings because it had a star. Everyone from Pope John Paul II to Nelson Mandela was moved by the lone nun. Anyone could feel for the small, skinny Italian sister facing off rebels who would have scared a Special Forces team, unable to save all her girls. That one gut-wrenching moment to haunt the rest of your life. But as I sat reading through archives, a batch of memories came screaming out of the cardboard box. Sister Rachele had done it before: 1996 was the *third time*.

In 1987, she'd cycled several miles into the bush to rescue Dina, a St. Mary's girl who been kidnapped, by a different mob of armed gunmen to the LRA incidentally, but still no government soldiers stopped them, and Dina had been snatched while on her way to the hospital with suspected appendicitis. Sister Rachele faced off a gunman who said, "Do you want me to slaughter you?" She met up with another nun, Sister Fernanda, and by complete coincidence, one of the kidnappers recognized Fernanda as his former nurse and handed over the schoolgirl, just in time for critical surgery.

In 1989, the raid was in broad daylight. The scene was chaos:

hundreds of girls running, leaping the school fences and tearing over twenty miles to hide in a cathedral. One hundred and three people had been taken—from St. Mary's, from the local seminary and from the primary school. Again Sister Rachele followed rebels into the bush unarmed. On her way, she found they'd killed five people and burned more than a hundred houses. She had to stop because government soldiers had found the rebels and started firing. But the soldiers simply fired their guns in the air. Six girls escaped in the chaos. Not Susan. The girls, one account noted, had all been raped, even the little ones from the primary school. After this incident, not one day went by without the nuns going out on bicycles or tractors to look for children.

Let's cut the army some slack. This is Africa, the saying goes: vehicles break down, parts are impossible to find in a hurry and fuel is constantly siphoned off. But in 1989, according to one contemporary account, the rebels had attacked a nearby secondary school in Ngai and left a message that Aboke St. Mary's was next. As soon as Sister Alba, the headmistress, heard this, she went to ask for protection—twice. Two weeks later the school was attacked. In 1996, I read, Sister Rachele asked for help days in advance and even gave petrol money.

Let's cut some slack for the soldiers who were shown where the LRA were camping the evening before the 1991 attack and said they wouldn't take action because "It's getting late." Let's say they'd bought lottery tickets and wanted to be back for the draw.

Let's cut the army some more slack and note that on the night of the 1996 abduction, Kony's rebels had attacked and crippled the local barracks at Iceme. Did the army tell the sister, "Sorry, we can't do this—send the girls home"? No. In fact, when the sisters asked, "Should we close the school?" the army's information officer urged them to keep it open. Why?

Let's cut some slack for the army's intelligence services and say the rebels were fiendishly brilliant. But according to a girl from Dorm Four, one of them stole a stethoscope from the school dispensary thinking it was a Walkman, and later dumped it complaining that it was broken.

Let's cut some slack for the three separate army officers who promised Rachele they'd send troops as that night in 1996 dragged nearer. Let's say they didn't think it appropriate to behave in a hysterical manner over a rumor. But one stated clearly that he knew St. Mary's was a main target.

Let's hand the army the entire ball of slack and say they're only human—they were too scared to face the rebels and save the girls. That's cool too. But at that point, it's a little unsporting to call yourself an army. Call yourself a group of similarly attired young men sitting in a nearby building who happen to have some weapons and ammunition they won't be using. This avoids the outside world mistaking you for people who might defend civilians.

I found an old school photograph of a girl labeled Judith.

This was the most disturbing part of the puzzle. Head girl of St. Mary's, Judith was the grand prize. The nuns had chosen Judith to take charge, and the rebels respected Sister Rachele enough to give her 109 girls back. Killing the nuns' girl was a slap in the face to even the rebels' own sense of decency. Judith's schoolfriend didn't have the heart to tell Sister Rachele how Judith died. Instead she described to Sister Alba the day Judith was fatally beaten with machetes, bicycle chains and sticks.

And there was a twist: the morning after the beating, Judith was still alive.

A week later, girls searching for firewood found Judith tied to a tree. Despite the extreme heat her body had not decomposed, indicating she had recently died.

Hillary was right, the girls' new life was "unspeakable." But Kony was the villain of the day, and endless newspaper articles ran about this photogenic, stylish psycho who no one could stop. Kony's powerless victim, the Ugandan government, still got paid. Hillary threw extra money at the situation, leveraging the World Bank to step in "to help people plagued by rebel activity... get jobs rebuilding their own community." The St. Mary's pupils who got away from Kony weren't rescued; they escaped, often risking their own lives during UPDF attacks. Some lived as sex slaves for years until their "husbands" defected. Out of 139 girls, the government army rescued Sylvia. Nun 109, Army 1.

"There are no easy answers," said Hillary Clinton. Fuck me, I wouldn't sit next to her in math class.

42

BECAUSE THEY ARE LESBIANS!

I spent the next few days locked in my room at the Hotel St. Jude, only going out to teach Marilyn. I thumped transcripts of assorted renegade priests and Sudanese-Chuck-Norris attack stories into my laptop. I felt useful; I'd done some actual work, and none of it involved Chihuahuas. To celebrate, I went out to look for frozen yogurt. This was a total bloody waste of time, so I called Helen the Dolly Parton fan to ask if she wanted to meet up for dinner.

"Sincerely!" said Helen. "I'll call you back!" She did call back, and told me we'd meet at her friend's house to watch the new DVDs from Nigeria. I say Helen called back, but strictly speaking she did something big in Africa: beeping. Beeping is where you call someone with your mobile and hang up before they answer, thereby saving the 5¢ cost of the call. I called back, as I had 5¢. However, most times, the other person can't spare 5¢ either, so they walk round to your house to see what you wanted. This is African instant messaging. That's nothing; in days gone by, to send a letter you'd give it to a post office runner, a man who ran 200 miles in 60 hours. Several runners didn't make it, having been attacked by wild animals or fallen in swamps.

"I paid for overnight delivery!"

"Yeah, according to your tracking number he was eaten by a lion."

"It's always something, isn't it?"

I waited for Helen under Mega FM, fearing the Nigerian DVDs.

Mega FM was your typical radio station, save for the gun-toting Amazonian guard manning the entrance. Helen led me down the back alleys into middle-class Gulu—small houses built around concrete gullies with kids doing the washing. Helen's friend Rose was like Helen, young and funky and worked for a local charity. Hanging plates painted with slogans about God decorated her walls. Everybody loved Jesus here. I'd mentioned in the Hotel St. Jude that I didn't go to church, and they still to this day think I'm joking. We found Rose singing along to concert footage of some American Christian stadium rock band that had a greasy, pregnant singer bellowing "Jesus, You Are My Best Friend," while middle-aged white cheerleaders with cornrows and PVC trousers did cartwheels behind her.

Dinner was roast chicken. During the couple of hours I was there, the hen went from a normal hen day to arse-in-the-air-on-a-plate. A friend called Freddie the Man popped by—he'd chosen the name to make himself easy to identify—and told me he knew a man I should meet. A man called Bill, a photojournalist with an adventurous streak who could help me if I wanted to go north to where the rebels were most active. Definitely, I burped.

After dinner, Rose pulled out a huge case of DVDs. Nollywood films were moralistic epics, apparently filmed using my old digital camera, and they starred the same actors over and over and the plots revolved around everyday witchcraft, romance and wife-beating. We watched a cautionary tale about a young girl who went to college only to fall in with a bad crowd—women in space jump suits with magic daggers who lured men home to slice their bits off, mocking the handful of gonads.

"Rose, why are they doing that?" I asked.

"Because they are lesbians," she replied. The jump-suited girls vaporized like Captain Kirk. So they were. I wasn't sure if it was a cautionary tale about homosexuality, having it off on a first date or further education.

I left Rose and Helen singing along to a Christian power ballad, "My God is an Awesome God," and went back to the hotel, finally feeling relaxed in Gulu. I was on to a big story, I was full of hot hen, and I knew how to spot a lesbian. But when

I got into the courtyard, I didn't need to turn the handle of my door to know the lock had been picked again. My computer was gone. The hen went cold in my stomach.

43

POLICE ACADEMY GULU

It was plain to see that I was under surveillance: who would want a brand new laptop? It was ten o'clock at night but I went to the police station. First things first, I wanted a police report for insurance purposes.

Gulu Police Station was empty apart from a five-inch spider with hairy orange legs shinning down a length of web. Below, someone had kicked a hole in the duty desk. As I waited, I read posters on the wall. The first, about how to run an election: "Make sure the following do not appear on the voting register! The noncitizens. The underage. The dead." The second, the official Red Cross laws of war, a list of dos and don'ts for armed combat, illustrated by jolly cartoons of soldiers committing war crimes, stealing goats, burning villages and so on:

"COMBATANTS, REMEMBER! Do not rape!" Oh shit, you're joking... Well, can I just finish this one... ?

The desk sergeant came in, a skinny cop in gumboots. His stripes were held on his jacket with staples. We both heard a terrible screaming from the cells to his left. Only one of us turned.

"Don't worry, it's the lunatics," said the desk sergeant. "Later we give them an injection. Can I help you?"

"Yes. Someone's stolen my computer," I said.

"Where is he? I'll shoot him in the head!"

"Can I just get a police report?"

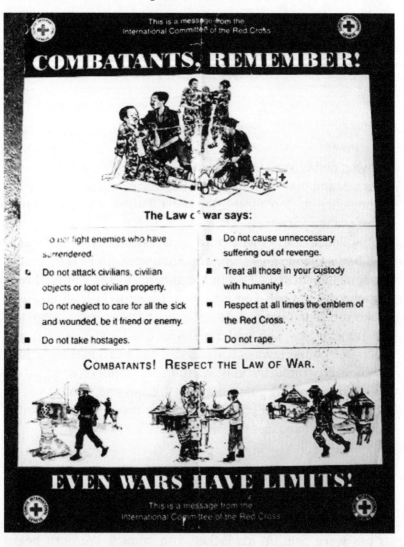

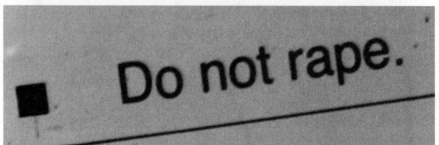

"Oh! It makes me so angry!" he said.

"Yes, but I don't want you to shoot him—" I said.

"Then I'll whip him and whip him and whip him—"

"What about my police report?" I ventured.

"Have you got one?" he said.

"No, I hoped you might have..."

"Madam," he said, suddenly strict, "we've only got one police report and we need it." He took pity on me. "Why don't you come back tomorrow? You can take it to the post office and get it photocopied."

"But... why should I have to go?"

"It's only ten minutes' walk to the post office!" he said. Then he calmed down and sunk over the counter on his elbows. "What I really want is to go to college." He sighed. "Madam, would you pay my tuition?"

I was weighing this up when I noticed a member of the public had come in and was standing next to me. He was naked from the waist down. He had quite a large penis for a lunatic.

Another cop came in. This one looked me up and down.

"Madam," said the new cop, "have you got children?"

"No," I said.

"Do you want children?" It was a nice offer but I'd had a busy evening and what I really wanted was to go home. I shook my head.

"Can you not have children?" he said.

"I don't know, I've never tried."

He picked up an old form, clicked a pen and wrote his mobile number on it, giving it to me with a sexy look. When I turned it over, the form read, "Does the hymen show signs of tearing?"

I was fighting off an uncontrollable horniness when another policeman walked in. The first two had a screaming match with him in Acholi. He seemed to have won and shooed the first two away. He noticed I was still there.

"Is there a problem?"

"Is there a problem? Yes, I've came all the way from Los Angeles and SOMEONE'S STOLEN MY CAMERA AND MY COMPUTER!"

A pause. The cop thought about this, analyzing the case,

mulling over the facts. I relaxed. He reached a conclusion.

"Los Angeles?" he said. "Can you help me find an agent? Because I've written a novel..."

The policeman disappeared and came back with a handbound manuscript in a blue plastic cover. On the front was an illustration of what looked like a turd. On the back was a list of people he gave thanks to. Two of them had been crossed out.

The policeman's novel was called *Across My Lips: the Burgles of Mortal Dignity.* I promised him I'd do my best to get it to a Hollywood agent and read a paragraph at random. I've reprinted it below. According to the book, this may infringe copyright.

> The brawny sexual abuser was wearing fur. He looked like a mighty chimpanzee with a lean and mean muscular stiffed genitals.

"If you like it," said the policeman, "I have another!"

As I left Gulu Police Station, I got a weird sixth sense—a sort of journalistic intuition—and it told me that these cops might not find my laptop.

44

I BET THEY JUST SAVE PEOPLE AND...

I tried being a foreign correspondent with no computer, working between Internet cafés, ants crawling out of the keyboard, running through tropical rain to grab a few minutes before they closed. Careering across smaller news websites, I read about what the child soldiers group and Laura had told me. It all checked out. The City of Children in the desert; Bashir denying that he supported the LRA while turning up to check on his child army breeding-by-proxy program; endless speeches from Clinton et al about the intolerable suffering of Marilyn's classmates without mentioning one glaring fact: the nuns knew the rebels were coming and the army never showed.

The army's iron fist had thumped down in 2002 and the LRA responded in kind: kids kidnapped faster than ever; sicker and sicker mutilations, including cutting off breasts and stitching up fannies. The kids caught the brunt of that iron fist: "when helicopters started bombing them," some mothers told me, "the small ones didn't know to run." But once again Kony got away. Like a spider, he saw the fist coming and fled. And the colonel still couldn't catch him.

"Madam, we're closing, please, we're very tired!"

"No! Just let me write my bullet points. Bullet points, very important. No, not bullets, bullet points!"

One hour later: the guys were desperate to leave. I was still typing. Clunk: Gulu goes dark. Across town all the lights go out, the music stops and your computer screen goes black. A power cut. All the guys flip their phones open to use them as torches. The Internet café owner turns to you with a long face.

"We have a generator in the back. But you saved your email, yes?" A very long pause. "I'll go and get the generator."

By the next evening I needed a large plate of fried butter with a rice garnish, pronto. I went to the Acholi Inn buffet. For all its dismal supermarket toilet air, the Acholi Inn was the party hub of town, and I spooned up fruit salad with the rest of the Westerners. The great investigative story that was going to save the children and definitely, unquestionably, make John fancy me was going to be cobbled together on old notebooks with no pictures, making it a lousy prospect to an editor. And what if it wasn't thieves? Was this anything to do with the Cleo incident? Then I remembered I'd left the adapter for my rubbish backup camera tangled in the laptop's cord. That meant my rubbish camera only had days to live. Then I remembered I was supposed to be teaching Marilyn the next day. I sat down to binge.

It was now night and the Acholi Inn's garden actually looked romantic. Worse, as always happens when I'm telling myself a plate of butter soaked stodge is a great night out, I found myself surrounded by couples. Worse, they were Useful Couples, back from the frontline after a hard day's standing up to injustice.

Doctors Without Borders. Bastards. I bet they just save people and fuck. I looked at my phone, wondering what time it was in Washington.

John answered.

"John, you know when you pissed off the government and got thrown out of Sudan... ?" I said, with the tone of a child who didn't want to turn the bedroom light off. "Is that a fairly common kind of thing to happen in Africa?"

"It wasn't just Sudan," John said with the tone of a dad saying tomorrow morning there'd be Cheerios as usual, before turning the bedroom light off. "I got thrown out of Zimbabwe." I looked around the Acholi Inn, feeling increasingly paranoid as John recounted his day in an airport, chuckling. "So I get to the check in counter, the guy looks down at my passport, looks up at me and runs away. Literally runs. The guys behind me were joking about it, "Did he leave the gas on?" Then he came back with some security thugs and physically dragged me to some kinda holding cell." I looked around. No one I recognized. "One guy came in and took a few shots, but—"

"Shots?"

"Punches, but—"

"Did it hurt?"

"Oh, yeah!" *God, that's so hot.* "But only in the body, over the course of the next few hours... They wanted the names of the people who'd been helping me investigate how Robert Mugabe fixed the election..."

"Did you tell them any names?"

"What? No, no, no. Eventually they put me on a plane to South Africa, just shoved me on. But here's what happened—the African passengers recognized me." John was laughing now. "I guess from CNN and the BBC. They literally gave me a standing ovation. It's a disgrace what the government has done to them in that country."

I was now watching the last frames of the widescreen Richard Attenborough adaptation of this story, and a tearful Tom Wilkinson stood up in his Business Class seat, knowing that his wife, Helen Hunt, hadn't died for nothing.

John apologized that he couldn't leave yet, but he was still tied up with the situation in Darfur. I wished him good luck resolving the terrible crisis.

Bloody Darfur. Fuck's sake, I bet that redhead Lindsay has coincidentally worked late... I bet she's knocking on his office door with a plate of chicken wings. Bitch! She doesn't even like chicken wings, she had a salad earlier... Don't let her in, you idiot...!

I bet Lindsay had a degree and only ate when she was hungry. I bet she wasn't sharing a flat. Perhaps I'd set my sights too high.

I went over to the Fanta Gang under the mango tree. Hanging out with army types who thought the colonel was doing a great job was better than watching altruists playing footsie.

Banya was there, and he was so nice about my missing electrical goods that I almost sat on his knee. Maybe a pensioner was the answer. All the reassurance against endless doubt you could ever want, *and* evenings on the sofa watching *Matlock* box sets. Sure, they might be falling apart, but the upside would be they'd have forgotten what a female arse should look like. You could look after them... Yeah, and you come home one day with a leaflet about prostate glands and find them doing someone who looked for all the world like Catherine Zeta-Jones in the stairlift. Balls. I was the worst journalist of all time. Before I drank myself to death, someone came to my rescue, an affable tall bloke called David Okidi. He was station manager of Mega FM.

"Why don't you come to the station? We'll put a message out about your computer. Maybe someone will hand it in," said David.

"You'd do that for a laptop?"

"Why not? Someone handed in a lost cow once." I imagined one of the cows with five-foot horns blundering through the Radio One building. It would have a job reading the news eventually.

45

WHAT YOU ARE DOING WITH THE RADIO
IS QUITE FANTASTIC

At Mega FM, the show just starting was *Come Home*, presented by Lachambel, the local Oprah. Whatever "It" is, Lachambel had enough spare to give away. He dressed in a lime green check shirt, yellow pants and golf shoes, a cross between Cliff Barnes from *Dallas* and Rupert the Bear. I could hear him on air, doing his intro, but there was no sign of him in the studio, so I assumed it was pre-recorded. I was going to go in and wait for him, but had learned my lesson the time one of us Radio One muppets had gone into an aging DJ's studio in similar circumstances.

"Do you mind?" the DJ ranted. "I'm building up to a gag!"

Suddenly I realized Lachambel was in the studio. He was under the desk. He popped up again with a crate of ginger beer, opened one, clicked his neck like a boxer, held his hands out in prayer, said "Amen" and sat down to finish his intro without missing a beat.

Lachambel could afford to large it; he was kicking serious ass in the ratings. Furthermore, the rebel kids in the bush tuned into *Come Home* every night.

"They call with requests," Lachambel said cheerfully. "Also, they listen because I have their friends on the show as guests— kids who escaped. They listen to hear that their friends got home safe. One time Kony called me and actually said, 'What you are doing with the radio is quite fantastic. We shall have to pray the Almighty keeps me until we meet physically.'"

I was about to leave, when Freddie the Man came sailing out of a cupboard. This cupboard, I later learned, was where he concealed the only good Internet in Uganda.

"Ah!" said Freddie. "So you have come to meet him. I will find Bill." He thought I'd come to find his intrepid photojournalist colleague and begin a brave adventure up to the frontline, rather than do a bleating shout-out about missing electrical goods. I didn't protest when he pelted off to get Bill.

Bill was a real reporter. He hunted down real news stories for a Ugandan newspaper. He was very short and younger than I'd expected, maybe twenty-one, but with the bearing and manner of a much older man, specifically Monty the World War II general. There was something weird about the way Bill held conversations, and after a while I realized it was because he thought before he spoke, something you never do in Los Angeles in case it interrupts your stream of lies.

Bill asked me what story I was working on. This is the exchange, from memory:

"I was writing a story about John—this peacemaker John Prendergast—going to do battle with Kony, sort of baiting a trap for the Most Evil Man in the World. Anyhow, John's not here—not because of me, he's... But now it's slanted the other way because I don't think people want to catch him. Kony. And then I talk to some priests and my camera gets stolen, then my laptop—this is in a different hotel—and this woman who says she's Betty Bigombe's niece and Betty doesn't have a niece called Cleo—sorry, the woman's name was Cleo—and... Listen, I know I'm paranoid, but is it possible that people could be listening to me?"

Bill thought about this, and said, "Let's talk somewhere else."

46

FUDGE PACT

The Green Light Café was empty apart from a few African men eating goat by lamplight. A very friendly waitress shuffled over and leaned on our table, arms framing a square of bosom.

"Just a cup of tea with milk, please," I said, closing the menu. "I'm on a diet."

"OK," said the very friendly waitress, writing, "Tea with milk."

"Do you have milk?" said Bill.

"Not really," said the waitress.

The waitress left and Bill moved closer.

"I think it is very good you want to write this story," said Bill. He told me that yes, things were not what they seemed in Gulu. I told him he sounded like a spy. He told me Gulu was rife with spies, real or imaginary—government agents, rebel collaborators. I told Bill about my frustrations at not being able to get an interview with the colonel. He said it must happen all the time in Hollywood, and I agreed, but in Hollywood when you can't get an interview with someone, you just pretend you met them and get quotes from the people around them: stylists, hairdressers and the stoner friend they call their consultant. We decided to interview the people around the colonel. It was his job to rescue kids from Kony, and I remembered Betty had mentioned a young woman who'd just been rescued. Bill was able to track down where she was being held. If we could talk to this girl, she'd be a real coup: Jenny was Kony's wife.

This partnership could be highly useful: he could take the pictures.

"So you're a photojournalist," I said.

"Yes."

"What kind of camera do you have?"

"I don't have a camera," he said, "but I'm hoping to get one."

No matter. I had a partner and we could bust this scandal wide open. Bill was so impressed to learn I was on assignment for the *Sunday Times* that I didn't feel it necessary to tell him that the peak of my investigative career was telling Rachel Hunter, "I have to ask you if you had an affair with Robbie Williams," and soliciting the reply "No, you don't." Bill also had something I didn't: integrity. He had planned on being a lawyer, but couldn't afford to sit the exams, so now he was a reporter who upheld the law instead. He had everyone's phone number and I was so grateful that I did my bit for the partnership, giving him tips on how to break into Western journalism. I felt faintly proud as I explained the art of fudging.

"And when you do a phoner, always ask what they're wearing, otherwise it sounds like you never met," I told Bill.

"But you didn't meet," he said. He was going to make me feel very, very old, but we were an investigative reporting team and he started by finding me a new hotel as our base. It had rooms named after British football stadiums. One had a bullet hole in the ceiling. Bill checked me into Upton Park for a fiver and promised we'd start first thing. Meantime, he let me use a computer in his office after hours. Yes, it was a low-end Crockett and Tubbs but it worked.

"Don't tell anyone you are here. The news team need it from 7 a.m.," he said. Later, the nightwatchman found me.

"Who are you?" the nightwatchman said.

I panicked. "I'm white?" I said.

"Oh, sorry," he said. Okay, I didn't say that, but I think it was implied.

47

DEAD FISH MONEY

Soon we were fully kitted out with a child's Leaning Tower of Pisa notebook and an old Instamatic camera borrowed from one of the child soldiers group's poor amputees. Must remember to send it back.

We walked up the road to where Jenny was being held, inside Gusco (Gulu Support the Children Organization), a large child soldier rehabilitation compound. I had two terrible thoughts about this poor beleaguered escapee. Firstly, whether I could trick her into going on record as saying that the colonel didn't want to catch Kony, in much the same manner as I fast-talked Christina Aguilera into going on record that she was knocked up (always go for the oblique: ME: "So, Christina, have you made any New Year's resolutions?" CHRISTINA: "That's the time I'll become a mommy, so—" PUBLICIST: "JANE!"). Secondly, that Jenny had better have a dynamite smile or no one would give a shit.

From the outside, Gusco looked like a maximum-security prison, its high fences iced with barbed wire. "Good," I thought. "At least Kony won't be able to snatch these kids back." A small face peeped at me over the fence. The tiny kid must have been standing on a table to see the outside world. Only at that point did it occur to me that the fence could also be protecting me from him.

The press spokesman was polite but frustrating. This was a government-run rehab center, I had no permit from the army to be investigating anything, and more to the point, army intelligence experts had first dibs on Jenny. She was exhausted after being debriefed for several days since her escape. In short, the interview wasn't going to happen. I hardballed the spokesman with the usual Hollywood lies—I was under deadline, I was leaving tomorrow, I was a great admirer of his work—but it didn't fly. I got up to leave, and almost without realizing, produced an old trick, an all-or-nothing lucky charm I only use about once a year in case its power wears out.

"That's fine, I totally understand," I said. Then, as a casual afterthought, "But is there any other child soldier rehabilitation center you think would benefit from the exposure? Full page in the *Sunday Times*... pictures... Sorry, I know you're busy..."

He said he'd arrange for me to speak to Jenny as soon as possible, and in the meantime, I could talk to a girl called Angela, wife of one of Kony's commanders. But I was very strictly briefed on how to handle a girl like this: "You can't take pictures. You can't use her real name. And you cannot use the term 'wife,'" he said.

"Why not?" I said, cockily.

He shrugged. "Because most of these girls were kidnapped as young as nine and given to a commander as old as fifty who raped them for years at knifepoint."

"Fiancée?" Okay, I didn't say that. But freedom of the press is the only thing between us and philistinism.

The press spokesman led me into a courtyard where an abandoned crutch lay on the dust. The inhabitants were mostly listless teenagers with toddlers. The spokesman went to find a translator, as Angela spoke Acholi. I waited on an old chair. A baby girl crawled up to me, put her hands on my knees and pulled herself to her feet. I smiled at her. She growled like a dog. I smiled at her again. She barked—literally barked—at me.

Angela was led in with her dad by an impassive lady social worker. Angela's dad sat in silence, seeing his daughter for the first time in nearly a decade. He looked sideswiped and was smiling into space.

Angela didn't make eye contact; she just played with her

baby's feet.

She was a tall, solid girl of nineteen, with a hexagonal face and bluish black skin; her baby was the scariest baby I'd ever seen, making Dog Baby look like an amateur. This baby had light brown skin and the expression of an old man who'd just been knocked down by a transit bus and was about to start on the bus driver with his walking stick.

The social worker told me the baby's dad was a commander called Ochen.

Ochen. The story was starting to form. Ochen was the short, fat, light skinned bastard who had killed Alan's brother in front of him as a warning about what it's like to have a brother killed in front of you...[20] Sure enough, Angela described her short, fat, light skinned husband.

"He told us he was thirty, but I think he looked a lot older," she said. Fortuitously, Ochen was in a profession that afforded short, fat liars not just one strapping teenage bride but nine. If one of them offended him, he beat all nine until they couldn't walk.

"Did you ever see Kony's magic powers?" I asked. She told me a story about a time when Kony called them to gather and pray.

"He told us to face eastwards and bend our heads. Then something came, like a rainbow, an orange light in the air about thirty feet away. People got scared and wanted to run away, but he said we should not fear that thing, it is an angel. An angel that has come to pray with us. We prayed and it left."

What was it? Did Angela really see it? I couldn't tell. She still wouldn't make eye contact. I asked the social worker what would happen to Angela when she was discharged from the rehab center.

"The first thing is looking after her child," said the social worker. "She thinks she can start a small business selling dried fish, but she doesn't have any capital." Angela told me she had been kidnapped at age twelve and she'd only just been rescued. Once abducted, she'd lived on the run from government

---

20. To misquote the UK's equivalent of the *Upright Citizens Brigade*, *The Comic Strip* [*The Comic Strip Presents: Dirty Movie*].

bombardment. A little unfair, given that the government troops had failed to stop her being abducted in the first place. The look on her face wasn't quietly stoic, it loudly said one thing, "This is how it is." The implications of that look made me furious. Struggling for dead fish money to feed a short, fat wife beater's baby after eight years on the run wasn't "how it is"; it was a series of decisions made by people who could have rescued her. Decisions that all reached one conclusion: let's not rescue her today. Not one person paid to be a diplomat had got Angela out as she was being beaten and raped for eight years. I changed the subject, trying to lighten the mood, at least my own. I asked her if she was happy to be going home after eight years—as a sex slave, after all—and Angela looked me straight in the eye and said, "No. Because the Man will find me."

On the way out, I buttonholed the spokesman. He told me she'd be okay, not to worry, she was traumatized, and if she needs food for her baby, well, the girls can come back and get it here for free.

"But she knows the rebels fairly well," I said. "And if she thinks they can find her..."

She'll be fine, he said. Yes, many children do get reabducted, but Angela was going to a protected village under army control.

As we left, I passed a line of girls waiting for their free food. The social worker casually mentioned that the food delivery was two weeks late. Seven thousand, eight hundred and thirty-seven kids had passed through Gusco. I swerved Scary Kid who was coming for me with his fists up and the guards closed the high gate on us.

Bill and I found a newspaper headline that cheered us up: CRIME RATE IN GULU REDUCES. Below, a smaller story: GULU JOURNALIST HAS LAPTOP STOLEN.

What would happen to Angela if Kony's men found her? I didn't know what a protected village entailed, but I doubted she'd be in a busy town with a reasonably well paid mum like Marilyn. I don't know what Angela's dad did, but he didn't look minted. The next morning, my stakeout of the colonel continued at the Acholi Inn, and I used the time to read up on the protected villages. The UPDF spokesman, Major Shaban Bantariza, had said in 2003, "The camps are a military strategy of the UPDF, designed to deny the rebels manpower and other resources." While I wouldn't trust the colonel to guard my lunch from pigeons, the villages weren't as bad as I'd feared, because the big international charities had stepped in—move over and leave this to us.

UNICEF were monitoring children, Canadian physicians were doing free vaccinations and fitting a health center with solar panels, while ActionAid were doing so much for the protected villages that their achievements ran the length of a whole half-page of newspaper. The villages were an emergency measure, but at least the people there got free food and medical care. The World Food Program spent millions of dollars a year on feeding people in the villages, according to one report, so Angela wouldn't live like Betty, growing up on one meal a day; and the International Rescue Committee sent free health workers, so she wouldn't end up like Faith, sitting in the dark after her money went to hospital bills. I'd seen kids chased out of school for being poor by their own headmaster. In the camps, the International Rescue Committee took educational supplies to hundreds of kids, ran free vocational training and even, in some places, savings and loan programs. Hopefully Angela could set herself up and get Scary Kid into school, or juvie.

I felt better; compared to what I'd seen in Uganda, the protected villages sounded like TGI Friday's. And regardless of whether or not Colonel Otema was doing his job, the villages were physically designed as safe zones to resist attack, placed strategically among their own army detachments. Kony's teenage rebels would have to fight their way through professionally trained soldiers to reach Angela.

The colonel wouldn't take my calls, but Gusco would. After some persistence, I was allowed back into the courtyard of crutches to see Kony's wife.

Jenny was a heavy set girl who seemed to have got her spark back. She knew firsthand who Kony was. Seventy wives, she said; 104 children. Kony will fight to the death. He did not want peace. But her answers were so robotic I couldn't tell if it was because she'd repeated them too many times already or she'd been given an official version, like the cast of *Alexander* insisting that the endless battle scenes manifested the hero adrift in an age of savagery, rather than Oliver Stone passing out in an edit suite. I resolved to find some kids who hadn't been quite so vigorously debriefed. Last word on the subject of babies: about this time, Kony had another baby; he called it George Bush.

No photo, no photo—Bill and I needed a photo of a former sex slave with a dynamite smile, but my rubbish backup camera was weakening by the hour. With no time to waste, I tried my luck at Gusco's rival rehab center, World Vision. World Vision is a large Christian charity funded by little old ladies from Wisconsin to West Ruislip. Their Gulu HQ was down a dirt track.

I waited in a hut, which was empty apart from two chairs and a table, while the social worker went to get a girl called Anna. I stared at the table, trying to think of tactful ways to phrase the order "Big smile, please," and gave up and read the paper. "More disappointing photos of the minister's daughter." The minister's daughter had disappointed by sitting on the floor, underwearless in a miniskirt, with some other drunk girls. The paper had pixelated her fanny, lending it a mysterious air, as though the pixels were hiding, say, a lizard or a tiny leprechaun.

Anna was a very pretty 15-year-old with short dreadlocks and a torn red dress. She was so nervous she never stopped smiling—a giant smile, like Paris Hilton, except pleasant. We chatted amicably.

"What do you want to be when you grow up?" I said, with the perkiness I usually save for asking actresses how fabulous they looked on a scale of one to ten.

"I want to be a doctor."

"Fantastic. There's a big hospital in Kampala—"

"I killed a boy called David," she blurted, her smile so wide it looked painful.

"Could I ask... why?"

"Because he was my friend," she said. "They caught him escaping. Because he was my friend they gave me the machete. They told me to cut off the back of his head, then the top of his head, then his leg, and then kill him. It was most unfortunate."

British colonialism. We gave them small arms and a lovely turn of phrase. Anna's smile didn't flinch. She curtseyed and left.

I went back to Gusco fast. I was too late. Angela had already been sent home to Kitgum Matidi, her protected village.

That night, back at the hotel, my mind was racing. What would happen to Angela if Kony's men found her? It was the colonel's job to protect these kids, but was he doing it? I couldn't sleep. I tried reading. From *Across My Lips: the Burgles of Mortal Dignity*, p. 45: "He caressed the free meat above his left shoulder... It quailed suddenly when he imagined the glimmering room, and its pleasurably feeling relatedness. Someone was hitting her cake."

It didn't help, so the next day I decided to go with Bill to visit Angela in her protected village, to see for myself how the colonel was protecting her.

48

LOVE ME TENDER

"I am not allowed in Kitgum without an escort," said the man from UNICEF, and by escort he did not mean Ryan Seacrest and a can of spunk. He meant seven armed soldiers in a pickup truck. Kitgum was right up in the north, where Kony's rebels were running free. Bill and I went round the charities, hoping for a ride with people who knew the terrain.

"Kitgum? You're too late," said the UN guy. "You wouldn't beat the curfew."

What did a curfew mean? It meant that if the rebels came after you between the hours of 4:30 p.m. and 9 a.m., the army would not be there to help, because they'd have gone home.

"Can we take a bus?" said Bill. The UN guy took a piece of paper from a pinboard.

"Let's ask the security briefing," he said, and read out the piece of paper: "'Wednesday, 0900hrs: shots fired at public bus.' Go in an AP vehicle."

"AP? I'm with Associated Press," I lied on autopilot. "I don't have my card, but—"

"Armor plated."

"But she's in a protected village. Why can't I take an ordinary vehicle?"

"Because they can't guarantee your protection." I bet he was from Logistics.

He suggested we fly: "It's only ninety dollars."

The travel agent shook her head at my credit cards. I couldn't tell if she meant they didn't take credit cards or didn't take my credit cards, which would have made her smarter than I thought.

We sat in a bar, the Travellers Inn, in silence. I had a beer; Bill had a banana. He really was a ridiculously noble person.

"You fly. I can take the bus," said Bill.

"Absolutely not. No way, Bill."

"The bus is not that bad," said Bill.

"You heard the fat bastard from the UN—you could get killed!"

"Well, you know death," Bill said, peeling a banana, "when you have to go, you have to go."

"But, Bill, for fifty pounds, we could stay!"

Bill went to his office to finish up a news story, and I stayed at the Travellers Inn to ask around, hoping Kony had something other than kidnapping on tonight. Fifty pounds. I no longer had fifty pounds. I could hear my mum's voice in my head. "Jane, it's fifty pounds! I'll give you fifty pounds!" I called Banya to ask for a lift—he was, after all, the only nice charity runner I'd met—but he wasn't in town.

"Excuse me. I can take you to Kitgum. I fly for Doctors Without Borders," said a stranger. I was suspicious, then felt guilty for being suspicious, as always happens in third-world countries. On your own soil, you can be as suspicious as you like.

"You are suspicious," said the stranger. "Good, that means you'll live a longer life." He was called Daniel, he really did work for Doctors Without Borders, and he was indeed a pilot. I was saved.

"I have space on the morning flight. But if you planned to leave later—"

"No, I'll take it. Oh, this is brilliant. Thank you. You have no idea."

"The plane is easy to find. If you meet me—" Suddenly a 6' 2" x 2' man in a Vegas lounge suit grabbed me. It was Walter, the Mayor of Gulu himself—Giant Elvis. He dragged me into the darkened club. Next thing I knew I was on the dance floor, squished in his tits. I was in a lake of black skin and the only light was coming from the fluorescent patterns on clothes. I was still too dumb to realize what was going on and wondered if I could survive by breathing through a straw between Walter's man boobs, like James Bond. The record ended and Walter led me outside. He nodded at the pilot.

"Be careful who you talk to," said Walter. "We will take you home."

"It's okay, he's from Doctors Without Borders," I said with a sinking feeling.

"He used to work for Doctors Without Borders; he probably kept his identity card. He is no good at all." I remembered all the classifieds in the back of the New Vision and the Monitor, mugshots posted by famous Western charities. One of which would probably read, "PUBLIC ANNOUNCEMENT: THE MAN CALLING HIMSELF DANIEL IS NO LONGER EMPLOYED BY DOCTORS WITHOUT BORDERS." I'm not sure what would have happened if I'd met Daniel the next morning by an airfield, but I probably wouldn't have ended up soaring across jungle with a hot neurosurgeon. My stomach kicked in. One of Walter's posse showed me to the loo, through a corridor lined with curtained rooms.

"Is this place...?" I asked.

"Walter is Chairman of Gulu!" he said.

"I know—" Two beefy young ladies dressed for Tuesdays at Bada Bing came out of one of the curtained rooms. "But are those girls... ?"

"Walter is very big man!"

"I'll say. But this place... ? Is this place—"

"Oh, yes. But if they shut it down, where would you get a drink, eh, sincerely?"

"Sincerely."

"And you have to agree the music is excellent." A banging tune fired up. I had to agree. The crowd went mental.

49

THAT ONE, HE WAS AMBUSHED

Well, that settled it, Bill and I were taking the bus. And all the bus had to do was leave no more than four hours late and we'd beat the curfew, not get shot and find Angela.

The next morning, Bill and I arrived at the bus park bright and early, bought lots of bottles of water, got on the Kitgum bus and waited.

And waited. I watched the shiny charity Land Cruisers tearing away, painted with two-foot-high initials: UN, UNHCR, ICRC. The international acronyms for "Don't shoot." But the kids who might shoot them had been snatched out of school, or bred to order by a man who studied the great philosopher Chuck Norris. The Land Cruisers would have been safer painted with MAN U.

And waited. Bus after bus left before us.

"Madam, I told you, we are the only bus going to Kitgum today," said our conductor, and slammed the door on me. Another bus left, the conductor yelling, "Kitgum!" I was losing my veneer of liberalism. I knew our driver needed the fare, but he'd get it anyway: every single bus ended up stuffed with hot flesh.

"Look, I'm not going shopping, I'm trying to get there to find someone. Please tell me, are we leaving in the next two hours?"

"I told you! We leave in twenty minutes!"

"Yes! You told me that an hour ago!"

The conductor turned away. He couldn't even begin to explain how wrong I was; he only had four hours to kill. OK, let me phrase it differently: how much extra would it cost for you to tell me the truth? I've noticed when you fly Business, the stewardesses think it's okay to tell you what's wrong with the baggage-handling system/holding pattern/gate allocation because you're rich, therefore less likely to start a riot. If you're poor, you can't handle the truth. If you fly Upper, they'll tell you where all the baggage went at Terminal 5. In the cockpit, they know the secret of eternal life, but that's a lot of Air Miles.

Very late morning, as the sun was turning the minibus into an oven tray full of human Yorkshire puddings, the Kitgum bus finally left the bus park, drove outside town and broke down.

I called Father Carlos and explained the situation. He told me to write down a phone number.

"I have a friend in Kitgum, Father Benedict. If you get into trouble. Very good man." I knew the drill by now. Emergency, what service do you require? Priest, please, I'll wait by the car.

"Bill, I'm sorry, we're not going to make it," I said.

"You don't know these buses," said Bill. Sure enough, the driver slammed the hood several times and the bus started again.

Soon we were plummeting north, taking corners at 90, chickens, charcoal and old newspapers flapping around inside. The passengers clung to each other, the man behind me clamped on my shoulder like a parrot with bad breath. Why do people with bad breath lean closer to you the farther you lean back? Like hell they don't know. We passed a tuberculosis control zone. What did tuberculosis do outside the control zone? We thumped over a pothole and Bill caught me trying to read the speedometer. He pointed out a burned-out truck at the roadside.

'That one, he was ambushed," said Bill. "If you see branches in the road, that is how they trap vehicles." *Missing in Action 2* or *Coming to America*?

I knew from the child soldiers group that the small soldiers would shoot the driver first. Up ahead—in the road—branches —right across—ow—can't anyone see them...? My heart clenched. I had two words in my head: "Oh bugger." But it was just a fallen tree. Then a child stepped out from the tall grass wearing a gun strap across his chest. I jumped back in my seat. It was a satchel. I looked back as we passed him. He was perhaps six.

Our driver was manifestly a nicer man than the conductor, as his rationale was either a) he'd kill his passengers in a high speed collision rather than let them live as sex slaves, or b) if he was shot dead while doing 90, his corpse would drive the truck far enough to give the passengers a head start when they got out and ran. Or maybe he was just a really shit driver.

50

CARMINA BURANA

A storm was brewing as we pulled into Kitgum. This fleabitten town felt angry. People were agitated, rushing to beat the curfew. We needed a boda boda instantly if we were going to make it to Angela's village, Kitgum Matidi, and Bill strode from bike to bike urging them to take us, but it was too far and profit was no longer an incentive. Kony said bicycles were a sin.

I called Father Benedict, feeling guilty, but dammit, he was a missionary. Surely saving people was what they'd come all the way from Europe for; I was making his day, possibly. Father Benedict told me to get to the church and waste no time.

At 4:30, dead on curfew, our motorbikes tore into a clearing. The winds of an electrical storm flattened the grass on all sides. In the middle was a huge, crumbling, painted Catholic church, the Vatican dropped from space into the African bush. As the storm rose, I could hear *Carmina Burana* in my head. I tried not to hear it, but it was persistent. I scanned the church for someone who could be Father Benedict and saw no one. I didn't plan on being stranded in the open. Around us in the fields, people were literally running for safety. Bill called to them. They carried on running. I asked the bodas to wait. They didn't. Not ideal. Then out of the corner of my eye I saw a little white man scuttling into a cloister. We reached him just as he got to the door.

Inside the missionaries' stark quarters, the anger was even higher. Wind whipped the red curtains into the room. This was a time capsule, decorated with missionary magazines, one of which was called the *Negro*. I don't know if Father Benedict had preserved this magazine since 1953 or if there was a jolly newspaper publisher somewhere still turning out 50s classics

like the *Negro* and an *FHM* prototype called *Salty Whores.*
Father Benedict bustled in with a packet of biscuits that he'd
probably been dying to open since the young Queen Elizabeth
stood him up.

"I am Father Benedict," he announced. France's mouthful-of-
pebbles vowels.

I thought I'd keep things light. "So! In Gulu, they tell me the
war is over," I said.

The little man swelled up with rage. "Rubbish! I say to you
again, rubbish! Sorry, it's to laugh. The rebels are completely
free to do what they like. Soldiers are just by the roadside, and
sometimes it looks like they are very fast to disappear when
there are problems."

Father Benedict had just got back from a hospital. He was
very, very angry for a very small man. "Anita was beaten in the
head and shoulders five times with a machete," he said. "This
place has a very big barracks. My question is, where were the
soldiers?"

Father Benedict read my thoughts.

"Let's go to another place, Kitgum Matidi," he said. Bill looked
at me. "On 27 May this year, the young men and women started
to go about some of their businesses. Eight were hacked to
death," he said. "So all these talks in the newspapers that there
is almost peace here, sorry, it is rubbish, it is a lie."

Father Benedict attacked a Fanta with a bottle opener. I
ventured on to peace talks; after all, my aging fancy man Banya
had said people's belief in the spirits would always stall them.

"Banya says—" I said. Father Benedict almost dropped the
Fanta.

"That is a lie! Banya is the biggest liar around. The Church
tried to make peace talks again and again. We had three times
peace talks, and it was going quite well. The army shot three
times and killed our men almost three times."

But... why would Banya lie? He was a captive too.

"Banya is taken around by the government and gets money to
say how good they are and so on," said Father Benedict. Banya
wasn't an ordinary abductee like the child soldiers group guys.

Or even an ordinary commander. He was Kony's Number Three, his military tactician, trained by the Russians. My head was reeling. That wasn't all: Banya didn't escape from Kony; he was captured. That meant if he had his way, he'd still be out there kidnapping.

Now, I'm a terrible judge of character. It runs in families. As I've said, my great grandparents were taken to Auschwitz. *This hotel is awful! And have you seen the showers?* My grandfather was a translator at the Nuremberg Trials, yet Simon Wiesenthal still had plenty of work. I, too, am a terrible judge of character, but my heritage shouldn't have led me to flirt with a war criminal.

Banya wasn't just following orders. This cuddly old granddad, according to a report commissioned by the United Nations, is "a man with a record of rape and torture... said to be responsible for countless sadistic rapes of underage female abductees in LRA captivity."[21]

"He is a real killer," said Father Benedict. "The people are all afraid when they see a group that is coming with Banya, you could be sure it would be bloody. The government took him to an area near here to talk, and one teacher stood up and said, 'You shut up now, you are the killer, you killed our children. I know if I talk like that I may not survive, but I will not keep quiet.'"

Thousands of miles from the yellow bricks of Metro-Goldwyn-Mayer Studios, I'd stumbled on the Wizard of Oz. If Kony was the Wonderful Wizard, protected by witches like Banya, little Father Benedict was Toto and I was a sugar-addled, shoe-worshipping Judy Garland as Dorothy. I'd fallen for Banya's lies, for a government patsy paid to find people like me, to spin me tales of snakes and leopards and spirit gods, so I'd go home and tell newspaper readers—including politicians reading the *Sunday Times*—about the impossible monster that was Kony, the enigma that no mere very well equipped army could catch.

Then I remembered something else. Banya ran Labora Farm. A residential work scheme for former abductees. Let me get this

---

21. Report compiled by UNICEF, OCHA, OHCHR, December 1, 2005.

straight: the problem here is kids being kidnapped. The solution is hiring a kidnapper as their babysitter. No wonder the kids at Labora looked glum. And as for keeping quiet because Kony was listening to them via his spirits, Banya was right there next to them, listening to them via his ears. And here is the strangest thing. Before he worked for Kony, Banya worked for Yoweri Museveni. He was his bodyguard while President Museveni was at the Ministry of Defense. "He's a very nice man," said Banya at the time of his capture.

I thought about Father Carlos's diary and the UPDF officer who called pretending to be a rebel. I wondered if Kony's ability to predict the arrival of UPDF helicopters came from the spirit of an Italian soldier or the outstanding coverage of Vodafone.

Even Bill was shocked. I could tell because his head was tilted back half an inch. And now I was really worried about Angela. Father Benedict went to find a driver who was prepared to run us back into town to find a bed for the night; we'd set out to find Angela first thing.

As we climbed into a pickup truck to leave, I looked back at Father Benedict, the small man in the clearing, his crumbling chunk of church stranded in a wasteland of shitty behavior.

"Why do you stay?" I said.

"We missionaries don't run," he chirruped and waved goodbye.

There was no way we'd be getting back to Gulu, so I bought Bill and me some toothbrushes and checked us into the Bomah, another ghastly hotel that should have been twinned with the Acholi Inn. The good old days of finding a bug on your car were long gone here; we'd have been lucky to find soup to go under our fly. The Bomah had another set of speakers playing full-volume ragga to an empty room and toilets apparently plumbed direct from the guests' bowels to those of hell. All the staff had sensibly fled to avoid association.

Around Kitgum, I visited a local parish priest to confirm Father Benedict's story. Yup, said Father Ernie, rebels all over the place, rampant kidnapping.

"But people came to these protected villages for protection," I said. "They could go home."

"That's not what happened at all," he said. Once again, here on the frontline there was a different story. Yes, when the massacres started, people wanted protection from Kony. Not everyone wanted to flee into camps. But the government broadcast orders on the radio: a 48-hour ultimatum to leave your home for the camps or face the army. This was a sweep, a clean-out—mobile ground troops moved from village to village spreading the ultimatum to people who hadn't heard it on the radio. In some places, like Kitgum, people were herded away from home by military chopper.

"Those who could not go into the protected villages within a given period were considered rebel collaborators," said Father Ernie. "Some were killed and their homesteads were burned."

Until this point, no newspaper, analyst or official source had mentioned that the protected villages weren't voluntary but this is what I was being told. This could throw everything into a new light: if any of these 1.6 million people were being held against their will, why were the charities helping? Bill and I had to get into the protected villages to see what was going on.

I bedded down with pillows over my head to save me from ragga. We'd get up early to collar an NGO and beg a lift to Angela's village.

At 8 a.m. we were waiting in the Bomah's lobby. The NGO vehicles would leave for the refugee camps the second curfew ended at 9 a.m., so negotiation had to be swift and conclusive. But there were no NGO workers around. This was highly stressful, as it was impossible to be a compulsive eater with the Bomah's service. No sooner had the Bomah staff brought me stale toast instead of what I'd compulsively ordered than a man from the Red Cross arrived. I dropped the dusty bread square on its plate and ran up to him.

"We can't carry journalists without permission from the army," he said. "Try UNICEF."

He smiled brightly, not seeming to hear the deafening alarm bells. I turned to see the waiter throwing my toast into the worst bin in Africa. Flies shot out of the bin in disgust.

A UNICEF guy came in. To my relief he was British; he'd feel some kind of allegiance to a fellow countryman.

"No. And you shouldn't go," said the UNICEF man.

I know that, but I am going, because no one is telling this story and my underwear tax is paying for a pedophile rapist to run a child rehab center, you altruist.

All the NGO vehicles started to leave for the field. Bill headed for the bus park to see if he could bargain a truck, and I went to grovel for charity at, er, the HQs of all the world's main charities.

At the Norwegian Refugee Council, a lumpen woman who looked like it would take 400,000,000,000 volts of electricity to trigger an original thought, let alone save a refugee, stared vacantly at me.

"You should take a plane. It's only ninety dollars," she said. "If you go by road and anything happens to you, you will be blamed." *If anything happens to me, the assignment of guilt will be the least of my problems, Brunhilda. And for the last time, $90 is a fortune to me right now, and I'm David Beckham compared to the mob you're supposed to be helping.*

The Danish International Development Assistance guy was not around. The Swedish Life & Peace Institute didn't operate here. What were all these Scandinavians doing in Africa? Was it some kind of Viking guilt? Rape counseling from the people who invented it?

The comfort of some of these charity workers was starting to really annoy me. That was how they seemed: comfortable, buffet-fed, okay with the situation, don't rock the boat. They didn't seem to be there to change anything. At best, they were merely there, attending a tragedy. At worst, they were there to make themselves feel good. They all smiled brightly as they told me they couldn't help. I hated the Useful People now, really hated their altruist guts.

Then a young logistics guy from UNICEF came pelting out of their compound, waving his arms.

"Wait! I know someone who can help you," he shouted, redeeming the entire concept of benevolence.

Shortly afterwards I found myself hiring a truck with seven armed soldiers in the back for $40. The driver was a jolly madman, an irrepressible "B.A." Baracus. His job was in some kind of irrigation, the truck he'd got from the Red Cross, the soldiers he'd found... somewhere.

"Are they... trained?" I said.

"I'm Nathan," he answered, pumping my hand. "Do you have a bulletproof vest?"

"No," I thought indignantly, "it's a Victoria's Secret Miracle Bra." He shrugged; he probably didn't have a bulletproof vest either.

"Where are we going?" he said.

I looked at our armed truck. *Coffee Bean on Sunset Boulevard. Shoot everybody.*

Nathan was a jolly driver and it was a jolly journey to find a former sex slave. The truck had happy face stickers on the glove box, was perfumed by an air freshener called Brings Back Memories of Love and we were playing Shania Twain's "Man! I Feel Like a Woman."

I asked Nathan if seven armed guards was perhaps half a dozen more than necessary.

"Feel my arm," he said. I touched his elbow. It had hard lumps in it.

"Are those... ?"

"Yes! Shot! I drove into an ambush, thirteen of them, all kids! Born in the bush, totally wild! They almost blew off my testicles!" His bullet-laden arm spun the steering wheel as we smacked through a swarm of dragonflies.

"Will we find Angela?" I said.

"We will find her," he said. I believed him.

We passed the Blue Moon nightclub, whose sign is below. Note the special offer on the sheet of paper.

51

GREAT WHEN YOU'RE YOUNG, BUT WHEN YOU'VE HAD FOUR KIDS THEY LOOK AWFUL

A brown smear appeared on the landscape. It got bigger. And bigger. The smear began to separate into brown blobs, thousands of round mud huts. This was Angela's protected village. I looked for the barriers holding off the rebels, but there was nothing. The army barracks full of trained soldiers I'd imagined didn't exist: protection was an army detachment of a few huts, huts sunk below ground for safety with only the round straw roofs visible, like giant Chinese coolie hats scattered on the soil. A dozen soldiers hung around. The soldiers looked young, and by young, I mean that if you were in high school, you wouldn't ask them to go to the liquor store for you. One of the soldiers was squatting in the road, playing with something. He was pushing a toy car.

Nathan, Bill and I left our armed escort and walked into the village. It was too vast to find anyone easily, so I looked for the flags and high-walled compounds of the big international charities. We found a local man in a shed. He was wearing an optimistic red baseball cap and introduced himself as the camp leader.

"Seventeen thousand, four hundred and forty-four people," said the camp leader. Bill logged it; he was on form, tracking every detail. I was leaning on doors made from old food aid cans, panting, and we'd only been out in the African air five minutes. Bill, trying to demonstrate how an actual reporter might operate, found the women's leader and told her we were looking for Angela.

"Can you describe this girl?" the women's leader asked.

I said, "She's about nineteen, she was kidnapped, she was a

commander's bride for eight years and she's got a baby." I swear to God the women's leader asked if she had any distinguishing features.

We followed the women's leader deeper into the village, past an old lady stirring a boiling vat. She'd just brewed several gallons of neat alcohol. This seemed an entirely appropriate response.

And here I have to stop this nonsense of calling it a village. I've been in villages, and even the ones without Morris dancers have plants and trees. We were on a seabed of blank mud: mud floor, mud walls and endless mud doorways. It felt as though something had swept through and taken the flowerbeds, the animals, all traces of life, except the survivors themselves, who now sat around wondering what the hell had just happened. It was open air, but seemed stuffy; this wasn't a place for living, it was for containment, which made it not a village but a camp.

I saw women with black eyes—60 percent of women in these camps had been domestically or sexually assaulted, they told me. What? Sixty percent? *Tuesday, took the rubbish out, domestically or sexually assaulted. Wednesday, got some milk, domestically or sexually assaulted... Or was I? No, that was Monday.*

The sun swooned over us as we went from hut to hut, asking for Angela, faces peering from the dark inside. One hour. Two hours. Bill had reams of notes. I had sunstroke. I'd resolved to get him into boozing if we ever got out of there. People told us three more girls Angela's age had just been kidnapped by Kony's men. A woman was quietly angry as she told us, "One girl, about nineteen, they found her stripped naked." The women didn't know if that was Angela. Where was she? Facing Kony's commanders? Were they looking for one of her friends to hold the machete?

Maybe she was in the clinic. I was glad the Canadian doctors had been fitting solar panels somewhere, but fitting a bloody doctor might have been a better place to start. There were 150 people flopping around and one young doctor walking among them. Gregory House, M.D., has more drugs in his urine than this guy had in his medicine cabinet. I asked the young man what his responsibilities were.

"Malaria," he said, which seemed a little unjust on a global scale. Then Nathan came running up. They'd found a girl.

I followed them to a round hut. She was sitting in the darkness with her back to me in an old orange T-shirt. I touched her and she turned round. It wasn't Angela. She told Bill her name was Victoria; she'd been abducted in 2002, impregnated by Kony's men and had escaped on March 7, 2005. She'd been discharged from Gusco three weeks ago, she said. She came home with her new baby to find both of her parents had been killed by the rebels. She was seventeen. "She says she has a headache," said Bill. I'll bet she did.

Victoria's aunt heard we were there, stumbled out of a hut to greet us and promptly collapsed on the floor. She was an old aunt; her life plan was to eat soft food for five years and die, not look after a teenage sex slave and her baby. The women's leader said, "The girl has no means of getting in touch with Gusco. She's had no counseling."

Victoria's baby went crawling off. Victoria got up unsteadily to catch her, then thought better of it and sat down again.

"Feel her skin," said Bill. Victoria was burning up with malaria. How come the millions of dollars the world had donated in aid couldn't buy this girl an aspirin? Water splashed on her arm and I thought the rain had started again. She was crying.

Perhaps it was hidden by the endless savings and loan outlets lining the camp alleys, but I couldn't see the millions of dollars worth of food. Other people were looking for it too. One woman in particular sticks in my mind. I finally cured my Tourette's when I met Edie the Matchbox Widow.

Edie had heard we were coming. By the time we reached her, she'd waited some time and her mouth was firm but her eyes couldn't keep it together much longer. They were pinned wide with stress, flashing around her.

"She was abducted in 1987; she got pregnant in the bush," said Nathan. "There were a lot of difficulties when she was sent back in 1999." I asked Nathan what she meant by a lot of difficulties. Edie was shaking by now. Nathan translated. "Her husband also came back from the bush in 1999 and they settled back home. Then one day they were riding bicycles and the LRA came. They thought she was rich because she had some business selling matchboxes. They killed the husband in her presence. She says they already had four children and they killed him in her presence," said Nathan.

"How did they kill him?" I asked.

Edie made the universal sign for a beheading, with a twist, flicking her fingers at her neck and down to the ground to show her husband's head tearing loose and rolling in the dirt at her feet. That day, she got back on her bicycle and rode home to her kids.

"She is requesting if at least someone would help her feed the children," said Nathan. "She's really bitter, that's why she's shaking," he explained. I fumbled in my purse and gave her everything I had: 23,000 shillings, or $12.76. How did I get to this age and all I have on me is $12.76? $12.76 is having failed at everything. The worst thing was Edie's shame. She was so, so embarrassed to take my $12.76 that she couldn't speak, only cry. Edie ran away to hide herself in the mud warren. Finally, nothing was funny.

Then our luck changed. A fat man on a bicycle wearing gold pimp shades, a safari hat and a safari suit with gold zip tags swinging on his nipples tinkled by. I looked at him. Bill looked at him. I looked again, and he was still there. A gold pimp on a bicycle is always a good omen, so we followed him. Somehow he led us to Angela's son.

"Grr," said Scary Kid, shaking his red head. Angela's father stepped out and scooped up the boy. He told me Angela had gone to collect firewood. I sat under a shea nut tree with Angela's mother, Lesley, waiting to see if she'd come back alive.

Finally Angela stepped into the camp, carrying a bunch of firewood.

Lesley looked like she'd won the lottery.

"Did you recognize Angela after nine years?" I said.

"She hasn't changed a bit. I'm very pleased she came back with a baby," said Lesley, cuddling Scary Kid, which just goes to show a grandmother's love really does know no bounds.

Angela sat down. This time she made eye contact. I asked her if she thought Kony could still win the war.

"Kony still has strength because there are many people who are still there with him," she said. "Above all, he has a certain spirit. What he predicts comes true." *The man who hears the colonel's army coming.* "When I look at him, I see somebody normal," she said. "A human being. But he tells one story to the top officials and a different story to us."

It was the same whiff of cynicism I'd caught at the child soldiers group. Now I had a better idea of who Angela was: a self-possessed girl who had somehow spent eight years running round with a machine gun.

Bill, Nathan and I would find someone to fetch Victoria. As for Angela, I've felt bad about leaving friends at rubbish parties in Muswell Hill; I didn't feel great about leaving a former kidnappee ringed by her former kidnappers. I explained about the *Sunday Times* piece, trying not to stare at the four-year-old girl by my shoulder with a giant swollen belly who looked like she might topple over. And then, like a stupid person, I said I'd try to help.

"I'll try to help," I said. The rank stupidity.

It was time to go. The camp leader and the women's leader came up again. They starting telling me about another four people who'd just been abducted from a neighboring camp, but my head was incapable of processing any more stupid, avoidable tragedy. This whole place was a sham. *We can't carry journalists without permission from the army.* A sham conveniently located in rebel territory; just enough attacks to keep it on the UN security briefing. This moment, however, turned out to be key.

"Isn't the colonel's army protecting you?" I asked the women's leader.

She shrugged.

"The trouble is, the soldiers use our girls as prostitutes and give them AIDS," she said. Now that was not, strictly speaking, protection.

"But... why don't their parents warn them?"

"Their parents ask them to do it," she said.

"But... why?" Incisive journalism.

"The World Food Program doesn't provide all the food we need," said the camp leader. "The people are only allowed to leave to dig their farms after 9 a.m. and they cannot go far from the camp." In Queenstown, I'd see them digging their cabbages at 6:30 a.m. "So now the families are hungry and they send out the girls—thirteen, twelve, eleven—to sleep with the soldiers."

"For how much?"

"For posho." For porridge. Cheap even by international child prostitute rates. It would cost you $2 in Phnom Penh (true, I was there). I was wrong, these places weren't camps, they were cash'n'carry brothels. Millions of dollars flying around, but all the world's aid had come down to a porridge fuck.

As we climbed in the truck, I noticed women were gathering to stare at an old tattoo on my leg. They pulled up their T-shirts to show me tribal scars on their stomachs and whispered amongst themselves.

"Bill, what are they saying?"

"They're saying they look great when you're young, but when you've had four kids they look awful," said Bill.

We rode the bus back to Gulu, quotes bouncing around my skull like a particularly cheap screensaver. *"My question is, where were the soldiers?"* This didn't make sense. The colonel's army had 40,000 soldiers; 200-242 protected villages; 165-200 soldiers per village. I hadn't seen 165-200 soldiers. I'd seen twelve, and one of them was pushing a toy car. What had the colonel got to hide? *"Look around you."* With girls being picked off like croissant crumbs, the colonel's army didn't seem to be trying to catch Kony. The St. Mary's abductions pointed to that. But what could be the colonel's motive for not doing everything in his power to catch his mortal enemy? Not the prostitution, there wasn't enough money in it. *"For posho."* Not much porridge, either, from the look of those girls. Where was all this aid money going?

For now, Angela was "fine." But I had not seen such a depressing sight as these camps since I caught my ex-boyfriend crying and wanking at the same time.[22]

---

22. Danny, 1997-1997. I changed the locks.

52

SOCIAL OBLIGATIONS

I got back to Gulu, and I was really rather cross about the porridge fuck. So I went visiting. I dropped in on the local rep of the World Food Program: Luis, nice man, airconditioned office. Compact fellow, bouncy.

The World Food Program spent millions a year on grain, he said, $30 million from Ugandan grain companies alone. I told Luis I'd seen children who looked malnourished in a camp fed by the WFP.

"They should be brought to a therapeutic feeding center," he said. "We have a very good hospital in Gulu."

"But if this child doesn't have the taxi fare?" I asked. *How can they afford to get to hospital when they can't afford fuck porridge?*

"If I see a child with a mother and the mother is asking for transport, I would offer them a seat in a WFP car," he said.

"I saw a large number of children who seemed obviously malnourished," I said.

"Was it severe or moderate…?" I wanted to tell him about the stick boy in Kitgum Matidi, grilling a single ear of sweetcorn, using a USAID food aid drum for a barbecue and an old office in-tray for a griddle. I wanted to tell him how, when the boy saw me, he grabbed the corn and ran up to me delighted, trying to sell me his dinner. I wanted to say, "Severe? Moderate? You tell me. You're the starving-people guy."

"I'm talking classic malnutrition babies, ones I remember from the television," is what I actually said.

"Maybe their mothers aren't bringing them in," he suggested.

"The boss of the camp told me there simply wasn't enough food."

"No. For supplemental feeding there is not enough food? No.

Maybe the children aren't eating three times a day," Luis said. World Food Program food, he explained, gave proper nutrition when eaten in three meals a day, not the traditional one-big-dinner system.

"But to cook some of that food, they need firewood, and when they go to get firewood…" *they can get macheted. And three times a day, well, that could get tedious.*

"We have started growing firewood trees," he said.

"But while those trees are growing, there's no chance the World Food Program would reconsider this three-meals-a-day policy?"

Luis stopped bouncing and folded his arms.

"As I have said, our food is for three meals a day," he said, adding that perhaps the refugees were selling the food to buy medicine for their kids, or worse: "They have to entertain their friends, so they would rather use all their monthly food rations in one night as part of their social obligation. Especially when there are relatives who died, and their relatives have to party with food."

"So you've just told me that one of the reasons for child poverty could be that the refugees are holding big parties?"

"No, not big parties. Other means of spending the food is what I said. And you have social obligations, like funerals of relatives."

I'm sorry, could you repeat that? Christ on a stick, he can't have said it, can he? Funerals.

I told him about the child mothers waiting two weeks for their food at Gusco. He told me someone should have told him. I wondered what Luis thought he was being paid to do, but as we left he showed me his new species of corn, and I realized what his job was: to fly to Uganda and improve the fatally flawed culture that had landed these hard-partying, massive-dinner-eating, funeral-celebrating refugees in camps. He was very proud of his ear of corn.

I carried on visiting. I dropped in on a UNICEF worker: nice man, who offered me a buffet lunch then paid for me and I let him. Hell, I was broke. He told me things were improving.

"Which is good actually," he said. "I can now get to twenty-three of the camps without an escort." I hoped against hope this was the setup to a joke. After a while I realized the punchline wasn't coming. We finished our enormous meal and he went back to work. He was a nice man.

I dug out the half-page article about ActionAid. It said, "ActionAid International Uganda has been using 'stepping stones' methodology which enables communities to own the process of identifying issues, and developing grassroots-led responses and solutions in the context of HIV/AIDS." If only I'd read the article more closely before I set out for the camps, I could have asked the women's leader if she'd considered "owning the process." If I'd read it more closely, I might have noticed it was a paid advertisement for the charity.

I could have written some stuff about starving people. But it would have been unprofessional to make the World Food Program look like a joke when Luis had done so well all by himself. Then once the rage had worn off, I thought about this. I was green. I'd seen people sick and hungry and I wanted to help. I'm British, I'd have given anything I had to make Edie the Matchbox Widow feel better. Same goes for Americans: outside Hollywood, you will find yourself trapped by people who refuse to stop feeding you their gourd based desserts. Look at the tsunami—the British and American public gave millions, at a time when they could have been paying off Christmas credit card bills. But in Uganda, there was something wrong with the picture. People were hungry in a fertile country, preventably sick in a nation that had a disproportionate amount of cash to spend on defense yet wasn't catching Kony. Yes, Africans like to celebrate funerals. They wouldn't normally have so many to celebrate. But why should Luis bring more food? Why should ActionAid be shipping in doctors? Why should the UNICEF rep be in danger from the same rebels who'd had the run of the place for twenty years?

Then someone gave me this document.

Signature intentionally obscured

It's a letter from the army ordering people out of their homes. What the priests had told me in Kitgum was true: the camps were not an option. They were created by a government that in some cases, Amnesty International claimed, had driven them in with mortar shells and beatings. Thousands came willingly for protection after big massacres, only to experience full-on LRA massacres *inside the camps*. In 2004, 337 died inside Barlonyo camp, and even Museveni putting the death toll at 84 hadn't brought the other 253 back to life. Ten years later the refugees were still inside, rotting. Instead of effectively protecting civilians, Human Rights Watch claimed, government UPDF soldiers sometimes beat, raped and even killed them.

Political activists said it was deliberate. They insisted that the northerners were Museveni's old tribal enemies and called it genocide, but I wouldn't, since genocide implies a clear manifesto and, frankly, hard work. If it were genocide then I'd call it a bone-idle one, but maybe that's the German in me.

And I'm green. Maybe the government was doing its best to look after its people. Then one very senior charity figure described to me what happened when a number of donors and UN agencies went to talk to Uganda's Minister for Disaster Preparedness, former Idi Amin honcho Moses Ali.

"We told him we were concerned about the implications of this military action on civilians—calling on people to leave their home areas," said the charity vet. "We said, 'If you do this, you're aware that these people's welfare is your responsibility?' He looked genuinely surprised and said, 'We're fighting the LRA. It's your job to do that.'" Despite these concerns, that's exactly what happened.

I stared at the Roundabout of the Useful People. The tenet of aid agencies is not to interfere, but they were interfering. Under Additional Protocol II of the Geneva Convention, Article 18, the moderate article, says agencies may offer "exclusively humanitarian and impartial" relief to civilians. However, sober Article 17 says "displacement of the civilian population shall not be ordered... unless (their) security or imperative military reasons so demand" with "all possible measures" ensuring shelter, health, safety and nutrition. Interestingly, the Geneva Convention never relieves states of their obligations to provide for their war affected population even if other agencies are providing relief. Sure, the charities might have meant well, and in these PC[23] days most make a point of helping people to help themselves. But by bringing in loads of new jobs, could they be accused of encouraging the government to keep Auschwitz open for business?

And why were some so sloppy about who they gave cash to? Even the government-loyal paper, *The New Vision*, reported that out of 35 billion shillings dispersed by the World Bank to help the

---

23. Post-Curtis, as in Comic Relief founder Richard Curtis.

poor in Gulu alone, only 21 billion was accounted for.[24] In total, I read, at least $1,562,000 went missing, at least half through embezzlement. Quite literally, free money. While the actual child soldiers of the child soldiers group couldn't get proper funding to do AIDS work in the camps, The Global Fund to Fight AIDS, Tuberculosis and Malaria gave $367 million in grants to Uganda only to have to suspend aid in 2005 when their audit showed millions had gone not to, er, people with AIDS, but to fake charities created by corrupt officials.[25] Global Fund money paid for trips to Paris, Oslo and a holiday with relatives in New York. The Global Fund for AIDS is the main beneficiary of Bono's Red Campaign money. The charities had helped people to help themselves all right.

This dismal status quo didn't make sense. There had to be an explanation. What was the point of these shitty camps? It wasn't genocide and they weren't really protecting people, but ten years later they still hadn't been shut down. Then I wondered if this *was* the point. In 2007, a man from the British government came to visit Uganda. He was taken to visit a camp so he could see the truth for himself. Afterwards, he said, "Today I have visited a camp for people displaced by the conflict and seen for myself the challenges that remain to ensure that people can access basic water and sanitation and have enough to eat." What did he do when he got back to Westminster? Recommend a joint operation between MI6 and the Ugandan secret service to track down Kony and arrest him? Recommend an envoy be sent to ensure peace talks were swiftly completed no matter what? Recommend Colonel Otema get the helicopter state-of-the-art enough to finally blow Kony off the face of the Earth? See the press release below.

---

24. *The New Vision*, 15 September 2005.
25. "A heap of garbage," was world's coolest judge James Ogoola's response to the health minister's explanation.

Department for International Development
24 November 2007

> Douglas Alexander, Secretary of State for International Development, today announced a new ten-year development partnership with Uganda worth at least £700 million in aid that will help continue the fight against poverty... Speaking from Gulu in northern Uganda, Douglas Alexander said: "I am delighted to announce this £700 million long-term commitment to support Uganda's development. The Development Partnership Arrangement is an indication of the UK's strong partnership with Uganda, and is based upon our shared values of reducing poverty, tackling corruption and having respect for human rights.

Regardless of Douglas Alexander's desire to help, a fat chunk of this aid money is paid directly into the coffers of the government that had been accused of driving its people into the camps in the first place, and leaving them there.[26]

There was barely any logic left in the atmosphere at all. Perhaps while I'd been away there had been a secret laboratory accident at MIT and some stoned math students had blown a hole in the world's rationale. Every charity I talked to was proud of their part in propping up the camps, as though the camps were in response to a natural disaster, like tents sheltering flood victims. Why couldn't they see that these were fake protected villages? And nobody in the outside world seemed to know.

I wanted to talk to someone about this, so I called John. He was back from Los Angeles and Uganda was on the agenda again—no fixed date, but John would be here. Never mind talking, he'd be here in the flesh soon. So I decided to get busy with the charities myself.

---

26. In 2007/08, £35 million of the £70 million commitment was provided as Poverty Reduction Budget Support (PRBS). PRBS is money that goes directly into the Ugandan government's budget, to be spent on poverty-reduction priorities identified by the government.

I went back to World Vision's rehab center. As I stood waiting for the boss, I felt something on my leg. It was yet another baby. I don't know how old—as I said, I don't like babies—but it was maybe the size of a large rabbit on its hind legs. It had a friend with a half-moon shaped chunk missing from its head. I didn't want to look like a baby-stealing mentalist, but it was persistent so I picked it up. Right on cue, the boss of World Vision came out.

He was an emotional man. He picked up both babies. "This is Moses; he is a battlefield baby," he said.

"Born on the battlefield?"

"Found on the battlefield in a pool of his mother's blood." *Jesus, that'll teach me to ask.* "He was trying to breastfeed; he didn't know she was dead." *OK, that'll do...* "The soldiers that brought him in said they were going to shoot him; they thought he was a trap! They said he is very lucky." I was too scared to ask how very lucky Moses's friend was. The boss gave me a tour, yawning to his deputy. "I had to take the Australian donors to a traditional dance last night," he said. "Muzungus dancing always makes me tired." For a Christian charity, this seemed a godforsaken place. I spotted a boy lying on a bed in a dark hut and asked the social worker why he was inside while all the other boys were having lessons.

"He's been shot through the testicles," said the nurse, while eating a huge lunch. "When he came back from hospital he was getting better and could walk again. Now he can't sit up." I asked her why they didn't take him back to the hospital, with a silent "for pity's sake," and she said they had a funding gap. I looked through the door. He was lying motionless.

"Is he in pain?" I said.

"Great pain," she said, and carried on eating. "But we believe God will save him."

I was in the Acholi Inn garden when a potbellied man in a pink pinstriped shirt approached me, holding a glass. In my memory he is drinking champagne from a flute, but this seems unlikely—I will have to check if they served it at the Acholi Inn. The pinstriped man asked me what I was doing and I told him.

He said, "You want to see women who have been cut? No lips? Noses? Yes?"

"Maybe in a few days," I said.

"OK. I bring them to your hotel. How many do you want?" I stared at this man in a manner I hoped would convey my moral outrage, then arranged to meet. Satisfied, he looked around him at the comparative flashness of the Acholi Inn and took a sip.

"Perhaps as I work for a charity I should not be in this place, but this is where you meet the people who matter, yes?" said the pinstriped man. "Mm, people are really suffering here." I swear to God that is what he said and that he was drinking as he said it. Wine or champagne, I don't know.

My new anti-aid sentiment was making me unpopular in Gulu. I talked about it in a pool hall with a beefy Aussie water engineer, ruddy and glowing after a day irrigating the camps. I asked him, with all these foreign charities, was this war costing President Museveni anything at all? He glared at me for fucking up his buzz and went off in a sulk.

Of course the former guerrillas turned government ministers stole the Global Fund money from AIDS victims; they're former guerrillas turned government ministers, that's what they do. If they thought there was a pound coin up their own back end they'd jam their hand in it and root around until they fell on the floor, an Ouroboros of greed. Charities, however, are a different story. I still saw people who needed cash—otherwise I wouldn't be giving bloody book profits to bloody former sex slaves, the bastards—and I'm green, but I'll say someone needs to take a fat look at what some of the world's biggest aid organizations are doing with the governments of the people they serve.

Of course they need the cooperation of the government in whatever country they are operating. And of course they could not sit on their hands while people are starving. But what if, by pouring aid in and not challenging the status quo, they are helping to prop up an irresponsible regime? Where should the line be drawn?

When I arrived in Uganda, the status quo seemed like a losing deal for donors like the American and British governments and the World Bank. But then I re-read the UK Department for International Development's press release; Uganda is held up as a success story, proof the donors invested wisely. *We're giving Uganda a helping hand while they get rid of Kony the bogeyman, and he'll be gone any day now, honest.* Charities and shit governments need success stories to stay in business or people stop giving.

Let's take a look at one particular success story. In the words of Hillary Clinton, the St. Mary's girls had been condemned to "a life of unspeakable horrors," so unspeakable she promised to persuade the World Bank to step up. The World Bank funded Labora Farm. Banya's identity and predilections were well known in the community, yet the World Bank employed the man instrumental in the girls' horror and gave him his slaves back. I couldn't deny the case of Banya was a success story, because in the words of Hillary Clinton, the World Bank had agreed to help Ugandans "rebuild their own communities," and LRA leader and sex-slave-keeper Banya did just that, in a nicer field, with a salary to boot.

But this goes beyond sloppy, for a reason: the Labora job courtesy of the World Bank made Banya look like a *good* person. When the International Criminal Court finally issued a list of arrest warrants for Kony and his men, his former Vice Chairman Banya—described by the UPDF themselves as "the heart and soul of the LRA"—mysteriously avoided all charges. Today, Brigadier Kenneth Banya is not a wanted man. He lives quietly around Gulu. Meanwhile, St. Mary's girl Catherine survived one month wandering in the jungle with a one-year-old baby after a bungled US-backed UPDF/Congolese bomb attack on Kony's Congo base. Kony himself learned of the raid with enough time to escape. According to the *New York Times*, Kony retaliated: his rebels killed at least 900 civilians, kidnapped more children and "even tried to twist off toddlers' heads." Incidentally, the *Times* reported that the US military gave the UPDF $1 million in gas money. Catherine made it out alive in the spring of 2009 after thirteen years in captivity. The last St. Mary's girl, Miriam, died in captivity shortly before Catherine's escape. I'm not accusing the Ugandan army of abandoning the St. Mary's girls to fate: quite the opposite. In February 2004, an army helicopter gunship found Jessica. It killed her, according to the girl looking after Jessica's five-year-old son at the time of the attack.

I carried on digging. Stilettos were an absurd memory, and I even looked like a reporter, if reporters had Hindu-bride henna feet from red dust. I'd gotten used to Africa, peeing twice a day instead of the usual six times to avoid the toilet, although this meant I was peeing nitric acid and could probably have carved my name in the porcelain. When something ran across me in the night, I squished it without even looking. God either approved or was disgusted, because things moved faster: I saw a headline in a paper.

It was a story on the Ugandan president's daughter, Patience Rwabwogo—something about a business deal. But I was intrigued by what her company, Corban, sold: Ugandan grain. I could hear Luis at the World Food Program again. "Thirty million dollars a year on grain from Ugandan grain companies." This was too obvious, and I was from *Your Life* magazine.

I got the number to the World Food Program's Kampala HQ

and made a call.

"Hi, I'd like a copy of your list of suppliers. The *Sunday Times*. Of Britain. Thank you." I gave them my email. Actually, since I had no printer, I gave them Kate's email and told them *InStyle* was a branch of the *Sunday Times*'s foreign desk. I didn't give a monkey's by now. While waiting for Kate to go mental, I skimmed the papers. One of my favorite stories from Uganda was:

> The Minister of Water, Lands and Environment, Maj. Gen. Kahinda Otafiire, crashed his car and drew a gun at a journalist, shouting, "Now, you stupid journalist, you are going to say I was drunk."

Kate went mental: the big attachment was totally crapping up her inbox, ousting endless e-vites from Elton John.

The World Food Program denied that they made grain purchases from the president's daughter. I mentioned the suppliers' list. This denial was subsequently revised. "The World Food Program did make a single purchase of some ninety metric tonnes of cereal from Corban," they said, stressing that this was only "twenty-seven thousand dollars, which is a relatively small amount compared to the WFP's humanitarian operation in Uganda."

Only a cynic would bring up the poo-smearing wage index, so I won't. The World Food Program told me they don't make moral distinctions between who does and who doesn't deserve charity—and rightly so. But maybe the WFP's "humanitarian operation" in Uganda wouldn't be necessary years later if the man responsible for getting people out of the camps, the Minister for Disaster Preparedness, Moses Ali, had a vested interest in doing so.

Of course the World Food Program didn't lie. It's the twenty-first century—they just didn't check they were telling the truth. Maybe they didn't know the president's daughter was boss of Corban Ltd. Maybe the one phone call it would have taken to find out would have put them over their peaktime minutes allowance.

One point six million people were living in outdoor brothels where Patience took a cut of the catering. Why would a president end a war if his family made a profit out of it? "The world's greatest neglected humanitarian crisis" was starting to look like a big fat bucket of con.

53

I DON'T HAVE A RELATIONSHIP TO THEM,
BUT I AM THEIR LEADER

Bill and I were having dinner outside the Green Light. The very friendly waitress came over and leaned on our table.

"I'll just get something small," I said, opening the menu. "What is French rice?"

"We're thinking of doing it," the waitress explained.

"Why is it French?" I said.

"We're not sure yet," she said.

Bill took the menu. "I'll take matoke," he said. "And simsim."

"What's that?"

"Sauce made from nuts and sesame seeds."

"Oh, no way," I said. Pause. Then, "Two of those."

Then I got the mystery phone call. It was a man, a voice I didn't recognize—because it was a mystery phone call—and the man didn't speak, he just laughed. He stopped laughing and said, "Jane, do you remember me? I was behind you on the bus. You work very hard... for a journalist."

Never mind the fact that I was being threatened and patronized at the same time, I was nervous. Nervous and sorry for whoever it was if they thought I was worth threatening. There was no way I was in the league of a real journalist... but if I kept introducing myself as one, it was understandable that people would get confused. And how did they get my number?

If it was someone watching me, what could they be trying to stop me from writing? In Hollywood, it was very simple: don't ask Kevin Spacey how he came to injure his head tripping over a ███ at 4 a.m. in a public park. Sorry, tripping over a terrier. But with Colonel Charles Otema, Military Intelligence Chief of Northern Uganda, I was a little out of my depth. The largest part of me, however, was now seriously hacked off. Clearly the Ugandan government didn't understand the principles of a free press. If you're worried about what I'm going to write, you don't make mystery phone calls, steal my equipment and send strange women called Cleo to spy on me. You send me free hair products. For one can of volumizing mousse, I wrote that the Sundance Film Festival was *fun*.

Bill was alarmed. "You took bribes?"

"No, just gifts and money. Well, I mean, not much money, like parking in their building would cost five bucks and I'd get twenty... and sometimes a coupon for a facial..." I drew a veil over the gifts of alcohol and hotel rooms, and resolved to go all-out to nail these bastards. My God, John Prendergast had better fancy me by now.

Back at the hotel, the maid said, "Did you see that man watching you at breakfast?"

I wasn't going to get worried. I know I'm a coward. I'm scared of Britney Spears and she's as nutty as a squirrel's turd. I asked the affable Dutch researcher if I should be worried.

"There was a girl staying here, she was researching something, they broke into her room," said the Dutch girl, matter-of-fact. "Turned it over."

"Who did?"

"Intelligence, I expect," she said. No wonder they could handle smoking weed all day without getting paranoid, nothing fazes the people of the flatlands. What if it was intelligence—the colonel's men—who had my computer? What if they'd bust my impossible password—"jane"—and read my sweaty, frantic interviews with cornered bishops, burnt priests and turncoat spies, all of whom I'd promised to help, not sell down the river to the Lint Marketing Board? I moved faster. I paid a visit to President Museveni's representative in Gulu, a man called Max Omeda.

I sat under Max's collection of passive-aggressive safety posters waiting for him. A picture warned me not to disturb the landmine in the filthy puddle where I got my drinking water. In these conditions, a mine would be a faster route to the same destination.

Max arrived, grumpy. He was a snappy dresser and a lot of thought had gone into his image, molded that day on Drunk Joan Collins: enormous shoulder pads, from which hung various garments in paisley and lime green. He frowned at my outfit: the Gap shirt that Benjamin, Kony's personal tailor, had adapted into a dress. Max clearly didn't rate the Gap's fresh twist on work wear, and I wasn't sure if I'd earned the interview. Then he relented.

"My name is Max Omeda. Sometimes I call myself Max O," he confided. "I represent his Excellency the President."

What Max didn't know was that I already had some information about him. According to some former kidnappees, Max had his hand in the till, and not just any till, but a rare till owned by child soldiers.

Rick was a former kidnappee who worked for the Former Child Soldiers Development Association, an organization not unlike the child soldiers group. But unlike the child soldiers group, Rick's association had received a fat grant of 15 million shillings from the Ugandan government. I went to meet Rick in his HQ. I wondered what kind of office 15 million shillings bought you. The Former Child Soldiers Development Association was an empty room. I called their number, but no one answered, possibly because the phone was locked in a drawer. A piece of paper tacked to a wall showed a list of the management committee's numbers; the numbers were dead, apart from one for someone called David. A woman answered. She told me David wasn't around, then long gone and finally that "The owner of this phone has died."

Rick arrived and told me the money had simply disappeared. Gone.

Why hadn't people complained? Rick gave me the kind of look you'd give someone who asked you to fetch their car keys from the middle of a minefield. A government representative had chosen David to look after the money and David had disappeared along with the bulk of it. Meanwhile, according to Rick, both the government representative and Max O had taken smaller amounts. In Max's case, a mere 400,000 shillings, but there was no record of it being returned.

"The president has been helping the returnees in so many ways, I cannot confine myself to fifteen million," said Max. "I don't look at it as a very important thing."

I said it might be fairly important to the child soldiers.

"It is misunderstood that the money is missing," he said. "The people who signed for that money are known. How do they come to delay? They hide themselves somewhere."

"That would be a crime then?" I said.

"Yes," said Max. Max looked fed up. This wasn't supposed to happen; he was facing a journalist in obviously homemade clothes.

"So what is your relationship to them?"

"I don't have a relationship to them, but I am their leader," he said, a line I plan to use a lot in Hollywood from now on.

"I heard money was taken in your name, Max."

"There is a young man called Joseph who took money in my name."

"What action have you taken to get the money back?"

"I've tried to get him on the phone," said Max, waving an example of the kind of phone he used.

I asked straight up if the president had ever bombed a peace talk. "He didn't bomb it," said Max firmly. "But if he did, I think there is a reason. He's an experienced president who has handled insurgencies."

I left Max under his posters. And as I walked home I realized my notebook was missing. Now I had nothing left to lose, literally. Never mind accusing Max, the president's man, of stealing from children to his face. Never mind that any day now someone in Gulu would find some old copy of a British Sunday supplement magazine and see my byline under Scarlett Johansson's slack-jawed trap. Now, I'd lost a whole notebook full of diagrams of war crimes with arrows pointing to a doodle of Colonel Otema. He was reading it now. Turning the pages with his whopper, with his foreskin, like an anteater. I was dead.

54

CRUISING FOR A BRUISING II

And then John Prendergast came back. Ostensibly to end the war, but plainly to save me.

"I know this is asking a lot," said John, "but would you mind leaving Gulu and meeting me in Kampala? In a hotel? The Sheraton. It's a pretty nice place..."

This was the final fucking straw. Where was I going to find a lip-plumping gel in Gulu?

I went trudging round pharmacies, defending myself to Bill in my head. I had to concede I hadn't finished the story; I hadn't saved the children or found out why the colonel couldn't stop Kony. But it was too late, I'd reverted to Girl Logic. Rather than actually finish the investigation, I'd tell John what I'd learned and John would fix everything. John had his big meeting with President Museveni on the night of our date, sorry, interview, when Museveni was finally going to read the peace proposal John had written with Betty. If Museveni was serious about peace, he might want to know what I thought the colonel was up to, and John could tell him. In short, a hero was coming to end a war, John would save the children, and I was going to do my bit by admiring him. God was rolling up his sleeves.

It started in a pharmacy, which was frankly poorly supplied with cosmetically enhancing mouth gels. I don't know how it happened, and I am not proud of it, but I spent a day going round African pharmacies saying, "Do you sell that stuff that gives you big lips?"

It continued that night, in a pine-stinky bathroom, getting ready for my big date—interview—with John. I found a tiny canker sore. Exactly why I thought this would affect our date, as though he'd pull my mouth open like a horse trader buying a mare, I don't know. But I decided to clean the tiny canker sore out. With a safety pin.

Next morning, on the day of my big date—interview—with John Prendergast, I woke at 3 a.m. from one of those dreams your body uses to tell you something is gravely wrong. I think Ben Affleck was in it. I ran to the bathroom and looked in the mirror. My lip was so swollen it looked like half a Twix had been forced under it. I knew the stories about getting an insect bite on holiday and, six months later, a cockroach eats its way out of the sole of your foot during a business meeting, but I went back to bed chanting, "Calm down, it's only a canker sore." About ten seconds later I got up and looked in the mirror again. The whole inside of my mouth, including the skin of my tongue, was peeling off to reveal a layer of yellow pus. I still had to wait hours for daylight.

Lacor Hospital: pride of the province. At 8 a.m. there were 200 people waiting on mats outside. Worse, they had brought picnics. Picnics in waiting areas are not a good omen. Today I was a Westerner and cut in line, although I chose Outpatients, not A&E, as a brave and selfless act.

"I'd like to thee a doctor," I said.

"What for?" said the lone receptionist.

"What f—?! Can I justh thee a doctor?"

A child walked past, then stopped dead.

"Madam!" said the child. "You look like baboon!"

"Yeth. Thank you."

"The doctor gets here at nine," said the receptionist.

"Well, ith he going to thee pathientth? Becausth he'th got quite a lot already."

"No," she said. "First he has to clean the hospital."

I called the only person I could think of. Father Carlos's truck rolled up in ten minutes flat.

"Why aren't there any doctorsth?" I said. Father Carlos sighed.

"This hospital has really gone downhill since the Ebola virus. Do you want to see where they buried the chief surgeon? Wonderful man. He caught Ebola through his eyes..."

It wasn't even 8:30 a.m.

Father Carlos took me round the back of the hospital to a secret priests' wing with secret priests like I've never seen. One, Father Amos, in gumboots and a dog collar, came blasting out of the building with his fingers splayed in a metal frame. I don't remember accurately, but I think it was because some of his fingers had been shot off. Either way, Father Amos was finished as a children's magician.

"There's been an ambush in Pader! Seven dead! You want to come?" he blurted.

"There wathn't anything about that in the newthpaper," I said.

"Of course not," said Father Carlos. "The war is over!" It's the closest a missionary comes to sarcasm.

A priest gave me a strip of giant pills that he said would fix my mouth. Father Carlos drove me home.

"Those are strong antibiotics," he said proudly. "Maximum dose. Take one now, and..." He noticed I'd eaten the whole lot. "Oh. OK. Maybe get some fresh air." And of course, they were penicillin, the one drug I'm allergic to. I'm sure Kate Adie often regales BBC colleagues with the tale of how she puked up priests' penicillin in a Ugandan toilet by sticking the only sterile object in her luggage down her mouth-ulcer-safety-pin-infected throat: an over-the-counter syringe for the removal of snake venom.

I went jogging to get some fresh air and perk up for my date. Sorry, interview. I jogged past some children.

"MUZUNGU!" screamed a child, probably scared by a five foot five-and-a-half jogging baboon. All I know is that I tripped on my tracksuit bottoms, took the skin off my hands and knees, and came to a stop in an open drain of shit.

But the worst thing, the worst thing, was that on the way to meet John I'd arranged to interview some women who'd had their lips cut off by Joseph Kony's men.

The smell in that hut was indescribable. I know the smell of fear; living in Hollywood, I smell it a lot. You know the smell of a child with a cold? Rheumy and disgusting, the smell of the body binding germs to mucus and hurling it out? It's like that, but with the top note of a pair of ski trousers your ex-ex-ex-boyfriend SIMON pissed in while drunk six months earlier and shoved in a wardrobe. The smell coming off the woman in the purple dress in that hut was not fear. It was not BO. It was not bad breath. It was an entire metabolism in meltdown; it was every cell screaming, "No, no, no. This is all wrong."

Ellen had a scar on her forehead where the surgeon had removed part of her skin to fashion a new nose. The nose was round and buttony. The rebels told her why they did it. "They said, 'You speak a lot; it seems you are the wife of a soldier. We are going to cut off your fingers, nose, mouth, breasts and ears,' but they never cut my fingers or breasts. It was two boys of twelve and an elderly commander of twenty." Ellen's teeth were exposed like a skull, but she was due to go back for more surgery. One day, Ellen was recovering at World Vision when she recognized a new returnee who'd just been admitted.

"I never felt pain when I saw the young boy, until he told me

I was lucky because they normally kill people," said Ellen. "And when I saw the commander, I was very bitter…"

I turned to the World Vision rep. "Excuse me, the people that did this were brought to live with her?" I said.

"Yes," said the rep.

"But that's… What… ? How come… ? Right." I turned back to Ellen. "So what did the commander say to you?"

The rep answered. "He does not think he has done anything wrong. He is making problems. We have moved him to the adult reception center, not the children and mothers center."

Well, aren't you the best, I should have said, but didn't.

As the rep walked me out, I asked, "Has anyone else talked to Ellen?"

"No," said the rep. The only person who had tried to help her was a celebrity hack who didn't know the difference between *Dawson's Creek* and *The OC*? Again, I promised I'd try to help.

Outside the hotel, the pinstriped man was back again, hopping from one foot to another. He was incapable of even standing in an honest way. He was still dressed in a pinstriped shirt with white collar and cuffs, but this time he had company.

"I have one for you," he said. Florence Akello was sitting in the shadows, pulling a cloth around herself. Same story. She was a warning to civilians, a massive PR campaign for the price of a razor blade. In Florence's case, not even a high quality razor blade.

"When the blade got blunt, the boy cut ears instead," she said, noting, "The commander made him do it. After cutting seven women the boy said he was getting really tired, but the commander told him to keep going." She quickly bent down and blotted a tissue to her lipless mouth so as not to be seen dribbling. Then she looked up; something was worrying her. Florence was, after all, Ugandan.

"What did you do to your lip?" she asked. "Are you OK?"

55

THE DATE

I arrived in Kampala to find the Red Chilli deserted apart from two girls dressed as Princess Michael. They were going to the Royal Ascot Goat Race, where the rest of the trustafarians were already watching goats in action. The trusties had shed their penniless hippie veneers for this popular annual charity event, but the trouble with the goat race was that goats don't have a racing gene, they have a stopping-at-the-side-of-the-track-to-eat-people's-trousers gene, and so the organizers had fitted the track with a board on wheels at goat-bum height. The spectators sweated in big Ascot hats, watching mystified goats being pushed round in circles by a trolley. Still, a good day out by all accounts. I wish I was a toff: it would be like being a pervert's retarded niece, your life mapped out and a carefree smile.

I got tarted up, put new sticking plasters on my infected hands and knees and went straight to the Sheraton in the cocktail dress the war criminal's tailor had made me. I asked a boda to stop somewhere so I could buy shoes.

"New shoes or old shoes?" he said. My God, he was working for my mother. We drove past the men selling piles of old shoes at the roadside, stopping at a mall, where I found shoes, although I'm not sure how new they were. The clunky red stilettos looked like they'd belonged to someone called Brenda from accounts until she lost them during a karaoke night and a bloke called Geoff had told her not to bother looking, he'd give her a lift home.

I will never forget walking into the Sheraton's lobby. It was all low lights, dark wood and cool air conditioning on my legs. I can still hear Brenda's horrible stilettos clacking on the floor.

"Meet me at the Sheraton..." John had told me. I'd imagined any one of the hotel suites I'd reviewed for the *Mail on Sunday*, randomly scattered with orchids, a bottle of champagne chilling, a balcony overlooking the lights of an exotic city. I cannot tell you how many stunning settings I have noted must be very romantic, and how many times I have told myself that experiencing the concept of romance is just as valid.

"... in the Rhino Pub," he concluded.

The large cartoon rhino that looked like Jack Black gave me the eye. But I was finally a foreign correspondent, and this was that sexy, dangerous drink in the exotic hotel in the obscure country with a sexy, dangerous man.

I kept trying to focus on the mission—tell him what you've learned, he can tell the president... *John'll be stone-cold sober, that's an enormous problem right there, he's not going to have a regrettable moment of weakness...* Focus on the issue of bombing kids, get a quote... *I think I'll run into the bathroom and put my hair up. I bet he likes women with their hair up.* Look, you have absolutely no idea what kind of woman he likes. *Well then, I'll just say nothing at all. That always works on blokes; they get paranoid.* Then how are you going to interview him, you raving idiot? FOCUS! Tell him the locals feel the military solution isn't working... *See? I know political stuff now; we'll understand each other. And this time tomorrow my whole life will be fixed.*[27]

I told myself it didn't matter anyway. I hadn't seen him in weeks; I probably wouldn't even fancy him any more, for fuck's sa—

Then John came in. He looked so unbelievably hot the room fell away. He'd pulled another all-nighter, and as he stepped in from the hot, dirty African evening into cold, clean hotel air, he looked like a man clinging to his sanity. Friends seemed to appear from nowhere, leaving conversations to shake his hand. He offered his phone and charger to the bar staff and there was

---

27. Note: this is not an advisable thought to have before anything, let alone a date with someone who doesn't know you fancy them.

a heated dispute over who'd plug it in for him. I thought they'd come to blows.

As he made it to the bar, I was waiting in Brenda's stilettos, Band-Aids on my hands and knees, wearing the school fabric dress and a fat lip. John was too polite to mention it, and kissed me on the cheek. He'd been trotting round Kampala talking to diplomats, charities and civil society groups about the Ugandan army, he said, trying to demand the people in the camps be guarded. Then the forty-eight-hour shift to get his draft treaty ready to meet the president. Looking back, it would have been okay to hug him. I gave him an orange juice.

"So, did you finith your peath proposal?" I said.

"Yup. I'm meeting President Museveni in one hour," he said.

"A hot date. Fantathtic. How do you feel?"

"Ah. You never get optimistic. It's just a small chance..." He looked a tiny bit happy.

"Tho can you tell me... could thith war ever end?"

"Yes. President Museveni is willing to make a deal."

"If ?"

"If he thought there was some value in it. If there was one iota of pressure..." Ah, the Rest of the World. The Donors. "But there is nothing."

And he explained it. "I tell you, of all the conflicts around the continent, I see this one as the simplest," he said. "It's a slam dunk, it's a no-brainer. The LRA lost any hope they would defeat this government long ago; they are just a mercenary band waiting for the right offer. So give it to them. Bribe them out..."

It was the greatest conversation of my life, soaring over Sudanese deserts and hideouts in the forests of the Congo. And it's lucky I was taping it, because the more complex the political theories he came out with, the less I was listening, and we were no longer in a dodgy hotel bar, but sitting on the verandah of a safari lodge at sunset to the sound of cicadas, or whichever tropical insect sounds cool but doesn't bite. Below us, elephants were walking home and we were about to go inside and see if the lodge's stereo worked.

Until John's phone rang. The bar staff looked at its screen and panicked. When he came back I knew what had happened.

56

THE SEXIEST THING I HAVE EVER SEEN

John sat opposite me again, but he couldn't see me. The shutters had come down; John was blazing in a world of memories it was best he didn't have.

"He stood you up," I said, but he couldn't hear me. John, this man who had the end of a war in his briefcase, went batshit with animal rage.

"If we were back in the White House I could finish this FUCKING war in thirty minutes," he said. "Go in Museveni's office with the World Bank, tell him the money is OVER until you sort it out." He looked around him. I wondered if he was going to punch someone. "Now this war will last another twenty years."

I stared. *This is the sexiest thing I have ever seen in my life.* Stop it, Jane! This man was going to end a war tonight, now he can't... *Well, then he's free later.* Stop it!

I knew that the last time a peace deal fell through, Kony warned Betty he might express his displeasure: one massacre took 300 when rebels swept through a crowded trading center.

John sat with his head bowed, saying nothing. I didn't know what he was thinking, but I bet he wanted to stop thinking it right there and then, and I bet it was one of those rare moments in a strong man's life when someone else could get in.

"I'm burning out," he said quietly. "When this is over, I gotta take two weeks off."

A safari. I should have put my hand on his shoulder. Then he looked up at me, and when I looked back at his knackered red eyes, which had seen more horror than anyone could imagine, I suddenly knew who his date was. It wasn't Angelina. And it wasn't me. His father sold corn dogs from the back of their car. "Never staying in one place more than three years, moving on to find people who hadn't gotten sick of corn dogs."

He felt for strangers because he'd been one. He belonged to the people that he couldn't even talk about. He belonged to Edie the Matchbox Widow; he was her date. I reached out my hand, but it came to rest on his glass, and I pushed what was left of his orange juice to him.

"Could the civil society groups or the diplomats stop Kony if he tries anything?" I said, a passing journalist once more.

"Someone needs to get everyone together and develop a strategy to protect these people," he said, and took the orange juice. "It's happening again," I thought, although I couldn't remember it ever happening as badly as this. I think I sounded chipper.

"Then you'd better get up early," I said.

"Yes. It's late. Thanks for sticking around. I hope this has been worth it," he said. I couldn't answer that, so I stood up and shook his hand.

"What are you going to do?" he said.

"Something. Look after yourself, eh?"

He kissed me, smiled his crinkly-eyed Clooney smile and walked out of the Sheraton. I watched him go. The door swung back and the Jack Black rhino gave me the eye again.

57

IT WASN'T ME II

I had $108, a fat lip and one contact lens. I looked like Marty Feldman. But this was my last chance to be a Useful Person, so I caught the post office bus back to Gulu with bags of letters and went straight to the United Nations. For some reason, I found I had an astonishing amount of pent-up energy.

"Hi, I'd like the latest security briefing, please," I said to the UN guy.

"I'm afraid I can't let you take it," replied the UN guy. "We don't release hard copies."

Don't fuck with me, my friend. I just did something noble and I am not happy about it.

"I need a hard copy. I've got to write a story about the security situation," I said. I did need it; I work in the media; I knew that statements from poor people and a somewhat emotional missionary wouldn't prove this war was a sham.

"I'm sorry, it's policy," the UN guy said. I marched out to the gate, hit on the guard and asked him to go and get it for me. I didn't give a fuck that the UN guy saw; I'd come a very long way to stand myself up on a date. The guard walked into reception, took the briefing off the wall in front of his boss and gave it to me.

According to the United Nations security briefing for that week in September, Kony rebels abducted three girls and a 19-year-old man, the army killed three Kony rebels, and a UPDF soldier who stole wages was killed by his own men. Kony 4, Army 3. Army shoots army soldier, own goal. Museveni said he was winning the war. Now I had a United Nations document that said in black and white that Kony was kidnapping civilians faster than the colonel could shoot them. The war is over? Sorry, it's to laugh.

Now I focused squarely on the good guys' excuses for not stopping Kony. But look, said the army's spokesman, we've captured their top commanders. Captured is an odd choice of word: Banya's drinking buddy in the Fanta Gang was the hard-faced, lean man under the mango tree. He had ulcers because the rebels got ulcers living in the bush. He was a brigadier all right, but he wasn't in the colonel's army; he was Brigadier Sam Kolo, Kony's spokesman, the Karl Rove of the LRA. Sam Kolo was living for free in the Acholi Inn, his Fanta tab being picked up by the Ugandan government. And by me, the British underwear buyer. I asked a father of a kidnapped girl what he thought about this. He fought tears as he told me, "We forgive. We just wanted the commanders still in the bush to see there was another life." The authorities had failed to honor this sentiment with one simple task: make the commanders still in the bush choose—another life, or a coffin. Why the authorities failed still foxed me. Meanwhile, the Fanta Gang were eating lunch with a guy from a large international charity.

I asked Sam Kolo for an interview.

"I'm saving it for a book deal," he said.

"But we'd love to hear your story," I said.

"Be careful!" He laughed. "I've got a knife! I'll cut off your lips!" Kolo walked away chuckling.

58

YOU HAVEN'T COME TO FIGHT HIM, HAVE YOU?

Having fallen for Banya's line about spirits particularly riled me. First things first, I wanted to demolish the idea that Kony had tapped into mystical forces no Westerner could understand. I played back Betty's interview, talking about the Holy Spirit Movement, the original possessed-by-spirits faith that had got Kony started. Betty mentioned the movement's founder, the witch doctor and military leader Alice Lakwena. Kony got many of his moves from Alice, including turning rocks into bombs.

"Alice is a nuisance," Betty had said. "She just wants money." Yet Alice could turn rocks into bombs; surely she could rustle up twenty bucks when she ran short?

The Holy Spirit Movement had started Kony's war. Admittedly, they'd won battles despite their small numbers and strange beliefs, and it had taken Museveni's artillery to finish them that day in the forest. So what exactly was the power of Lakwena, the Italian spirit, canny enough to bail out of Alice at the right time and possess Kony, much as Denise Richards left Charlie Sheen before finding Richie Sambora? Lakwena had even possessed Alice's dad to see how that might work out. And Lakwena/Kony still controlled hundreds, possibly thousands of child soldiers, whether they believed in his power or not. Steven the former spy told me that deep in the backstreets of Gulu, I could see the Holy Spirit Movement for myself. Somewhere I would find a tiny church, and in it a root cause of this twenty-year war: a man called Father Severino, Holy Spirit Movement practitioner, former warrior and the father of Alice herself. He was nicknamed Otong-tong, one who chops victims to pieces. Just in case, I took some antiseptic wipes, in a top pocket should he get my hands.

Steven, now on fine form, led Bill and me into the slums. We jumped over an open drain, through back alleys and over muddy paths where the bare feet of children slithered on wet earth. Steven was in ultra-spy mode: "Not this place. We move... Not this place. We move..." We finally moved round in a circle and ended up behind the market of marble wash jeans. Deep in the middle of all this was a very small church. You couldn't find it unless a former spy took you.

Inside, the air was tangy with incense. It smelled like a rave. The teal wall was painted with strange religious symbols, and underneath, a skinny old white-haired man in a white robe was waving his thin arms in prayer. The congregation was a couple of tutting women in the back, some bored children at the front and by the door, and one devout follower, a stunningly beautiful girl so deep in prayer she looked addled. I wondered if this was "the rapture." If it was, it was indistinguishable from the faces of the gay guys in my spin class, the really gay ones who yell, "YEAAAAAH!" when we climbed imaginary hills to Mary J. Blige.

Father Severino's young, prodigiously smelly assistant priest came up to me. "You haven't come to fight him, have you?" he said. "Only last week we had a German lady who came to fight."

The ladies tutted at me.

"No, no, just to talk about Lakwena." I beamed, and on cue Father Severino spun to greet me. He smiled, showing an explosion of teeth, as though someone had said, "Open your mouth, the teeth are coming!" and twelve had plummeted into his gums at random.

"Where is the spirit? It is here! In me! It is talking to you right now!" he railed. The spirit that had started this whole thing was talking to me right now. I didn't see an Italian army medic. I saw a skinny black man with crazy hair in a long white robe, flailing to a group of bored children. I told this late-period Michael Jackson that Kony was quite insistent that Lakwena was in him now. Father Severino/Lakwena scowled, and the women at the back tutted again.

"Why this messiah claim he is having the spirit? Are you not listening to me?"

"But if Kony has no spirit to protect him, why haven't they caught him?" I asked Father Severino/Lakwena.

"Don't ask of me, ask the spirits. Are you not listening to me? John, chapter 8, verses 42-8. Write it down! He arrested this body," he explained, pointing to himself. "It was beaten for ten months, on hot fire for ninety-two days! Am I not right? Am I not right?"

"That is right," said the ladies, glaring at me. I wasn't about to point out that ten months wasn't ninety-two days. I could sense I was already in enough trouble as it was.

"People shouldn't fight, they should love," he continued.

I asked him how he explained all the people massacred by Alice.

"Because they accept to die in the name of Jesus. Because they will come back. Have you not been listening?" Father Severino/ Lakwena shook his head, perplexed. "It was to cleanse the people! You are branch of river, I am whole river. This is Cain and Abel..." And off he went like a loon outside Grand Central Station.

It struck me that this is how dull it must have been for Kony's child soldiers, listening to his marathon religious lectures in the desert of Sudan.

Then Father Severino/Lakwena took a sudden swerve.

"... My wife stoned me to death on 11 November 1984."

"—Pardon?" As proof of this domestic violence, he showed me his teeth, which did indeed seem to have leaped out of his mouth, possibly as the result of a stoning, before falling back in again. "Your wife killed you? But you're still..."

"Then I rose from the dead," he explained. I was the stupidest woman he'd ever had to preach to.

Soon, he'd been on full rant for an hour and Bill was reading the paper. "That one needs the prodigal son," muttered Father Severino/Lakwena, frowning at Bill and gathering up a pile of stones to represent the people living in the camps, or a pile of stones.

Was this it? Was this the satanic face of Africa that Western diplomats were afraid to tackle? The dark mystic force academics respectfully honored? This bonkers old twit pushing pebbles around in his nightie? I scanned the tiny church. Maybe I'd missed something. Maybe the Holy Spirit Movement's spiritual cleansing helped round here. The beautiful girl was still stooped in prayer, sucking everything she could from Father Severino's speech. I didn't want to brand Africans as simpletons—I live in LA, I've simpletoned after all manner of leaders and their cleanses, from Robert Atkins (Atkins Diet; 250 pounds at death "caused by water retention") to Judy Mazel (Beverly Hills pineapple diet, dead at sixty-three from vascular disease, so screw antioxidants) to S. Daniel Abraham (Slim-Fast Diet, the Angus Deayton shoes incident). But here in Uganda, the only people I'd heard about who wanted cleansing were Kony's kidnapped kids and, strictly speaking, it wasn't original sin they were washing away, it was sin committed on the orders of Kony's Holy Spirit Movement/Lord's Resistance Army itself.

The prodigiously smelly assistant opened a door in the wall and, with the determination of Vanna White smiling through a series of wrong guesses, produced a teaspoon of clay and walked toward Bill and me with it. I backed away into the beautiful girl, who looked up at me, and I realized she was mentally handicapped. Well, that did it: the Holy Spirit Movement was a crock.

59

WHOREOBICS

If powerful black magic wasn't driving Kony, what was? A friend told me someone wanted to meet me. This time it was highly confidential. He led Bill and me on another journey, this time to the Traveller's Inn brothel-cum-disco. In a back room, girls were performing a dancercise routine to no one. There, waiting for me at a side table, was the man they said was Joseph Kony's cousin.

Our friend introduced him as Philip, a chunky man in a red top with a peevish, low-energy manner. I studied Philip's face for signs of a family resemblance. Philip had high cheekbones like Kony, but none of Kony's Rick James flair. If Kony was the prodigal son, Philip was the dull straight relative. I didn't care, so long as he would reveal what drove his cousin.

But Philip was in a sulk. After a while, it transpired the government had promised him some money and it hadn't arrived. Maybe the person bringing it had stolen it, he said. But the point was, he hadn't been given any money, or his own house. Why should Philip have been given money and a free house? Because Kony expected it: it was proof that Kony too would get money and a free house if he surrendered.

In Hollywood screenwriting classes, they teach you the importance of subtext in dialogue—the subtle slips of the tongue, the wafer-thin hints revealing your character's secret ambition. See if you can spot Philip's subtext when I asked him what was standing in the way of peace. Our friend translated.

"The family of Kony don't have money. They don't have a house. Kony is losing hope: how are the family being handled? Kony says, 'Now I come home, but I sent my family to the government; the government will not take care of me.' Museveni is a good person; he used to send money to family of Kony. But the people sent with the money used to just go away with it. The president hugged me and told [local MP] Betty Akech to give me some money, 'Take Mr. Philip to the barracks; I want to meet him and I have small money to assist him.' But Betty refused completely... The Kony rings me and I tell him we don't have nothing here, they just give us some beans and so on. So the Man get annoyed: 'Maybe if I come there you cannot handle me.'"

Where's our money?

The Whoreobics was getting louder. I asked Philip if he knew why the girls were there.

"No," he said, turning to the girls. "EH! SHUT UP!"

But what about the magic, the spirits? Kony's cousin shrugged. "One day Kony got water in a small plate and the water got dry completely," he said, flopping his hand across the table to indicate another miracle. Bored, he looked at the hos, who were now doing some kind of grim Spice Girls "2 Become 1" routine.

"As we are talking now, Kony knows what's happening, about our talk," he added. Kony's cousin posed for a couple of pictures, muttering that the peace talks should be in another country, say, America, and that he should be invited. "I was supposed to be on that committee but they threw me out," he said, smarting at the injustice.

Money to go away. Not taking over the government, not restoring Uganda to the Ten Commandments. Just money to go away. Museveni, Kony's bitter enemy, was "a good person" when he was sending money to "family of Kony." If this was true, the kids weren't just soldiers, they were hostages, and now Kony wanted his ransom. The Most Evil Man in the World? Kony was a con artist. A Ken Lay chancer using kids as his meal ticket. A Chuck Norris fan who got his moves from the Blockbuster bargain bin. Black magic, mystic powers, an impossibly fiendish enemy—all a con, and I had fallen for it. Meanwhile, there was nothing mystical about Kony's cock as it raped six dozen kidnapped girls in rotation.

So if Kony was just a man, why hadn't the colonel caught him? What was I missing? I didn't think defending Patience the president's daughter and her marginal grain profits would motivate a man of the colonel's ego.

I made another futile trip to the Acholi Inn. I'd worked out why the colonel annoyed me: it was my $75 underwear tax. He was the horse Britain backed; my underwear tax had been bet on him stopping Kony. If I throw money away, I expect it to go to vodka distilleries, not helicopter gunship raids on children. Yes, I once lent $75 to a junkie friend who said she needed it for rent; however, as junkies make lousy helicopter gunship pilots, I'm fairly sure she only spent it on smack.

And now I was out of time. I stood at the counter of Gulu bank staring at my eight cards fanned out on the counter. The extremely upbeat teller studied them too. I was powerless to make them produce money, powerless to make the colonel talk to me, powerless to crack the secret of Kony's success. *I'm in a third-world country and I can't borrow money at an extortionate interest rate or get an interview with a dangerous military officer. I'm a pedophile who can't get it up at a kids' fancy dress party, sitting in an armchair bitterly twisting balloon giraffes. There is no point to me.*

"Good news! This one still works," said the extremely upbeat teller.

"Oh! Can I get two hundred—"

"No. I am afraid not. We can't give you money. Barclays Bank in Kampala might. The bus takes no more than eight hours," said the extremely upbeat teller.

We can't give you money. Why open a bank if you can't give money? Oh! You want money! Money's off. We've got waxy pens, deposit slips and a patronizing leaflet about mortgages for Indian families. Would you like to apply for a credit card? No, I'd really rather have some of my money if that's alright by you. And why did it take the cashier twenty minutes to finish with one person in front of me? Is she actually trying to incur interest? Is she reading a deposit slip or Harry Potter? Is she sitting on a chair or a toilet?

I went on an eight-hour bus journey to take money out on the only credit cards of mine that hadn't been stopped. I shouldn't have even got on the bus: the bus station was heaving with bad omens. One bus was called *It Wasn't Me*, and not just It *Wasn't Me*, but *It Wasn't Me II*. By now, this was a sign even to someone with a third eye as myopic as mine.

On the way back, there were twenty-six people on my minibus, seats for fourteen, and I was between the only two fat people in Uganda. I was a thong. Someone had wrapped the seats in plastic to stop them from being pissed on, but it still smelled of piss. How can seats wrapped in plastic smell of piss? Did someone piss first, and seal it later? Did they think, "That's some good piss, I'm keeping that"? And now the diarrhea I'd had since the hen-print donut chapatti Rolex had turned into a fever and I was percolating, sitting on a plastic seat in a puddle of sweat so that when I moved, my foreign correspondent dress farted. Everyone was looking at me.

The journey refused to end. We stopped so a woman could go shopping at a meat shack where a man was macheteing a carcass that rippled with flies.

"Two thousand is too cheap," a passenger chided when she came back. "It must be old, or sick."

"I don't care!" said the woman. That was some good beef and she was keeping it. I should have bought a chunk off her and eaten it raw to combat the stomach bug—fight fire with fire. There'll be nothing left of me, just a bumhole with an eyeball on a stalk, looking around.

As we got up to 70 miles per hour a cockroach crawled in through the window and landed on my lap. How? Cockroaches are the SWAT team of insects.

The man on my left turned to the woman on my right and said, "Have you been saved?"

"Oh, how marvelous! I have! I too have been saved!" she said. I was being spit-roasted by Born Again Christians. They both turned to me.

"Have you been saved?" No, but my inner child had been taken into protective custody.

But what about Angela? What about Victoria? What about all those girls, alone in that camp? I had a chance, an actual chance to do something. And I failed. I called John. He couldn't stop because he was on his way to dinner. With Angelina Jolie.

And then the bus broke down in the middle of nowhere, and we all got out to push. I was pushing the godforsaken heap of bear piss down the road when I called my sister.

"Kate, sorry, I'm running out of minutes. Can you call British Airways? I wanna come home." Kate called BA.

"British Airways say they can't change it without your booking reference," she said.

I stopped pushing the bus to fumble in my bag. *My God, I've been away from home so long my bag has BO. How? I didn't lend it to* ███████. I found a filthy piece of paper with flight info on it and read it to Kate.

"British Airways said that's not a booking reference, that's an e-ticket number," said Kate. Another scramble. I found another fever-sweat-soaked number.

"British Airways said that's not a booking reference, that's a confirmation code."

"Why don't you tell British Airways I know they're looking at my booking reference on their computer screen, so bloody tell me it?"

"They said they can't, privacy laws."

"Tell British Airways I will remember those privacy laws next time I'm going through security and a giant Helga feels my tits in front of everybody..."

Then I noticed the bus had started to roll. The Born Again Christians were jumping in as it rolled away, leaving me at the side of the road in front of a crippled baboon and a big crowd of kids. The kids pointed at my foreign correspondent dress, concerned.

"Madam, your dress is wet!"

"Yes. I know. I'm sick..."

Then it hit me. I was alone in the middle of Africa. Yet still talking on a BlackBerry like a wanker. I'd been abandoned— by Jesus—and a bunch of starving African kids thought I'd shat myself.

Kate came back on.

"British Airways have got one seat left tomorrow morning. Do you want it? Hurry up, I'm at the Jimmy Choo sale; it's a war zone," she said.

I stared down the endless road. If I went back to LA there'd be a job for me. I knew the exclusive everyone wanted: I could ask Whitney Houston if she's trying for a baby. Not since she found out crack babies aren't really made of crack, but that's another story. It was a clear-cut choice: stay in Uganda and tell the world about children getting bombed on our shilling, or go home and tell the world, "Whitney's back and stronger than ever."

For the first time in my life, I didn't run away. What the hell, I was never going to marry John Prendergast anyway. I told my sister I was staying in Uganda.

By a miracle, the bus stopped to wait for me.

I made one last call. By a second miracle, the colonel answered.

"STOP BOTHERING ME!" he screamed. "YOU WANT TO INTERVIEW ME? OK! WE GO TO PADER. MEET ME TOMORROW MORNING AT THE ACHOLI INN!"

The colonel wanted to take me to Pader. Pader was the middle of nowhere. No mobile-phone reception, no electricity, no running water. No one went to Pader, because if you went to Pader you got shot. In other words, it's a scoop! Kate Adie would be so proud of me if she had any idea who I was! I picked up my stinking bag and ran after the bus.

60

A NICE BRIGHT GOAT

The night before my date with the colonel, I had a celebratory drink in the Acholi Inn, buying drinks for everyone who'd helped me in Gulu. This was the third and final date: Ashton, John and now Colonel Charles Otema, Military Intelligence Chief of the Ugandan People's Defense Force. But everyone was telling me not to go.

"Colonel very bad man," said a journalist.

"You know, a man like the colonel, he can go crazy at any time," reflected a social worker.

Trying to change the subject, I turned to a friend of Bill's at the bar, pumping his hand.

"I'm Jane. What do you do?" I said.

"I am a lawyer," said the lawyer.

"Oh, yeah? What are you working on?" I said, recklessly.

"We are investigating allegations against the UPDF," he beamed. I sighed.

"What have you got?"

"Ten murders, sixteen cases of torture and twenty rapes. In six weeks," he replied.

"Peak season?" I said. Sam Kolo walked past.

"It's the girl," Kolo said. "Small but dangerous." I don't think I'll ever hear such high praise from a man again, and I don't know if it's more or less flattering coming from a rapist war criminal.

Another friend of Bill's turned up, a very sharp guy called Anthony, the only Ugandan I'd met in Gulu who liked a drink. It turned out Anthony worked at a night shelter and, to my embarrassment, I had to admit I'd spent all these weeks watching the kids flood into them every night yet never stepped inside one. So on my last night alive, we went to see the bedtime of the night commuters.

As Anthony and I walked to his shelter, it was raining stair rods. The shelter was across a muddy field and hundreds of kids and I were slipping in the mud. This time the armed guards let me in.

The shelter had a girls' shed and a boys' shed, and an office with boxes of malaria medicine and, surprisingly, dozens of hyper-realistic clay animals.

Anthony pushed a thin boy called Michael through the door— he was the kid who'd made all the animals. I commissioned one.

"I paint the goat any color," he said. "What color goat would you like?"

"Make it in the national colors of Uganda," I said. A nice bright goat painted red, black and yellow.

I went into the girls' shed and a tiny girl in a big frilly mauve and white party dress crawled on my knee and clung to me to get warm. She was soaking wet from walking to the shelter. I asked why they didn't have any food or warm beds for the kids.

"They're called pull factors," said Anthony. "We're not allowed to offer anything that would make this better than their own homes."

Yet the kids loved it there; this was a great club where they sang songs, played games and did exercises. I asked if they'd seen any rebels.

"Yes!" exclaimed a boy called Francis. "They have unkempt hair and they are smelly and they move with clubs. Their eyes are red like a killer!" Ten of the boys had been chased by rebels. I did a quick survey. Of the fifty-one boys, forty-one had had no dinner, thirty-six no lunch and Christopher and a boy called Theo, lying prone on the ground, had had nothing to eat that day. I asked the kids what their biggest problem was, expecting some highly quotable line about a lack of lasting peace in their troubled region. Instead a little kid bounded to his feet with his hand up. He had a hole in his shorts and no underwear. He said, "I need clothes."

Fired up to do the right thing and keep my date with the colonel, I shouldn't really have stopped at the Internet café. How do foreign correspondents get their information? Kate Adie must have some secret database.

Ladies! How to tell if he's the one! Google his name + human rights violations.

[DOC] 10/3/2005
File Format: Microsoft Word - View as HTML
I would like to seriously draw your attention to the rampant violation of **human rights** by some section of the UPDF. I draw your attention in particular to...
www.fdcuganda.org/pages/publications/10.doc -
Similar pages

ABDUCTED AND ABUSED:
V. HUMAN RIGHTS VIOLATIONS BY UGANDAN
GOVERNMENT FORCES... In early October 2002 **Colonel Otema** allegedly told the prisoners that they would be released...
www.hrw.org/reports/2003/uganda0703/uganda0703a-05.htm - 14k -Cached - Similar pages

Accord: Initiatives to end the violence in northern Uganda
Human rights abuses were important in the origins of the war in Acholiland.... Kuteesa and Lt **Colonel** Julius Aine conceded that **violations** may have occurred...
www.c-r.org/accord/uganda/accord11/peaceprocess.shtml - 31k - Cached - Similar pages

Northern Uganda: Chronology
The NRA allegedly commits **human rights violations**, including extrajudicial killings. 18 prominent politicians and local leaders from Acholi and Lango are...

Jane Bussmann

ology.php - 46k - Cached - Similar pages

Uganda-CAN » Archive
Human rights violations committed by military forces had
led to increased... **Colonel Otema** further said that five LRA
fighters surrendered earlier...
www.ugandacan.org/archive/1/2005-08 - 206k -
Cached - Similar pages

Uganda-CAN » Archive
The army has been criticised for committing human rights
abuses against... Speaking yesterday after the death, **Colonel
Otema** Awany, the army chief of the...
www.ugandacan.org/archive/1/2005-12 - 144k - Cached -
Similar pages

RRIA - Forum - RRIA - Forum - RRIA - Forum
The incumbent President and his governmet accuse you and
your government of 1980-85 of committing atrocities and
grave **violations** of **human rights**,...
www.flok.de/foren/guestbook313072.php?sn=6 —
102k - Cached - Similar pages

Colonel Otema—the horse we back—and his unit are linked
by Human Rights Watch to beatings, a gang rape and the
shooting of a suspect at point-blank range. In the back.

At 7 a.m. on the day I was due to die, Michael was waiting
for me outside the Green Light carrying a life-size clay goat.
The paint was still wet because he'd been up all night to have
it ready in time. He hadn't understood the national colors
of Uganda thing; it looked like someone had puked on it and
Michael thought I was mad. The goat was heavy, and its creator
was skinny and tired.

"Have you had any breakfast?" I asked him. He shook his
head. "Dinner?" Michael shook his head. I could have carried
on—does this egg jog your memory?—but I bought him a
chapatti and he was so silently grateful I couldn't speak either.

I looked at the puke-covered goat, thinking, "Goat. I'm going to meet the colonel, but I will be back for you." (I have to tell you, in a film this animal would never have seen me again.) It really was a fantastic piece of work. The boy had carved every hair on its fur, he'd finessed the texture of its hooves, he'd even put a real leaf in its mouth. There is a picture of Michael's goat on the next page.

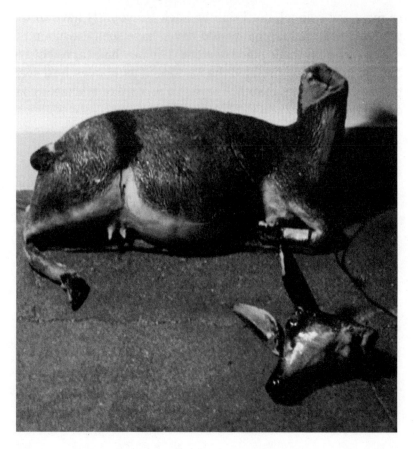

Fucking baggage handlers.

61

THIS IS ASHTON KUTCHER'S DOING

I waited for the colonel in the bar of the Acholi Inn. I was ready for some serious war reporting—I had my kid's Instamatic camera, my safari dress and a travel-size bottle of baby shampoo. I had to go, because in this story I'd missed something. If I knew one thing about Colonel Otema, it was that he didn't like people laughing at him, and Kony was laughing in his face. Otema wasn't going to look like an idiot every day just so his boss's daughter could make a few bucks. Was he up to mischief? *Look around you.* The kids who might not talk in riddles were miles away from Banya in the heart of the beast. Who better to take me than Colonel Otema, the man in charge? And hey, a date's a date. I sensed any kind of husband wouldn't have let me go. So it was just as well I didn't have one.

Then Steven, former LRA spy, texted. "I will go with you," he wrote, "you not go alone." I called him.

"Steven, you're a former LRA spy; don't you think this might be a bad idea?"

"No, I come. Fifteen minutes. You not go alone."

It got worse. Bill called. "I'll come with you. I'll ask my boss for the day off."

But it was too late. Colonel Otema's pickup crunched up to the hotel and the colonel got out. From behind, I could see that he walked with his arms out, lifting his legs. *Oh my God. He's got massive balls as well. Jesus, no wonder he's angry; it must be like trying to walk home from Safeway with a bag of oranges tied to your belt. Why did I do this?*

I had a weird thought and gave my new notebook to the barman.

"Would you keep this for me?"

"Are you not coming back?" My guts made a horrific sound. The diarrhea was kicking in. *I should not have had that goat. I could be at Entebbe Airport having a nice martini, on the toilet.*

I called Bill.

"Bill, I think we're off—"

"I am so sorry, I have to work. Will you be OK?"

"We go now!" bellowed Colonel Otema.

"I'll be fine," I said. I called Steven the former spy.

"The telephone number you have called is not available at the moment," said the treacle lady. "Please try again later."

I got in the colonel's truck and we set off. The colonel was in the front, his tiny corporal was driving and in the back were seven of his UPDF unit. My peripheral vision was full of gun muzzles.

I'd got all my questions ready, but the colonel didn't want to chat. He was saying something to the corporal in a language I didn't understand. *I know, I'll secretly tape them and get Bill to translate.* I slowly unzipped my bag, slowly pressed record and slowly held the recorder behind his back. Then I saw that behind my head there was a window in the pickup, and outside the window were seven of the colonel's soldiers in their rain ponchos. Did they notice? I wouldn't know till we got to Pader.

Now the colonel was looking at me in the rearview mirror, angry. I knew it was his facial holding pattern, but my brain seized. *This isn't an interview, is it? Oh my God. I bet he's got my computer, my camera and my notebook. He was taking me out into the middle of nowhere to shoot me in the head. Ashton Kutcher's lawyer. This has Marty Singer's stamp all over it.*

I thought about all those Westerners Prendergast said never came out alive. If they're going to say I was killed by the rebels, they'll probably have to mutilate me. What does it feel like to eat your own lips? Sashimi? Great, I was going to go down in history not as a war reporter but as the English girl who learned about cannibalism the hard way. I sent my sister the following text message: "Hi, Kate. Everything's fine, but if I'm found dead it was Colonel Charles Otema, not Joseph Kony (the child kidnapper). P.S. Don't tell Mum." She deleted it.[28] My phone reception died.

The truck bumped over potholes and I clutched my guts. I was thinking two things. Firstly, everything I've ever done is irrelevant now. All the times I stayed up till 6 a.m. to finish something; all the times I wouldn't eat the dinner Mum cooked because I was on the no-lamb diet; all that underwear I swapped the price tags on at Macy's—none of it mattered, it was all going to end today in some field in Uganda, all that had ever mattered was what you could see in front of you right now. Secondly, I really needed the loo. If I hadn't been so close to shitting myself, I would have been shitting myself.

Finally the colonel pulled over outside a concrete building at the side of the road. Is this it? Is this the building where I'm going to die? Well, where's the toilet? The colonel got out of the truck. The Ugandan People's Defense Force stared as I bolted into a privy. And sure enough, there was no toilet paper. *This* was the final straw. I was finally over this foreign correspondent bullshit.

28.

From: Kate Bussmann
Subject: Re: book
Date: July 23, 2008
To: Jane Bussmann

i didn't delete that text!

THINGS I HAVE
USED AS
TOILET PAPER

① notebook

② skirt

③ ties of a wrap
shirt

④ sock

⑤ press release
for "ALEXANDER"

1. Obviously.

2. Everyone's done this.[29]

3. This I learned from the Duchess of Kent.

4. Surprisingly hard to flush.

5. A three-hour movie about bum sex and elephants. Colin Farrell, who is your daddy now?

I went back to face the colonel. He looked down. I had one bare foot. I put my shoe back on, sockless. On the one side, him: thirty years' experience in an African army, six foot two, 200 pounds, most of it whopper. On the other, me: fifteen years in

---

29. Haven't they?

celebrity journalism, 5 foot 5½, 112–144 pounds. This was it. And I can tell you one thing about the moment you think you're going to die: your mind is an empty husk. All intelligent thought—gone.

So naturally I said, "You're in amazing shape, Colonel. What's your secret?" He stared at me, not quite sure he'd heard right. And then, I swear to God, his whole face changed.

"Exercise! Every day I run for one hour! It is the only way to keep fit!" he said.

I stared at him, not quite sure I'd heard right. Not only did the magic celebrity question work, but a heavily armed Ugandan military officer was the only person who had ever given me an honest answer.

"I bet you get up really early," I said.

"Five o'clock!" he exclaimed, looking rattled. "How did you know?"

"Look. We all know what the Ugandan People's Defense Force is most famous for," I ventured, "but how does it make you feel when you're not appreciated for your inner talents?"

The colonel thought about the question and said, "Well, this morning we killed a rebel. You want to see?"

We went hunting for the corpse. It was the best interview in years. We strolled in a field of sweetcorn. The colonel poked around in the plants.

"So, Colonel, have you ever been to London?"

"Yes, I go to Marks & Spencer Oxford Street," he replied.

"I... I bet they have no idea what an important colonel is shopping there!" I said.

"They do when I pay five hundred dollars for their casual clothes!" he said. Then, miffed, he added, "But they always try to make me get a store card. Anyway, I prefer the (under) pants at Next." It was a good quote, but it wasn't going to indict him for war crimes.

Then we came to a tomato patch. The colonel was staring down at a fresh shallow grave, bordered by tomato plants.

"Oh dear," said the colonel. "I think they buried him already."

"Well, then they had better dig him up," I said. AS A JOKE. Be careful what you wish for.

The villagers brought a hoe and started thwacking the soft soil away with the blade. Careful, that hoe's sharp, I wanted to say, then realized the bloke was already dead. The hoe hit something and the villagers started scraping instead of thwacking. The hoe caught on a handful of fingers. A small man was lying on his back in the soil tray, his arm flopping backward and forward on the hoe.

The colonel spoke to the very short corporal, who told him that the man was killed at 5 a.m. when rebels crossed the road, about fifteen to twenty of them, looting. Rebels are often killed when they come out of hiding for something to eat. These are people prepared to eat leaves; they must have been really hungry.

"The army did a deception: a raincoat on a stick," said the colonel. "The rebel shot the raincoat, and as he raised a gun they shot him. There's the bloodstain." The very short corporal gestured to something scattered across the bloodstain in the road. "He was looting food, look," said the colonel. The rebel had been killed for some nuts.

I jumped in the grave. The skinny little person with gray skin looked up at me from cloudy eyes. He could have been thirty. I wondered if he'd been a kidnapped child. I wondered if he'd been a bastard commander with fifteen wives. If anyone missed the small man in the tomato patch, or wanted him brought to trial, it was too late now. They couldn't have killed him for my benefit, could they? I felt waves of guilt, but then I always do, and all I could think was that I had to log details as fast as possible and work out if the colonel was telling the truth. *His mouth is open. His chest is hollow.*

"Sudanese uniform," said the colonel, glancing in the open grave, but the uniform was a piece of shirt loosely strung round his neck. "That means he was probably a commander. Kony's finished. We kill so many of his men."

"Wow!" I said. "You sure he's not Kony?"

"Not this time. Soon."

"Who identified him as a commander?" I asked.

"The army," said the colonel.

"No one else?"

"No."

"And now you've buried him."

"Of course. It's a hot day." That breaks international law. Probably. I needed better Intel, and fast, because I also needed a pee again and the only place to hide was this grave, which really would have been the final insult.

"So you're doing really well: you've almost beaten Kony," I said to the colonel. "Do you still have time to rescue any children?"

"We are rescuing them all the time," he said. The colonel was relaxed now, showing off. "Would you like to see some children we just rescued?" I looked up from the corpse—bingo.

The deal was done. The next day the colonel would drive me to a child soldier rehabilitation center. These kids, I hoped, would be different: fresh out of the bush, hopefully not too debriefed and hopefully not hovered over by any Banyas. But first, we'd get some sleep.

"We go to PADER!" boomed the colonel. We set off to bed down for the night at the end of the Earth.

62

THE MOON PEOPLE

And Pader was the end of the Earth. No electricity, no running water, it was simply a red dirt road to nowhere. The colonel told me to wait for him at a hotel called God's Given House. As I stepped inside God's Given courtyard, I found four Europeans. They were Useful People, but good Useful People; they had to be: it turned out they'd been there for nine months—four strangers thrown together on the moon. If the rebels took Pader, the nearest help was 30 miles away. It would be a siege: all water came in jerry cans, and when they were empty, that was that. As I walked in, the Moon People turned to me—*muzungu!*

There was a tall Frenchman who worked with children, a Polish woman writing poems about conflict and a Hungarian man with a beard who didn't say one word all night. I wondered if anyone knew what he was doing there. He might have killed a man, but he was probably from Save the Children. The last Moon Man was a short, convivial Russian who worked for the Red Cross. He was very easy to like, keen to tell me every story he'd presumably only got to tell once in nine months, and showed me the only book he'd brought with him from the Ukraine, about a rabbit that wants to kill himself.

"Poor fucking rabbit," he said, laughing uproariously.

The Moon People made a four course meal and we had a dinner party on the moon. Every night, it seemed, they sat down and cooked themselves a starter in the middle of an African war zone. The Hungarian even silently made espresso, and I have no idea how. We ate by candlelight, because when we ran light bulbs, flying ants two inches long kept hitting them, losing a piece of wing but still flying on. We talked about politics while picking long black wings out of our avocado and beetroot salad.

As we were talking, some odd pointy animal flicked past. A mongoose?

I drank too much espresso and woke up in the middle of the night needing an additional piss. I went out in flip-flops and tripped over a loaded gun—the colonel had three soldiers sleeping outside his room. Even Graham Norton doesn't have that. One of the soldiers grabbed his gun.

"It's OK! Going to the latrine!" I know, I know, broke the rule of two. The Russian was still up.

"Do you want to go to a nightclub? We can take the Land Cruiser. I call it a Kalashnikov on wheels," he said. One hot chat-up line from a Russian.

The Toyota Land Cruiser is a fuck-off top-of-the-range people saver. He had a special Red Cross edition. His squad car was white and eight feet tall. Boy, was he useful. It had a fat black air pipe coming out of the engine, so you could escape from militia through rivers up to six inches below the top of the windshield. The antenna was as thick as a post, and not for listening to *All Things Considered*. It made the whole car a radio station broadcasting useful information 185 miles away.

"Is it armor plated?"

"Same as the bad people who want to steal it." He smiled. We drove to the nightclub. It was 200 feet away.

"We take the Land Cruiser, because this is Pader," he said.

At night the generators had kicked in and little shops had become pools of colored light, green reflecting off the felt of a pool table, orange from the coals of a pork joint, blue from a TV.

The nightclub was closing, so we ended up watching TV in a bar. For some reason, the only DVD they had was a Matthew Perry movie. I should write to Matthew Perry really and tell him: he might stop getting so munted he crashes his car into his own head.

We went back to God's Given House and I bedded down again, but an infernal snoring kept me awake. I realized the colonel was in the next room. His snoring sounded like a razorback pig getting fucked by a lion. Exactly like that.

The next morning I got up for a look at where we were. Morning shock is the best thing about travel. I once spent a night driving through a forest in Transylvania with suicidal Romanian peasants. That evening, they were too sad to respond to even the perkiest chat and too proud to take the fruit I'd kept from the plane. Morning shock revealed they were jet-lagged Americans, who were really fed up with perky chat and plane food.

Pader at sunrise was beautiful and smelled like breakfast. The huge African sun was breaking through the mist. At the side of the road to nowhere, frybuns were cooking. A vendor racked up cushions of white dough on a bench, then dropped them into oil, where they puffed up like jellyfish.

I gave a stall owner a dime, and while he rolled my dough flat with a greasy piece of old cardboard, I sat next to him with the Instamatic camera, waiting for the perfect picture. There were no sounds apart from frying dough and the rhythmic stamping of the colonel's soldiers on their morning run.

This is a perfect morning, and if I have TB it hasn't kicked in yet. Then, from nowhere, a perfect little girl stepped out of the dawn, naked apart from a belly chain, the sun's rays shooting out from her, a walking baby Jesus. It was one of the most arresting images I've ever seen. As I wound on the camera, the little girl squatted down and did a perfect yellow circle of diarrhea right in the middle of the road.

This would be my lucky poo.

Then I saw the frybun man's paper.

I could not make this shit up. The Born Again Christians were right, I *was* saved. Note, the paper says it's business as usual at Entebbe International Airport; it's only the roof.

63

OUT OF A JOB

We got in the colonel's truck and set out to meet the children. The colonel was proving to be strangely endearing. To hear him talk, he hadn't lost a war with Kony for twenty years, he'd won it in slow motion. As we drove, the colonel riffed about success.

"See? The civilians feel free to move," he said, indicating some women farming. "They can easily grow food... The rebels smell because they give up on life; they are like animals, they don't bathe... We support our infantry with helicopters, state-of-the-art helicopters; last year the rebels were attacking every day, but now..."

We arrived at the child soldier rehab center. The colonel handed me over to a man from Child Protection, who sat me down and brought me kids. He seemed familiar, although I couldn't be sure, because I'd met a lot of child wranglers in Uganda. Everyone was relaxed now.

I said to the colonel, "It must be hard for a man like you, when you have to fight the rebels and child soldiers get accidentally shot?"

"No, no, no," said the colonel. "The army only shoots to scare these days."

Of the eight children I interviewed, six were ignorant of this policy shift. Especially the ones with bullet holes. Cathy was a 14-year-old who said she'd been in a group of sixty soldiers, most under the age of sixteen.

"Some of us were released, some killed. Firing is to frighten," she said. "But when you are running away they shoot to kill."

Tim, aged thirteen, and George, aged fifteen, had huge two-inch ulcers on their legs. I thought they were mosquito bites gone septic.

"From the battle," they said. They were bullet wounds.

Bosco had sores all down his leg. There were a hundred rebels in Bosco's group when he escaped in March this year: "Most like me, most now wounded," he said, rubbing the wounds on his shins with his fingers.

George said, "We were attacked by the army sometimes twice in a month. Some died. It hurts," he said, gaze steady, looking nowhere.

Like Hollywood celebrities, these kids were in a state of arrested development. But instead of being frozen at the age they were when Kony struck, they'd become pensioners. As I talked to George I had the feeling I was talking to an old, old man on his deathbed, who'd realized there would never be anything else for him now. I tried to change the subject. I should have learned a new change-the-subject question.

"Are you happy to be going home now?"

"I don't know if my parents are dead." *Shit. OK, how about...*

"George, how is your health?"

"It hurts," he repeated.

"What does?"

"The bullet." He rubbed his arm. I turned to the rep from the army's Child Protection Unit. "Is George getting any medication for this... bullet?"

"First I've heard of it," said the rep.

"Don't they go to the hospital?"

"We take them as soon as they raise a complaint."

Raise a complaint? They've spent years slicing boys called David without raising a complaint about that.

"Right, right. Well, I expect you're pretty busy," I said.

After I left the center, some representatives from the charity came up to me. "All the children get medicals," they said. "He didn't understand what you were asking him. They don't speak good English. They are very—"

"Traumatized. I know." Now I understood why these people were familiar to me. They were publicists.

You may think this proves nothing. And in journalistic terms it doesn't. Who knows who shot George? I wasn't there. Shouldn't this interview be conducted by a real foreign correspondent, not some half-arsed Ashton Kutcher-praising hack? That's a very fair point, and believe me, I agree with you.

Here's what happened when a real foreign correspondent, Callum Macrae, spent a day with Colonel Otema:

> There are few things which can prepare you for the terrible reality of witnessing a "military victory" against the kidnapped child soldiers of Uganda's Lord's Resistance Army (LRA).
>
> I was in the northern town of Gulu, filming for the forthcoming BBC2 special, *A Day of War*, when Lt Col. Charles Otema, the incongruously genial head of military intelligence for the area, contacted me.
>
> He said government troops from the Uganda People's Defense Force (UPDF) had scored a "significant blow" against the rebels. He told me the LRA's second-in-command, Vincent Otti, had been injured in the battle, fifty-five rebels had been killed—and that, as we spoke, government forces were pursuing the rest through the bush.
>
> He invited me to come and see the evidence for myself.
>
> In a tiny military helicopter, we flew 85 kilometres northwest, towards the Sudanese border.
>
> Our helicopter touched down in a village which had been taken over as a forward base for the Ugandan army. The helicopter could get no nearer and we had to cover the remaining 4 kilometres on foot.
>
> And then we arrived at the site of the battle.
>
> It was a scene of terrible carnage. Dozens of bodies lay scattered around the undergrowth where they had fallen.
>
> The first body I saw, the first of these fifty-five dead rebels, was about four years old.
>
> Almost certainly he had been born in captivity, probably,

like so many others, the product of a forced marriage between an older rebel and a young abducted girl.

Some 10 metres away, just such a girl lay, dead, stripped to the waist. She may have been the child's mother.

In the shade of a clump of trees was another group of corpses—a couple of kids, barely teenagers, an older man and a couple of women. One of the women was huddled against a tree, clutching it as if for protection, her head bowed. She looked as though she was still alive, until I walked round and, from the other side, I could see the top two-thirds of her head had gone, blown away by rockets from one of the Ugandan army's new helicopter gunships.

This, I was told, was the group which had been sitting with Vincent Otti, deputy commander of this brutal rag-tag army of stolen children.

According to survivors, he had been injured in the attack and carried away into the bush on a stretcher.

The other dead woman in this group was, I was told, one of Vincent Otti's wives. His three-year-old daughter had been found alive, wandering through the carnage.

We were moving quickly through the bodies—the area was not entirely safe—when I heard a soldier say, "This one's alive!"

He was a boy, of fighting age certainly, so perhaps fourteen. He was lying semiconscious, his chest shuddering. He had lain there, unattended, for nearly twenty-four hours.

"Can't we get medical attention for him?" I asked.

"We will carry him back and treat him," I was told.

But then five minutes later a soldier brought the news he was dead.

"Too bad," said Lt Col. Otema. "But at least you know we wanted to rescue him."

This is, truly, an awful war.

Few would deny that military action is needed to contain the LRA and protect local people—but in that bloody battlefield near Sudan, it was equally clear to me that the price of a purely military solution is unacceptably high. It is very difficult to defend the slaughter of four-year-olds in the cause of peace.

Serious international pressure might force both sides into

peace negotiations, but it has been slow in coming.

Last year the LRA abducted 9,000 young people.

It is tempting to think that if they had been stealing oil rather than children, the rest of the world would have paid more attention.

I got back in the colonel's truck and I asked him the real question. "Colonel, are you winning the war?"

He said, "Of course. Kony can't get the manpower. He can't kidnap any more."

I told him about the seven girls kidnapped in Kitgum. I told him that even the United Nations security briefing said Kony was still kidnapping. And the colonel said, quote: "Ah, well, you know, these UN officials lie. Because if the war is over, they are out of a job."

As a journalist, you know when you've got your quote, and that was it. So with these words ringing in my head, we drove back to the Acholi Inn.

The colonel was warm, affable. "How did you sleep?" he said.

"Great," I lied, adding, "you giant razorback pig getting fucked by a lion," but silently, because I'm a coward.

"I know," he said, not listening. "I don't trust the sheets. I don't trust the towels. And if you want to go for a short call, it's out in the back." So that was Colonel Otema's Achilles heel: hygiene. When he wasn't snoring, he lay awake at night wondering if he was rolling in biscuit crumbs or ticks.

I stopped off briefly at the Sister Rachele Center, a rehab facility named in honor of the Italian nun. To my relief, it was great. The kids were cared for, they got proper lessons, and the food wasn't two weeks late. There were no emotional men offering up armfuls of babies with head injuries to me, and no kids with perforated testicles being left to the great pediatrician Jehovah. These were the people I'd send to find Victoria.

64

LOOK AROUND YOU

The colonel's quote was still ringing in my head as I sat at the bar of the Acholi Inn with Bill. I was cleaned up and ready to fly home. I vowed to get the story out somehow. After all the time I'd spent chasing the colonel, his motive was pretty simple after all. I'd over-analyzed this military man: he was just a buffoon who liked fighting. His job was war, and if he let Kony escape, it was because he loved his job.

Bill and I said our goodbyes. I promised to put his byline on the *Sunday Times* article—it would read, "By Jane Bussmann and Bill Mulindwe in Gulu." He went back to work and I turned to the worst job in journalism, counting your receipts. I managed to keep going for literally minutes before I switched to hitting on the barman, with limited success.

"This is a fantastic Coke, Roger! Let's go find your boss and tell him how fantastic you are!" The barman didn't like that idea.

"No... you cannot," he said.

"Why not? Not just because you've got self-respect," I said.

"I don't think he would like it," said Roger.

"Go on, what's his name?"

The barman pointed into the garden, where a man was striding out to join the Fanta Gang, dressed no longer in combat fatigues, but the casual spring styles of Marks & Spencer.

"Otema," said the barman.

His boss, the owner of the Acholi Inn, was Colonel Charles Otema. And I looked around me at all the Westerners come to save the children, all on expense accounts, all paying straight to the colonel. There under the mango tree was the Fanta Gang, the government army drinking with Sam Kolo and Banya and

Western charity representatives. I'd wondered why the colonel hadn't caught Kony yet. And there on the bar in front of me was my own pile of receipts from the Acholi Inn.

65

THE WILLIES OF ZEUS

I flew to London to file the *Sunday Times* piece. On the way home, I went to see the choir in Queenstown. They were so happy to see me they sang me a song. Half of them were missing—I dunno, AIDS—but they still had the baritones.

I'd finally got my police report from the Gulu cops, and amazingly they'd filled it in wrong, so the insurance sent me two cameras and Bill got a real one at last.

Leaving the bubble of Africa to rejoin the first world, I expected to feel showered and calm. But we hadn't even taken off from Entebbe when it became clear that the Reverse Logic zombies had won. More and more random new laws had been put in place by nonelected bodies, starting with the Government of British Airways. First, we'd all be sprayed with insecticide.

"The spray is essential," the stewardess explained. *To whom? Under what law? Which medical truth?* "It is not harmful to humans but it may affect you, so please cover your mouth and eyes." *What? What? Has logic fucked itself inside out?* The cabin flooded with a fug of lilac, a made-up smell. Then before we landed, we went round and round in circles.

"I'm afraid we're still waiting for the OK from ground control to land," said the pilot. *Why? Why? Did you not tell them you were coming? Did you think, "I'll just turn up and hope for the best"?*

"Madam, blankets have to be stowed under your seat." *Yes, yes, in case I'm hiding box cutters under it, but the horse has bolted and right now we're landing, which is when you turn the aircon to freezing to keep us alert for a crash, because we are so stupid our 747 falling out of the sky wouldn't wake us...*

She stared at me until I complied. I looked into her side-parted Kingdom of Leather face and knew something had shifted. I had heard so much grand scale bullshit in Africa that I no longer had patience for the trivial.

At least Mum was the same as ever when I rang the doorbell. I think I'd told her I was coming home, but I'd been quite busy.

"Hi, Mum! I've been a foreign correspondent," I said.

My mum replied, and I quote: "That's nice! I'm just doing the washing; have you got any dark clothes?"

The *Mail on Sunday* sent me straight to Rhodes—result!—so I found myself packing again as I called the *Sunday Times*.

"Listen, this story is bigger than John Prendergast. It's kids getting bombed, it's the army letting a kidnapper run free and it's Britain and America funding them," I blurted in some shape or form.

Sean Ryan, coolest foreign editor in the world, said, "Sounds interesting. Email me your bullet points today. Two thousand words by Thursday."

"You'll run it?"

"We'll run it next weekend."

Two thousand words in the *Sunday Times*? That's a full fucking page! Holy... bullet points! Shit!

I was still writing the bullet points as my plane for Rhodes began early boarding. With a minicab hooting outside, I was hammering my brother's iBook. *Argh! It's only 256 megabytes! Tom, why didn't you buy more RAM, you inconsiderate silky haired bastard. Shit!* The minicab office started calling. *Fuck, fuck, fuck! I'll have to send it in webmail...* The minicab driver was ringing the bell. *UPLOAD, you fuck—no, don't drive off—*I hit SEND and made it onto the Rhodes plane.

Thursday, Friday, Saturday: in a flamboyant celebrity astrologer's Greek villa, using a friend's spare laptop held together with duct tape, I busted a gut to write more than I had ever written. Normally 2,000 words was no problem, but these had to be true, and it was really, really hard. The story would fall into place. President Museveni said Kony was the problem. What happened to the people who were getting rid of the problem? Father Carlos, who fixed it for kids to come out, no bullets fired; the army almost burned him alive. Betty Bigombe, who spent her own kid's school fees on phone bills to ask Kony for peace; they blew up the phone so she couldn't finish the conversation. John Prendergast, who sleeps four hours so he can write peace proposals to end wars; Museveni was too busy to meet him for a month. Another month of ambushes and mutilations. Even Papilloma the publicist might feel bad about that. Meanwhile, Kony built a whole city of children in the desert, where anyone could have found them but only a nun did.

Museveni said he was sending the army to catch Kony—40,000 troops. But Kony is still alive, because 40,000 troops weren't looking for Kony. *"Where were the soldiers?"* They were next door, in the Congo, full of gold and diamonds, in a feeding frenzy. Never mind a hotel, Otema's colleagues in the UPDF ran their own mining operations in the Congo, mines scraping up coltan for mobile phones, laptops and computer games. Local villagers who didn't comply got a visit from the kind of men John Prendergast said, "Weeell," about: Congo militia, the creative rapists, armed and trained by Uganda's UPDF. Meantime, the cash kept coming: we paid Museveni's grocery bills—43 percent of his budget comes from foreign aid—and with the money he saved, he bought Mambas and attack helicopters and rocket-propelled grenades. His army firebombed a few of Kony's kids to justify them, then nipped over the border for some duty-free shopping. The cash kept coming.

When Kony was kidnapping at his fastest, Uganda managed to export over $100 million more gold than it actually, as it were, had. In 2005, the IMF announced Uganda would get 100% debt relief under the Multilateral Debt Relief Initiative. In 2006 the International Court of Justice found Uganda guilty of war crimes in the Congo. But the cash kept coming. Uganda's government had the war under control, but not in the way you'd think.

Sunday, Monday, Tuesday: I wrote between coach trips to sherry distilleries and pottery kilns. While middle-aged ladies painted Zeus's willy on souvenir plates, I transcribed Angela, Marilyn, Father Benedict... My hands were packing up, but John said a page in a quality paper would be useful. People in power would read it. Useful. I carried on.

Two thousand words. Would I have enough? Wednesday morning, I did a word count: 100,000 words. I'd accidentally written a novel in four days. Shit! You tell me which AIDS-ravaged-kidnapped-child-soldier-sex-slave-lips-hacked-off-prostitute-toddler I cut out now? It was killing me. I couldn't take out Ellen, I couldn't take out Laura, I couldn't take out Victoria. *Sophie's Choice* was a piece of piss: there were only two of them.

Thursday morning, *Red* magazine called: Did I *know* my column about my glamorous life in Hollywood was a week late? What? What? OK, fine. "Today, went to a party, saw Eve taking a piss." SEND. Actually, I think I sent them something about celebrity babies, figuring celebrities were probably having them, but I did go to a party and see hip-hop star Eve taking a piss. She was wearing furry boots, like she'd stepped in a pair of beavers.

Finally, Thursday afternoon, 6 p.m. GMT, hands crippled into Cornelius paws, I'd got it down to 7,000 words—that's nearly 2,000. I emailed the *Sunday Times*: "I wondered if you'd had a chance to look at my bullet points because I'm nearly done."

Sean Ryan emailed back, "Jane, I never got these bullet points."

That day, on my brother's ailing iBook, instead of emailing Sean dot Ryan, foreign editor of the *Sunday Times* of Britain, I had emailed those bullet points to Sean Hayes, flamboyant supporting star of TV's *Will & Grace*.

Sean Hayes advised me to concentrate on the history of the Lord's Resistance Army. No, Sean Hayes did nothing of the sort; he never got the email either. My story was quite justifiably killed.

Now I was worse than useless, I'd done actual damage, because I told those kids I'd help them.

Touching down in Hollywood, I was in the right mood for a mission: GET THE STORY OUT.

Most of my days began at 6 a.m., with me on the phone saying, "Hi, I was calling back about the peacemaker and the kidnapped children feature... OK, I will try the *Sunday Times*. Thanks."

"Hi, I'd submitted a story about children in Africa. You would?" A long pause. "I can totally see your point, but Angelina Jolie wasn't there." A shorter pause. "No, not Madonna either. There weren't really celebrities there at all."

A Sunday supplement went for it, and I spent three weeks writing the piece. Then they announced they'd had a makeover, and it "didn't fit with the new direction."

"If only you'd been able to get some quotes from, I dunno, Angelina Jolie," said the Sunday supplement. Outside the window, a man on a pogo stick bounced clean out of sight.

I got an email from Bill Clinton's office. A quote from Bill Clinton about John. "Too little too late, I'm afraid, Jane," said the Sunday supplement's editor. Story of my life, and probably Bill's too.

No one wanted the story. Then one day I came home to find a message on my answering machine, and it wasn't from Marty Singer.

"Jane? This is Tony Grant. Got your message and I'd like to

talk to you..." His voice sounded Old World British, as though whatever bombs were falling, he understood and there was no point getting hysterical about it. I somehow knew Tony Grant wouldn't demand I travel back in time and take Angelina Jolie with me to Gulu. Tony Grant was, in fact, one of Radio 4's most seasoned producers. "Call me back when you get a chance," he said, "and we'll talk about Fooc..." Fooc? FOOC!

I drove to one of the BBC's LA studios, in an old movie lot in Silverlake. The BBC's venerable LA and Baghdad correspondent David Willis taught me to sound really, really posh. Willis is the only man who could recall Baghdad as "Baggers." Willis cranked up an elderly microphone and somehow I got the colonel's story into it. As long as I'd lived, I never thought I'd turn on the radio and hear Kate Adie say, "Good morning. Today on *From Our Own Correspondent...* Jane Bussmann, who's just back from Uganda..." Unbelievably, I really was a foreign correspondent. For four minutes and forty seconds.

But I kept getting texts from the child soldiers group. "How are you? I am fine. My sister dieth of malaria, my brother dieth too..." The war was still going on, Kony was still kidnapping and kids were still being dumped in camps. I still had several hundred sex-slave prostitute toddlers on my conscience—an overcrowded place at the best of times—and I had promised I'd help. But how? Then something Tony Grant said got me thinking.

"Why did you run it?" I had asked him, honestly at a loss after every single media outlet had nixed the story.

"I liked it," said Tony. "It had a real celebrity journalism feel to it." I took another look at the failed documentary about John. Reels of footage of this insanely hot man being trailed through the corridors of power by a loser love bunny. There was something in there; it wasn't pretty, and it certainly wasn't searing current affairs. Two quotes floated up.

Slut at Channel 4: "We can't use this. It looks like she fancies him."

Man from Sunday supplement: "We can't run it. If only you could have got some celebrities..."

I tore the whole documentary apart and recut it as a comedy. Instead of the noble story of John going to save the children from the Most Evil Man in the World, I told the ignobler story of me trying to date out of my league. I stuffed it full of every celebrity I'd ever interviewed, overpraised and lied about. With no more money for filming, I'd have to do it live on stage, but John, the fool, had sent me footage for the documentary, serious footage of him and Don Cheadle going round the camps in Uganda. I would use it totally out of context for a bad-taste comedy, which would be projected behind me onstage. I tried to tell John, but he was busy. Well, "tried to tell"; I sent him an email saying, "Would it be okay to do a show about being inspired to go to Uganda by the world's coolest peacemaker?" And he said, "Go for it." What do you want? I'm a coward.

How hard could it be to act in, produce and direct a stage show? I could have answered that six months later, doubled over in psychosomatic gut pain in the toilet of an Off Broadway theater, and by then I had a professional team to take the heat off me. The show opened in Manland, sadly not a gay disco but sitcom star Sean Maguire's outdoor den, and I realized glumly through a triple vodka that it was going to be three hours long and an unmitigated disaster. Then Robbie Williams walked in singing "Sergeant Pepper's Lonely Hearts Club Band," which I took to be an omen, though of what I was unclear, and I decided to keep going.

I hired the only theater in Hollywood I could afford, which was tiny and smelled of wee. Then one night, a comedy writer friend turned up with his agent. This really was an unmitigated disaster: I'd transferred to the theater's Room 209, an even smaller room with nine chairs that smelled not of regular wee but tramp wee, the Wild Turkey of wee.

The show wasn't ready to be seen by any agent, let alone an agent like this, a heavy-hitting British comedy specialist from the Pentagon agency with the security guards, the one where the old black guy cleaned the agents' shoes on their feet. More to the point, this particular agent hated me. We'd met just a few days earlier in Las Vegas, on the one evening all year I chose to do no writing and instead take vast quantities of very strong magic mushrooms with one of the agency's most valuable clients, before regaling the agent with uproarious true tales about being pulled over by the Nevada Highway Patrol on the freeway outside Pahrump in the superstar client's sports car with a boot full of psychedelics. Tales that the agent didn't find funny.

However, by a big, fat, impossible Hollywood miracle, the agent had also been to Uganda and knew what I was talking about. He'd even come unstuck with a bunch of hill pygmies, and I think the show must have triggered a suppressed memory.

The day after the show, the agent became unhinged. He turned into some kind of phone-hammering, feral-eyed madman. He got the show into the Edinburgh Festival. We started with two nights in New York, in an Off Broadway theater that smelled not of wee but fine wine. More on that particular opening night later, as it turned out to be quite significant. My favorite review was "I hope if she gets gangraped she knows about it."

Things went from surreal to surrealer. The Soho Theatre offered to put it on in London. Despite my going onstage blind drunk every night in terror, the show sold out and the irrepressible agent and his irrepressible London colleague invited a bunch of movie people. They asked me a question. Could I pitch it as a movie? By a ridiculous series of events, I was now, all these years later, going inside the Magic Kingdom for that meeting with 21st Century Fox.

IT'S EVERYTHING MEETS EVERYTHING

Back in Hollywood, I had to be groomed for entry into the castle keep. I was sent to work on the pitch with a Hollywood Player. When you tell a movie studio executive your idea for a movie, you think you've told him an exciting story. Don't kid yourself. You've asked him to spend $80 million of his boss's money on something that doesn't exist, and you are not Clint Eastwood. So the pitch is not an ambling "wouldn't-it-be-fun-if?", it's a tightly written, impeccably rehearsed twenty-minute show about why your movie won't get him fired and why you are the Next Big Thing. In other words, it's excruciating.

The Hollywood Player assigned to help me work on the pitch lived behind a Beverly Hills Zen statuary garden; I didn't know whether to pray to it or pee in it. All I knew about the Kingdom was that inside, there lived two kinds of studio executives: Inscrutables and Cockwavers. Inscrutables, they're self-explanatory; meetings where you give up trying to guess what they're thinking and become aware of everything that's wrong with your idea, your outfit, your approach to romantic relationships and frankly your hopes of a future. Cockwavers are much more entertaining. Cockwaving is an art form in Hollywood, the rudest town on the planet. Humans are basically nice, unless hungry or threatened. In LA, everyone's dieting and thinks they're being replaced by someone hotter. Those that do eat are largely living off protein and bananas, like chimps, so are belligerent and cockwaving. Cockwavers use the most obviously made-up industry jargon, ask your opinion so they can tell you why it's wrong and, above all, invite you to come in for an Ignoring. To work out your position in Hollywood, count the number of minutes you are ignored after they've invited you into their office and add 1,000. Congratulations, you are the 1,011th most important person in show business. Here is a meeting with a Cockwaver. (The worst Cockwavers, by the way, are women. Thin women.)

"Josh, send her in."

You walk into her office.

"So let's see what you've got. Let's see the reel." Your showreel starts playing. Josh immediately buzzes the Cockwaver on the intercom, as he has been trained to do.

"I have Harvey," Josh says.

"Excuse me, I have to take this..." Now don't think for a minute you are being ignored for Harvey Weinstein. Are you *high*? "Harvey, I specifically told your guys, I want the sign in the *middle of the door...*" You will then be ignored for eight to nineteen minutes for a conversation with a house painter.

Another Cockwaver, another meeting. The Ignoring finally over, the Cockwaver will hang up, sigh and turn to you.

"So. Tell me about you. Tell me about your show. Who do you see working in it?"

"Bill Nighy—"

"No. That won't work. The studio won't want that. The network won't want that. The audience won't want that. What else would you like to write about? You can do anything you like."

"Maybe a love story—"

"No. No. If you don't bring anything to the picnic, you can expect to feel the cold..." They gesture to a signed cast photo of a hit show. This was their work, they developed it, they alone told the network that the show's creator was a genius, unless it tanks next season, in which case the cast photo will be removed and they will recount how they warned the show's creator where he was going wrong, but the creator is *legendarily* difficult and wouldn't listen.

You think I'm embellishing, don't you? No, I'm playing it down. During the first meeting, the Cockwaver left during the phone call and never came back.

If the Cockwaver really has got to speak to the real Harvey Weinstein first, you'll wait in a conference room with a view of the ocean and a table the size of a lifeboat, but less accommodating to women and children. Thrilled Man will be sent in. Thrilled Man is an exec with a vague job, whose main duty is sitting in conference rooms asking guests if their hotel is nice and if they've had a chance to see any shows while they're in town. They are paid to stop you getting angry about being ignored, but they didn't get a law degree at Harvard for this, so they flatter you in suicidal hyperbole.

"We are so thrilled you could meet with us; we think you're amazingly talented," says Thrilled Man, his eyes squinting from depression. "And *you're* amazing..." *Is that a single tear behind the Dior frames? God, you hope not...* "Yours is a truly original voice that we can't wait to... to..." He remembers his youthful hopes and dreams and falls face down on the mahogany table, keening in psychic pain.

"Amazing," by the way, is suicidal hyperbole for "I'm still listening." "You think you might go to Disneyland while you're here? Disneyland is amazing. We saw your reel. Amazing."

The Hollywood Player was going to help me prepare for these meetings by Working on My Pitch, and he didn't waste any time. He had brown eyes, a black tie and I think his years working as Thrilled Man had left his voice permanently damaged, because when his eyebrows tried to drag his face up into a smile, his voice never raised from a monotone of depression.

"First off: you need to compare it to two similar movies that made a lot of money."

"Um, *The Constant Gardener* did OK…"

"Only in Europe. It was a disaster here. Thirty-four million? God, a disaster. Fuck," he said brightly. "Any more?"

"There aren't really any comedies about… war criminals… er, Africa, kidnapping…"

"Doesn't matter. There's a journalism angle, so you should be thinking *The Devil Wears Prada*, that's your ideal scenario. Had you thought about Reese Witherspoon?"

"I'll definitely think about that," I said, and meant it.

"You should. She's someone every studio wants to be in bed with. So what have you got?"

I told him. I felt excited after I'd finished, and so did he.

"Amazing. It sounds like a guy movie. Joseph Kony, now *that* is a villain."

"He's bad. He's kidnapped twenty thousand kids."

"Kids. Ah. You see, then it's a woman's movie. If you had a woman in peril and a guy coming to rescue her, it could be *Romancing the Stone*."

"What would she need rescuing from?"

"Africa. Meryl Streep waiting for Redford to get her *Out of Africa*. I'm joking," he said, suddenly suicidal. "But they should remake that… Reese Witherspoon… I think we both know the real problem you've got here. Does it *have* to be in Africa? It's not me saying this."

"It's… it's about a real person," I said. "The kids are real; he's holding them hostage—right now in the Congo." His expression changed to faint optimism, so I carried on. "The Congo's in Africa," I said.

"Oh," he said, disappointed. "Maybe if you open in Hollywood… end in Hollywood… Will there be a *lot* of Africans in it? I'm on your side."

"You sort of need Joseph Kony. The war criminal."

"But does he have to be a criminal? Could he be a cop? An ex-cop sent to protect this girl? Then you've got your Chris-Rock-Jamie-Foxx. Ah, but then there's the problem of if they fuck. I mean, it's Jamie Foxx, he's gonna wanna fuck, but is the audience gonna wanna see a black guy and a white woman?

No. It's not me saying this. Fuck, I would find that hot as fuck. But they're very racist in Europe. Chris Rock can't even go to Europe. I mean, he can fly there, but he can't get off the plane."

Now we were both sad. We both searched for a solution. I found one.

"Oh! What if... she goes to Africa to look for Kony and some bloke helps her, just as friends?" Bill wouldn't mind, surely. The Hollywood Player's eyebrows hoiked up his mouth, happy again.

"So it's *Rush Hour 2*," he said.

To work on the pitch, I put my stuff in storage and moved into a friend's flat. Because, of course, being Hollywood, there has to be adversity. The credit cards came home to roost about the same time as I realized why Donald Trump famously doesn't invest in theater productions. I was in big trouble.

It was during a heat wave in a bijou studio apartment and the first thing I did was break the window frame so it wouldn't open. Worse, I was officially cat-sitting and I couldn't open the door in case the cat escaped. Monster was old with a belly that flapped as it ran, ratty gray hair that fell out, one working eye, a scabby raisin for the other and giant paws like a platypus.

"I love cats," I said. "Allergic?! No! No, no! I've got a cold."

"Even you will love her. She's so affectionate, she loves to hug," said my friend.

I spent three weeks dodging the hug, my eyes streaming, sneezing, walking through shimmering clouds of dander as Monster bounced after me like the Easter Bunny of germs. I paced the tiny room, learning my lines. It's *Romancing the Stone* meets... *The couple run away, she sees a lion, obviously if this was* Out of Africa *he could shoot it, but now he just scares it off...* Bridget Jones *meets... and this is a Trailer Moment—bang bang bang, they are firebombed by helicopters...* James Cameron, of course, just goes in with "It's everything meets everything."

After a day or two I gave up pacing and took my laptop under the covers to hide from the love-struck Monster. Every time I looked up from under the duvet it would be peering down at me, giving me the one eye. But I didn't know the hairy sex pest could use its platypus feet to pull back the covers. I never felt a thing. One night I got hotter and hotter until I pulled off the duvet to find the cat was spooning me, its paws wrapped round my back, so blissed out to be finally in body contact that a big warm circle of cat piss was spreading under the pair of us.

I was groomed. The pitch was groomed. It was *Romancing the Stone* meets *Bridget Jones's Diary* meets *Private Benjamin*, and I was going to pitch it to the Queen of Girlcentric Comedy and the King of Edgy Blockbusters. These were serious, heavyweight meetings.

I pulled up to the studio gate, where a nice man looked at my ID and told me to turn left.

"Left. Thanks. Brilliant. Left," I said, turning right.

I was inside the castle, headed for the keep. It was full of posters for movies you'd heard of. I met up with the producers who'd be producing our movie if the Queen liked the pitch. They were nice producers and they did this all the time. If they realized I was limping because I couldn't afford to reheel my boots, they didn't mention it. I was more worried about the fact that I only had an hour before my face cracked as I'd run out of foundation and was wearing extremely absorbent stage make-up.

We had an Ignoring outside the Queen of Girlcentric Comedy's office for thirty minutes or so, and then her assistant invited us to go in for some more. I could feel my face cracking, and leaned my cheek on one hand in an air I hoped looked casual, but which felt inexorably like Harpo Marx as the minutes dragged on.

The Queen of Girlcentric Comedy finally strode in, dressed apparently for golf with Agatha Christie, and stared at us wildeyed.

"Hello—" began the producer.

"Don't sit there! That's not the pitching chair!" said the Queen. "*I* sit there, *you* sit *there*, the producer sits *there*, and *she* sits *there*." The producer chuckled amicably; we all thought she was joking. To prove she wasn't, she left the room. We swapped chairs and started again. Incidentally, the office was decorated with Zen executive toys.

Afterwards, the producers asked her what she thought of the pitch.

"They won't like it," she said. "We're not in the business of throwing stuff at walls to see what sticks." *No, but I expect you eat lots of bananas*, I should have said.

No matter. There was still the King of Edgy Blockbusters. I rehearsed until I was dreaming Bridget Jones analogies. I pulled up to the studio gate, thinking, "Remember this moment. You're not a journalist, not a tourist, you're actually having a meeting in a movie studio." A nice old man at the gate looked at my ID and told me to turn left. I turned right. I was inside the Magic Kingdom and I was completely bloody lost. For an hour I searched, driving past endless studio roads named after people like Muddy Waters, people carrying chunks of stage set and a 30-foot-high Kelsey Grammar. I finally found an office. It was decorated with full-size posters of movies you've heard of. A nice young man gave me a bottle of water. Something made me stop before I drank it all, as if I knew I was going to need it.

The King of Edgy Blockbusters didn't keep me waiting, wasn't dressed for between-wars golf and gave away no aggression. I got my hopes up. Then I realized he gave away nothing at all.

"So, tell me all about it," he said. As I started speaking, I realized I had no idea what he was thinking. All I knew was that I was wearing too much make-up and too much perfume. *Why is my skirt so short? I shouldn't have worn fishnets. Oh God, I bet he can see my underwear through the holes, not that he's interested when I look this revolting and am obviously mentally ill. Please let him be gay. Why am I speaking in pathetic reviews of my own show? Why did I let that bloke who said, 'I did that for you, don't ask me to do that again,' have my apartment keys? Why did I sell that place in Queen's Park? I'll never own my own home again...* I finally made it to the Bridget Jones analogy and dried up.

He stared at me for a few seconds without speaking. I held a relaxed pose and missed my mouth with the water bottle. As I blotted my miniskirt, the King of Edgy Blockbusters said, "I love the story, but this way of doing it wouldn't really... It's not what we're about here. *The Constant Gardener,* which did great box office internationally, that is an ideal model for us." He smiled the Don't Give Up smile. "But you look amazing."

68

SIXTEEN CENTS

The great thing about the phrase "It can't get any worse" is that it's an invitation to worsery. I moved into a flat with cockroaches and a cat rat—a rat nose-to-tail the length of a cat—and three big guys who sat on my windowsill all night talking about jail. I finally pulled up the blinds and saw not three big guys but three lovely young ladies. I don't know if they knew Eddie Murphy, but again, it was Hollywood. What were the chances?

It got worser. Two Posh Young Producers reneged on payment for scripts, and the cashier in the bank explained that I'd gone too far this time.

"I haven't used my card," I snapped back boldly, little realizing that by going into debt, I had given another person the right to use my card, namely the bank. She showed me a printout.

"But... you fined me for being fined," I said.

"You make a deal with the credit card companies."

The customer behind me tutted. I gave up and did something Donald Trump rarely does: I put a bag of pennies on the counter.

"Can I get dollar bills for this?" I said, another thing I doubt Donald Trump ever says, except of his ex-wife.

"You have to roll the coins. We don't do that." She handed me some paper tubes. I sat in the middle of the bank, in front of the customers, putting pennies in the tubes. I thought my neck was going to snap from nonchalantly holding my head up. Nine dollars and sixteen cents. I bought $9 of gas and drove to one last meeting about child soldier comedy.

"We would never tell you to make it like *Sex and the City*," they said, "but *Sex and the City* was huge. And you're the one that refuses to get in touch with your feminine side..."

"I..." I said.

"The female lead—she's got to have a baby that died," they said. "Because otherwise the audience are not going to buy that she would want to go to Africa."

"A dead baby... in a sitcom... I—" I said.

"We've been over this! She's got a fiancé at home; why would she leave him?"

"He's a git. I—"

"No. She's got a man. She'd never leave him. Now with you, you didn't have a man and there was a man in Africa, that's totally relatable..."

I went to bed that night on a pile of boxes, since I hadn't had time to unpack and had just thrown a futon on top of everything. I rolled over and a box collapsed under me. I told myself it hadn't happened.

I got out of the boxes at 6 a.m. to find my upstairs neighbor's bathroom had leaked in the night and I had been sleeping in a puddle.

I went jogging past the homeless people and told myself I was lucky. Then I came to a stop. I'd slept in a pile of cardboard boxes and a stranger had pissed on me as I slept. It was over.

I went home for Christmas and walked the West End to make sense of things. On December 22, I was kicking down Little Mortimer Street, wondering if it was too late to travel back in time and start my life again with a wet look perm and a job as Woooo Gary Davies's PA, when my phone rang. It was the boss of a cool film company, British this time.

"How did it go in America?" he said.

"Oh my God, it was a total bloody nightmare," I said. In the Golden Age of Stupid I would have said, "It was brilliant," but by this point I was past caring. "They said, 'Are there going to be lots of Africans in it?' And when I said she had a black friend, they said, 'So it's *Rush Hour 2*?'"

"Ha!" laughed the film company boss. "Well, we'll do it then."

69

FIFTEEN PAIR GUMBOOTS

That Christmas, knowing that most films, let alone child-soldier comedies, don't get made in the end, but deciding to acknowledge the fact that at least someone with a real job had said he'd like to make this one, I got on a plane to see the child soldiers group.

I arrived to find them in great shape. Things were looking up in Gulu. Banya had got fired from his job as babysitter, after an exposé written by a hot, fiery-eyed reporter at the *Monitor*. The child soldiers announced that I too would have a job title; they had made me their international coordinator. Patently they hadn't read my CV but how hard could it be to internationally coordinate a group of Ugandan former child soldiers and sex slaves?

First off, they wanted me to talk to a man from a British charity who had visited them. I internationally coordinated a meal in a Japanese restaurant with the charity rep, who was younger than I expected and extremely sensible. The British charity was going to fund the child soldiers group; now they'd have an office that wasn't in a panel-beating shop and motorbikes to get to the camps.

Over a beer, I laughed to the man about how paranoid Uganda had made me, convinced I was hounded by secret police when my laptop was stolen. The man told a man he knew in Gulu about it. The man in Gulu told the colonel.

"It's OK," the colonel apparently told the man in Gulu. "She can have it back now."

And I got a text message:

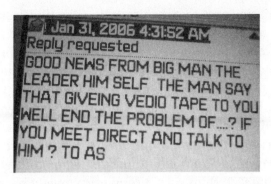

Joseph Kony wanted to meet me for an interview in southern Sudan, in return for "25lb. beans, 100lb. rice, torch batteries, antibiotics, 15 pair shocks [sic] and 15 pair gumboots." I didn't do the interview. The official word from the editor was that their man in Uganda "says the LRA have his numbers and if Kony wants to do a BBC interview, which he thinks very, very unlikely, they would contact BBC people in Africa directly." Of course, Kony did do an interview not long after with another freelancer. But to be honest, I'd already bought drinks for Banya the war criminal, and fifteen pair gumboots for Big Man the Leader Himself would have tipped my karma into the abyss.

I hadn't seen John since that night at the Sheraton, but I knew it was just a question of right time, right place; I had high hopes for genocide in Darfur.

Now back to the opening night of two nights Off Broadway.

The show was opening in the swanky 59E59 Theaters in midtown Manhattan. It was all chrome and glass and audiences drinking fancy red wine while they waited for the show, which was a minor one in a calendar of much fancier productions. I was, as usual, in the bog. Things had not cleared up since Uganda, far from it; things had got so bad that I was on the phone to my mother discussing my doc's receptionist in London and my missing arse test results. It was the third conversation we'd had on this particular subject, since I knew my illness wasn't psychosomatic, and it went something like this:

"How can she have lost my poo? OK, mislaid, how do you mislay poo? Mum, tell her I can't just 'pop back in,' I'm in New York. I could bend over and take aim at London if you like. I'm not being disgusting; it's not even poo any more, it's Coca-Cola. I've got an unnatural arse condition. No—Mum—listen! I've got to go onstage and do a comedy about children getting blown up and the audience thinks it's a romantic comedy because there are tits on the poster. LISTEN! They're out there now... I know it's my fault. OK, all I want to know is, do they think it's cancer? Because it's either arse cancer or a parasite the size of a condor. I'm scared to eat in case it leaps out and grabs my fork. I'm not shouting at you... I'm not shouting at anyone, Mum, but it's her job to collect poo, she's a poo collector, and she lost my poo... Hang on, I've got another call..."

I'd recognize John's number anywhere, even though I'd barely dialed it. This didn't help with the in-no-way-psychosomatic stomach condition. Because while I'd emailed to tell him I was doing a show about him, he still had 500 emails a night to attend to, 499 of which made more sense than mine, and despite this, the show had to go on.

One day I'd gotten an email back. "So my friend says there's this show in New York and I'm kind of... in it?" John really was a diplomat.

I hit TALK on my phone.

"Hey, it's John," he said.

"Where are you?" I said.

"I think I'm outside the theater."

I asked him to come straight to the stage and not talk to anybody because I had a couple of things to tell him first. I got my shit together, or what was left of it, and waited for him on the empty stage. Imagine how I felt when he walked in. I hadn't seen him since Uganda. I was now wearing the DKNY safari dress to do the show, like a character from a Monty Python sketch. He was in a blue shirt, I think—I could barely see at this point and my guts were stabbing me. He looked worried. I told him to sit down.

I could have told him I'd never been a real journalist. Or that I had no right to follow him into Kofi Annan's boardroom, let alone round Uganda. John certainly should have been told there was a whole stage show playing in London, LA, Edinburgh and a couple of other places about how I fancied him. But with ten minutes to curtain up on opening night in New York City, I had to pick my battles.

"John, three things. One, that Uganda footage you made with Don Cheadle and sent me? I'm using it all." John didn't flinch. "Two, it's a comedy." Now he flinched. "And three, I do not have a stalker crush on you." Now imagine how *he* felt. Three, by the way, was partly true.

The show started, and I walked out to do a lot of deeply questionable material about having a crush on him to his face. After one minute of terrifying hush, I heard him laugh. Then the audience laughed. The slideshow didn't work: there was a very deaf man in the audience who said, "Whadishesay?" every time people laughed, and his wife would tell him, so I could hear my own lines on a delay. But we got away with it, and when the show ended, John came out of the audience and hugged me. "This is a plant," thought the audience. "This is the longest route to a cuddle ever," I thought, wrapped up in aftershave, clean bloke shirt and renegade muscle. He was quite a lot taller than me. John, of course, was mobbed by the audience, students, ladies and geeks making goo-goo eyes as I smiled at him from across the room. It was the worst date I'd ever been on, but it ended well.

And on the last page I realized this story has a Hollywood ending, because I learned that one person can make a difference. Yes, Ashton Kutcher's lawyer doesn't know it yet, but I sponsored Angela and Victoria and their two rape babies in his name: the Marty Singer Scholarship. You only screwed me once, Marty, and now you have four kids. And they're all black.

EPILOGUE

THE BURGLES OF HOLLYWOOD

The hoo-ha around the show meant I ended up having breakfast at the Polo Lounge with the Most Powerful Agent in Hollywood. He represents the top people in comedy. The Polo Lounge was gloriously fuddy-duddy, with heavy silver cutlery and plates under plates, and a view of an old-fashioned Hollywood garden.

The Most Powerful Agent in Hollywood arrived, tall, trim, with perfectly toned skin. He knew exactly where he wanted to sit, even though the place was empty. He ordered grapefruit juice, turkey bacon, a bowl of blackberries mixed with blueberries and a single egg on a plate—the breakfast of a man who was going to kick Tinseltown into shape that morning. I ordered three muffins, a jug of hot chocolate and three coffees, the breakfast of someone who was going to have mood swings and write a sitcom about AIDS.

Sitting there facing him, it was clear that this was a dream opportunity. Everyone in Hollywood would have fought for this make-or-break chance to big themselves up as the greatest writer of all time. I figured I was never going to be the top people of comedy, but I could at least make good on a promise.

I took out my battered copy of *Across My Lips: the Burgles of Mortal Dignity* and showed it to him. The Most Powerful Agent in Hollywood, being an industry professional who never passes by a Next Big Thing, read the passage that ended, "He looked like a mighty chimpanzee with a lean and mean muscular stiffed genitals." He put down his blueberries.

"It's amazing," I said, looking the Most Powerful Agent square in the eye, with all the sincerity in Hollywood. "But you'd better move fast because Mel Gibson's trying to option it." *What the hell. There goes my career.*

"He is?!" said the Most Powerful Agent in Hollywood, turning back to the page.

APPENDIX

BRIEF HISTORY OF UGANDA

Here is a map. Uganda is in the middle of Africa, between Rwanda, Sudan, the Congo and Kenya: genocide, genocide, genocide, coffee.

0—1888: Ugandans farming and hunter-gathering. Lots of ethnic groups, mostly getting on, the odd flare-up.

1888: British give Uganda to the British East Africa Company, the Halliburton of men in pith helmets. Britain divides whole country into north and south. Decides north is home of tall, dark, scary people (mostly Acholi, Langi and Alur people) and makes them join the army. Decides south is home of lighterskinned, shorter, more trustworthy people (mostly Bantu people) and gives them jobs in government. When the King objects, they depose him and replace him with his baby son.

1888—1962: North and south get pissed off at each other.

1962: The British leave, by which time north and south are very pissed off at each other.

1962—85: Various bastards killing everyone, most colorfully Idi Amin, who got away with it in Uganda because he used extreme violence, and got away with it internationally because he was funny and great with the press. No shit. On the Queen's Silver Jubilee, Amin asked our monarch to send him her "twenty-five-year-old underwear." Meanwhile, Amin's prison "elimination chambers" were "littered with loose eyes."[30]

1986: New president Yoweri Museveni gets in. Britain and America trust him and give him money. By 2005, Britain had given Museveni $1.2 billion.

1987: Religious nut-job Joseph Kony declares war on Museveni, attacking fellow Acholis to teach them a lesson about supporting Museveni, even when they didn't and it made no sense. Nonetheless, Kony forcibly recruits an army of several thousand children, which creates havoc across the north.

2014: More than twenty-five years later, Museveni still hasn't managed to catch Kony.

---

30. *Time* magazine.

GLOSSARY

Behr, Dani: British entertainment institution. See also Armando Iannucci, Chris Morris, Bill Nighy, Graham Norton, Sally Phillips, David Quantick.

boffin: egghead, professor.

bollocks: testicles.

Brass Eye: legendary British current affairs satire show.

chat up: to hit on.

chilblains: red or purple swelling of the skin on the toes, fingers or face caused by cold. Associated with mountaineers and parents recounting stories of the Old Days.

cobblers: nonsense, inaccurate statements (to talk cobblers).

cock-up: fuck-up.

cunt: vagina. British term of affection in second person ("you cunt"), unspeakable human being in third person ("he's a cunt").

Deayton, Angus: TV host and actor known for upscale satire shows

gobstoppers: jawbreaker candy

GP (General Practitioner): family doctor.

knickers: women's underwear, panties.

lorries: trucks.

morris dancers: traditional English folk dancers, skipping and kicking in formation while wearing bells on their lower legs and waving handkerchiefs.

munted: extremely on drugs.

pissed: drunk, shitfaced.

privy: toilet.

shagging: fornicating.

spunk: sperm.

toff: member of the upper class. Infers idiocy, inbreeding, arrogance.

tosser: masturbator but more derogatory than wanker. Tool, asshole, etc.

twat: vagina or imbecile.

wanker: masturbator, doofus, jerk. (**wanking**: masturbating.)

willy: penis, pecker.

Woo Gary Davies: former BBC Radio One DJ famous for white shorts, bouffant hair and jingle "woo Gary Davies on your radio yeah."

JANE BUSSMANN has written for *South Park* and over fifty comedy shows, including legendary British *Daily Show* antecedent *Brass Eye,* the most complained-about program in TV history. She performs the award-winning comedy of this book to sold-out audiences from Mombassa to New York.

www.JaneBussmann.com